Freud and the Rat Man

Patrick J. Mahony

Freud and the Rat Man

With a Foreword by
Otto F. Kernberg, M.D.

Yale University Press
New Haven and London

Copyright © 1986 by Yale University.
All rights reserved.
This book may not be reproduced, in whole
or in part, in any form (beyond that
copying permitted by Sections 107 and 108
of the U.S. Copyright Law and except by
reviewers for the public press), without
written permission from the publishers.

Designed by Sally Harris
and set in Plantin type by
Brevis Press, Bethany, Ct.
Printed in the United States of America by
Vail-Ballou Press, Binghamton, N.Y.

Part of Chapter 5 originally appeared in somewhat different form as "The Oral Tradition, Freud, and Psychoanalytic Writing" in *Freud: Appraisals and Reappraisals—Contributions to Freud Studies, Volume 1*, edited by Paul E. Stepansky © 1986 by The Analytic Press, Hillside, N.J.

Library of Congress Cataloging-in-Publication Data

Mahony, Patrick, 1937–
 Freud and the Rat Man.

 Bibliography: p.
 Includes index.
  1. Lanzer, Ernst—Mental health. 2. Obsessive-compulsive neurosis—Case studies. 3. Psychoanalysis—Case studies. 4. Freud, Sigmund, 1856–1939. I. Title.
 RC533.M34   1987   616.85'227'09   86–11022
 ISBN 0–300–03694–9 (alk. paper)

The paper in this book meets the guidelines for
permanence and durability of the Committee on
Production Guidelines for Book Longevity
of the Council on Library Resources.

10 9 8 7 6 5 4 3 2 1

To Pierrette,
our children,
and those ever more preciously near

I read one day that the gold the devil
gives his victims regularly turns into
excrement; and the next day Mr. E.,
who reports that his nurse had money
deliria, suddenly told me [by way of
. . . *Dukatenscheisser*] that Louise's
money always was excrement.
                    Freud letter to Fliess,
                        January 24, 1897

Ham. [*Drawing.*] How now? A rat?
Dead for a ducat, dead! [*Kills
Polonius through the arras.*]
                    Hamlet, act 3, scene 4

Contents

Foreword	ix
Prefatory Note	xiii
1 Erratic Design	1
Important Events in the Life of the Rat Man	24
2 Taking Apart the Psychic Apparatus	28
3 The Rat Man's Treatment: General Facts and Questions	69
4 Freud's Technique: Tracing Its Historical and Clinical Features	89
5 Freud's Technique: The Rationale of a Particular Practice	133
6 Freud's Theory of Obsessional Neurosis	151
7 The Art and Strategy of Freud's Exposition	174
8 Conclusions and Reiterations	212
References	229
Index	239

Foreword

One of the most exciting developments in psychoanalytic theory and technique has been the growing understanding of how linguistic style and structure and verbal expression reveal unconscious conflict. The psychoanalytic understanding of linguistics serves to enrich the analysis of the communicated content. Thus it is an understanding that has relevance for psychoanalytic technique as well as for theory.

Patrick Mahony's contribution to this field is an exploration of Freud's published cases through a study of Freud's literary style, his rhetorical stance, and his verbal expression. As Mahony reexamines the life histories of these patients, their transference developments, Freud's evolving clinical understanding and theoretical formulations, and the potential implications for countertransference, his focus is firmly on the fit between content and narrative account.

This methodological approach, masterfully developed in Mahony's earlier books *Freud as a Writer* and *Cries of the Wolf Man*, reaches a new height with *Freud and the Rat Man*. On the basis of a careful analysis of all the available material, including Freud's original process notes and the published case history of the Rat Man, Mahony gives us a stimulating and highly sophisticated account of the patient's dynamics. He points to the striking relationship between Freud's discoveries regarding the unconscious conflicts and defensive operations of obsessive-compulsive neurosis, and the particular characteristics of this clinical report.

There is a rapidly growing awareness on the part of the non-German-speaking readers of Freud's works that the uniformity of style and language in the *Standard Edition* is a far cry from the narrative expression to be found in the original texts. *Freud and the Rat Man* offers new evidence of the discrepancies between Freud's German and the *Standard Edition* and an explicit analysis of the problems with the Strachey translation that is both informative and informed. Mahony thereby helps the English-speaking reader to experience the richness and complexity of Freud's original style.

Mahony's thorough knowledge of German, his understanding of Freud's thinking at the time he was treating the Rat Man, his objective and critical analysis of Freud's writing, and his full appreciation of Freud's creative and intellectual genius combine to take the reader on an exciting voyage through psychoanalytic theory and its application to treatment.

His account of the complex and multiple ways in which anal eroticism and the defenses against it infiltrate the Rat Man's communicative style in the analytic sessions is impressive; he shows how Freud's countertransference responses accentuate the importance of these dynamics in the transference. The relationships between defensive isolation, disconnectedness in the patient's communications, disruption of continuity within the case study, and Freud's own complaints about his writing style in this work illuminate those concepts—the defenses and unconscious conflicts—with which Freud himself was struggling at that time.

Mahony demonstrates his general thesis that the patient's linguistic style expresses his dominant conflicts in detailed and highly convincing close-ups of the Rat Man's interactions with Freud. For example, he points to the patient's utterances as symbolic extensions of his corporal schema; he describes how the Rat Man manipulates the dialogue with Freud so as to engineer a reconstruction of the rat torture in the acoustical sphere; and he illustrates how the patient's disconnected, fragmentary communication infiltrates Freud's own style, so that isolation is inscribed in Freud's very text.

A detailed analysis of the early sessions of the treatment of the Rat Man is the starting point for an analysis of Freud's technique at that stage in his theoretical and clinical discoveries. The notion of transference—a relatively recent discovery at the time of the Rat Man's treatment—is approached intermittently rather than conceived as a pervasive phenomenon. The active interventions that occur reflect both the immaturity of the technique of psychoanalysis and some particular consequences of the transference-countertransference developments in this treatment. Mahony suggests that Freud lost his habitual control over his expository style and charges this loss to the effects of the patient's obsessive mechanisms, particularly isolation and disconnectedness, on the analyst.

In this book, then, we have in a single creative, bold stroke a reexamination of one of Freud's important clinical reports; an introduction to the richness and complexity of Freud's actual style, previously obscured by Strachey's homogenized translation; and a masterful application of psychoanalytic textual analysis. The high expectations raised by Mahony's earlier books are more than fulfilled in the present volume.

Otto F. Kernberg, M.D.

Prefatory Note

Immediately there are two facts worth stressing. First, it is commonly accepted that of all the intellectual giants who have lived in the twentieth century, Freud has had the greatest cultural influence. Second, as Henry Murray has declared, the material amassed on Freud is the most precise and penetrating body of data that exists on the life of any individual in history. Yet, curiously, there has never been any comprehensive attempt to study Freud's case histories of his patients.

And now to backtrack. I was convinced that Freud's rhetorical stance and verbal expression are deeply implicated in his very way of understanding psychoanalysis, a consideration cavalierly dismissed by most analysts as being superficial or merely belletristic. I set out to demonstrate the central value of my thesis in *Freud as a Writer* (1982), which dealt with the Freudian corpus. Later I decided to apply the concerns treated comprehensively in *Freud as a Writer* to the challenging and more focalized area of his case histories, especially since various levels of psychoanalytic theory are held to be ultimately grounded in that clinical experience. My new task, then, was to concentrate on the fit between the patient's life story, Freud's clinical understanding of it, and his ensuing narrative account. In carrying out this enterprise, it was appropriate that I began with writing *Cries of the Wolf Man* (1984), a monograph on Freud's most famous patient. The current book on the Rat Man is the second in a planned trilogy, which will culminate in a study of Dora and Freud's other female patients. For obvious reasons I resolved to examine neither little Hans nor Schreber: Freud saw little Hans only once and then conducted the boy's therapy indirectly through his father. As for Schreber, Freud never saw him at all but rather analyzed his writings and other germane material.

In my study of the Rat Man I have drawn on all available source material in order to write a coherent narrative enlightened by a synthesis of psychoanalytic, historical, literary, and textual approaches. A most useful document proved to be a photocopy of Freud's process notes on the Rat Man, which is readily obtainable from the Library of Congress. In August of 1984 I took advantage of an invitation to lecture on Freud in Budapest and, following up previous correspondence, went to Vienna to consult the staff of various archival departments and examine their resources; I also traveled to the summer resort region in Upper Austria in order to get some idea of what the Rat Man saw there. Complementing my archival research, I read all substantial psychoanalytic commentary on the Rat Man in English, French, and German. Soon I became aware, to my surprise, that no one previously had made a thorough analysis of the differences between Freud's process notes and their final composition in the case history. Gradually a host of questions began to confront me. How reliable was Strachey's chronological table of the Rat Man's life? How faithful was his translation of Freud's report? Did he give an accurate description of what he chose not to translate—namely, the first third of Freud's daily notes on the Rat Man? How well did Freud's comments on the Rat Man conform to external evidence? To what extent was there internal inconsistency and even intentional confabulation in Freud's case history of the Rat Man?

In addition to answering these questions, my research has enabled me to identify the Rat Man and to bring forward new documentation about his family and his own academic, military, and professional life; to discover, on two pages of the *Minutes of the*

Vienna Psychoanalytic Society, a hitherto undetected commentary by Freud on his patient; and to adduce further evidence that two dreams in *The Interpretation of Dreams* belong to the Rat Man. I hope I have also made contributions to the history, theory, and practice of psychoanalysis in general and in particular, to the clinical understanding of obsessional neurosis, the appreciation of the creative genius of Freud as clinician and writer, the psychoanalytic comprehension of the Rat Man, and the contemporary explorations of translation, reading, and semiotics. In many ways the set piece of my book is the session in which the Rat Man tried to describe the rat torture, a scene I analyze from the angle of Freud's overdetermined technique (chapter 4) and overdetermined exposition (chapter 7).

My ultimate aim is not to write a book on the Rat Man that will be accepted as a terminus ad quem but rather to present a discussion that will incite readers to return to the original text and study Freud for themselves. I am convinced that we are very far from grasping many textual implications in reading Freud. That said, two preliminary comments about my study are in order. First, even when supplemented by other documentation, Freud's texts about the Rat Man remain often intriguingly incomplete; that circumstance prevents me in the biographical chapter 1 from elaborating on many points, such as the sequel of a childhood attempt to maim a sibling, a painful amatory rejection, and the identification of a life-saving confidant. On another score, I should add that since the use of Freud's correspondence is incidental in my study, I have for the convenience of the unilingual English reader referred to the readily available received translations. Nevertheless, I have of course checked them against the originals, and in a few necessary instances I have supplied modifications.

The initial crucial factor in my research consisted in obtaining and examining a copy of Freud's process notes, for they start off by mentioning the Rat Man's real name and age. Having this basic identification, I then explored various archival sources and sought the aid of so many informative people. It is now a wonderful pleasure to reexpress my gratitude to Ms. Susan Rotter of the Israelitische Kultusgemeinde in Vienna, and to the staff of the Österreichischer Rechtsanwaltskammertag, Archiv der Universität Wien, Österreichisches Staatsarchiv—Kriegsarchiv, Salzburger Museum Carolino Augusteum, Ausschuss der Steiermärkischen Rechtsanwaltskammer in Graz, Magistrat der Stadt Wien (Wiener Stadt- und Landesarchiv), Stadtamt Leoben, and Rollettmuseum der Stadtgemeinde Baden. I am also grateful for the kind assistance of Dr. Kurt Eissler, Dr. Hanns Jäger-Sunstenau, Mrs. Claire Wittkower, and Dr. George Canisius, director of the Austrian Trade Commission in Montreal. Dr. Abraham Freedman's extended commentary on chapters 2 and 4 remains a memorable gesture of thoughtfulness and generosity.

I happily thank Ms. Gladys Topkis, Cecile Watters, and Cynthia Wells of Yale University Press for the especial editorial scrutiny they intelligently devoted to each chapter. Last but not least, I am indebted to Drs. Darius Ornston, Otto Kernberg, and Pierrette Senay, who also read the entire manuscript and gave me invaluable counsel, so much more cherished for the kindnesses gracing its transmission.

Freud and the Rat Man

1

Erratic Design

It is Vienna, 1878. In Brücke's laboratory Freud is conducting zoological research. After five years of study he is still not a medical doctor—as a matter of fact he will take the exceptional period of another three years before receiving the title. Meanwhile the young Freud is plunging into the evolutionary debate; he has already finished two zoological papers justifying the stand that low animal life gradually evolves into higher forms; significantly, a third paper has announced his personal discovery of testes in the mature male eel, an uncanny harbinger of the revelation of sexual concealments among humans in the decades ahead. Two other events in Freud's life in 1878 interest us. We learn that the three brothers of Gisela Fluss, Freud's adolescent love, arrive in Vienna and stir up the feelings of our wistful hero. Next, we place ourselves on August 6 alongside Wilhelm Knöpfmacher as he opens an envelope from Freud. In gratitude for a loan, which he quickly repaid, Freud forwarded to his benefactor two published articles of his own, including the one on the eel's testes. Turning to the accompanying letter, our eyes fix on Freud's remarks about money and his growing preference for operating on animals rather than on humans:

Dear Friend
   It is unfair of you to jeer at my haste. The filthy lucre runs through my fingers at such frightening speed that, with the honest man's fear of failing in my duties, I was trying to place

2 Erratic Design

my riches in your safe-keeping. By doing this today the proverbial weight is taken off my mind.

I thank you for the friendly way in which you helped me out of my embarrassment. If there is a God He will take note of your deed and repay you a thousandfold. . . . During these holidays I have moved into another laboratory, where I am preparing myself for my real profession: "flaying of animals or torturing of human beings," and I find myself more and more in favour of the former. (Freud, 1960, p. 24)

Again the scene shifts. We are still in 1878 but in another part of Vienna. There a certain male baby is born. The future will see him procrastinating over and constantly struggling with the daily decisions of life—it will take him the unusual time of five years after finishing his courses in law, or ten years in all, before he finally obtains his doctor juris in 1907. In that year, after reading some psychoanalytic writing, he will go to see its author and eventually mention a Gisela Fluss, a name followed in Freud's notes of the day by three exclamation marks. With Freud we listen to his patient's complaint that he is plagued by irrational obsessions—he's a rat, babies are rats, rats are both the biting tormentors and the victims. He even bestializes Freud's announced fee into the reflection, kept silent for months afterwards, "So many florins, so many rats." The patient goes on to talk about his parents, his beloved "lady," his undescended testicle, and his immoderate fears of castration. Freud's operation will be a delicate one: to extract the rat and save the other party.

Let us now go back and gather up the scattered information on the life history of the Rat Man, the subject of Freud's "Notes on a Case of Obsessional Neurosis," which came out of the printer's shop in mid-1909. Naturally Freud's publication did not contain his patient's real name, which may now be revealed for the first time—Dr. Ernst Lanzer. This native Viennese began his life on January 22, 1878, in a household already populated with three children. Three more were to follow. By the time Ernst's parents, Heinrich and Rosa, had their last child, they were respectively sixty-one and forty-two.[1] The comforts of a middle-class standing were not sufficient to prevent the paterfamilias from raising his hands in despair with the arrival of each new child. But burdened though they were, the parents enjoyed a reportedly very happy marriage. Rosa had come from an impoverished family and was subsequently adopted by her distant cousins, the rich Saborskys, who nevertheless raised her rather harshly. Also born into a family of limited means, Heinrich had previously courted a "penniless" woman, whom he left for his cousin and future wife. Upon their union, he was taken into the large industrial concern of the Saborskys—a financial advantage that Rosa would not let him forget for years afterward.

Although head of a Jewish family, Heinrich apparently did not practice his religion in a formal sense and did not particularly resist assimilation. His character was a mixture of impulsiveness, self-assertion, unpretentiousness, and a happy-go-lucky quality. Once, as a noncommissioned officer, he had spent some of his unit's funds on gambling, and if it were not for economic assistance from one of his disgruntled companions, he would have been in a perilous position with his superiors. True to character, he often attempted to institute sound fiscal policies in his own home but usually soon abandoned them. He was generous by nature, even to the point of secretly paying the rent of his first lodger. "By all accounts," Freud emphasizes, "our patient's father was a most excellent man . . . distinguished by a hearty sense of humour and a kindly tolerance towards his fellow-men." In consequence, we are not surprised to hear Ernst saying that he and

---

1. Henceforth I shall use the real names of Ernst's siblings in place of Strachey's pseudonyms, which are indicated in parentheses: Hedwig (Hilde); Camilla (Katherine); Gertrud (Gerda); Rosalie (Constanze); Robert (Hans); Olga (Julie). Similarly, Dr. Palatzer (Dr. Springer); Lieutenant David (Lieutenant A); Dr. Jacob Freundlich (Bob St.); Fräuleins Rudolf (Peter) and Paula (Lina); Saborsky (Rubensky).

his father were each other's best friend. And with Ernst we may want to remember the story of how once, when heavy snow prevented the train from entering Pressburg, his father mustered out shovels to Jews, who cleared the market area to which they were ordinarily forbidden entry. When the officer in charge of the commissariat congratulated Heinrich for the well-executed task, the latter stalwartly retorted: "You rotter! You call me 'old comrade' now because I have helped you, but you treated me very differently in the past."

A certain down-to-earthness in Heinrich's character had its appealing and unappealing sides within his family. To his grown-up children he forthrightly and good-naturedly owned up to his failures and misfortunes in life. Yet Ernst was embarrassed by his father's simple, soldierly personality and his lack of education, such as his mixing the words for "layman" (*Laie*) and "tepid male" (*Laue*). Heinrich also annoyed his wife by his habits of breaking wind and using words like "arse" and "shit." And he occasionally responded to the naughtiness of his children impulsively and with severe punishment. One such occasion occurred around the time of his daughter Camilla's fatal illness: while being beaten by his father, Ernst hurled back the triadic insult "You lamp! You towel! You plate!" Shaken by the vocalized fury of his son, Heinrich stopped beating him and pronounced: "The child will be either a great man or a great criminal."[2] On other occasions, though, Ernst would only recede before his father's anger.

In the Lanzer home there seems to have been abundant verbalization—let us bear in mind that individual households, like historical epochs and cultural regions, differ in their prolixity and taciturnity. The verbalization of the Lanzers, moreover, tended to the exclamatory sort. An interesting indication of this stems from Ernst's seeing a performance of *Die Meistersinger von*

---

2. Reflecting in a footnote upon the father's having omitted a third and more common outcome of such forceful passions, Freud unforgettably adds, "a neurosis."

Nürnberg. In the first act of Wagner's comic opera, a familiar dramatic device is used when the name of Albrecht Dürer's painting *David* is exclaimed; that happens also to be the name of a ridiculed personage, who unexpectedly responds to the call of his name. Ernst went home, described the humorous scene, and thereafter used the David motif as a laughable exclamation in his family. This joined "On my soul" and "I swear on my soul," emotional utterances that were repeatedly heard at home. Heinrich Lanzer's good-humored conversation also contributed to the animated family atmosphere. It must be said, however, that Ernst tended not to say much to his mother.

As a budding sensualist, the four- or five-year-old Ernst begged his governess, Fräulein Rudolf, to be allowed under her dress to cry; upon her assent, he fingered her genitals. At six, he "always suffered" from erections, and from that time onward, he had the feeling that his parents could read his thoughts—he explained this by supposing that he spoke them aloud without hearing them himself. An early and persistent wish to see girls naked set in along with the uncanny feeling that something might happen as a result, such as his father dying. Then, in addition to more sexual experiences with Fräulein Paula, a succeeding governess, there came an unforgettable experience in the already plightful life of our growing protagonist. One evening he and his younger brother, Robert, were in the company of the female domestics—the governess, the cook, and another servant girl. Suddenly Ernst caught the governess's sexually humiliating comparison: "It could be done with the little one; but Ernst is too clumsy, he would be sure to miss it." Ernst did not clearly understand the meaning, but he grasped enough to cry and remember his crying. Pertinently, at the age of eight, when Ernst started school, his jealousy toward his more handsome brother, Robert, took the form of an ocular punishment: he loaded his toy gun and pulled the trigger as Robert compliantly looked in the barrel.

I have not forgotten Mrs. Lanzer, but the truth is that very little information is given of her, necessitating measured use of the available evidence. The fact that she figured in the "greatest fright" of our young hero is hardly accidental: as Ernst was running with a stuffed bird taken from his mother's hat, the wings suddenly moved, giving testimony to the terrified boy that the dead could return to life. As part and parcel of a number of impressionable episodes dealing with the rectum and feces, he was content to be a "dirty pig"; on one occasion he asked his mother to wash his "arse," only to be saved by her from his infuriated father. Ernst in turn was also offended by his mother's eructations[3] and grew up to be meticulously overclean; he became all the more piqued by his mother's economical excuses for her refusal to bathe and thus control the foul odors coming from her genitals because of an abdominal disorder. There was likewise from this early time a memory of seeing worms in his cousin's stool.

As an adolescent, Ernst was lastingly pained by an older male companion who befriended him strictly for the purpose of gaining access to the Lanzer home so as to court one of the daughters. The utilitarian relationship affronted Ernst's moral sensibility, much as had his father's economically motivated marriage. When the twelve-year-old Ernst was "platonically" in love with a small girl, he was plagued by the return of the obsessional wish that his sexual prohibitor, his father, would die. Up to the age of fourteen or fifteen Ernst was devoutly religious; some time around

---

3. After the mention of eructation, Strachey's translation continues: Ernst "could not eat on account of his parents" (p. 296). This is a misreading of *Eltern* (parents) for *Ekel* (disgust)—cf. Hawelka's edition, p. 190, a reading I have corroborated in my own photocopy of Freud's manuscript; thus we should understand that Ernst directs his hostility toward his mother alone. From now on, a simple indication of a page number without further identification will automatically mean a reference to Strachey's version of the Rat Man in the *Standard Edition*, vol. 10; when that page number is followed by a slash and another page number, I am then referring to the counterpart passage in the *Gesammelte Werke* (*G.W.*), vol. 7. I shall use a simple *H* to indicate a reference to Hawelka's edition.

the end of that period, he focused his sexual expression on looking and on periodic masturbation.

In 1897 the nineteen-year-old Ernst enrolled in the standard four-year course in the University of Vienna's Law Faculty, but little did the new student know the drastic events that were awaiting him. The next year his family employed an affection-starved dressmaker; she asked Ernst if he was fond of her and, not having received an assuring reply, killed herself; had he given an affirmative answer, Ernst omnipotently thought, he could have prevented her suicide. At around the same period he met Gisela Adler, a slightly younger cousin, with whom he would carry on an indecisive and tormenting courtship for twelve years before finally marrying her. Cousin or not, Heinrich Lanzer found the poor and sickly girl an unsuitable match for his son and counseled him not to make a fool of himself. The rebuked student, financially constrained like most students then and now, silently thought, "My father's death might make me rich enough to marry her."

In the following year an event occurred that would have lifelong, even posthumous, consequences for Ernst: Gisela, his "revered lady," underwent an ovariectomy. If Ernst blurred the fact that it was bilateral, he clearly recalled his jealousy when he was visiting Gisela in a sanatorium and a young doctor on rounds reached his inspecting hand under her bedclothes. As if he were living in a dream, the same year also fulfilled a wish: Heinrich Lanzer died on July 20. Ernst reacted in two ways, by resuming masturbation and by denying his father's death. For instance, on hearing a good joke, he would reflect, "I must tell Father that;" and on hearing a knock at the door, he would often think, "Here comes Father." Ernst was not yet disturbed in his study habits, however, and could organize his life well in some respects. In September he took and passed the first of three state examinations that were prerequisites to admission into civil service. He voluntarily entered the army two days later in order to satisfy the year's military service that was obligatory for university students.

Ernst Lanzer's performance in the Third Regiment of the Tyrolean Riflemen of the Imperial Army is a matter of record. His military dossier of 1900 contains this humdrum march of laudatory terms:

> Quiet, serious [ernst], very diligent character, good intellectual gifts with like comprehension. Conforms to the requirements of his official position, and leads his section decisively and also independently both in fighting and in formation, and is skilled in train service [*im Fahrdienste gewandt*], orients himself well in the terrain. Reliable and smart behavior on the front, well instructed in the matters of weapons and firearms, can use his knowledge practically, shoots fairly well, . . . eager and industrious, . . . obedient and ready toward his superiors. Very friendly and companionable with his equals. And suitable by his good influence on subordinates.

Elsewhere the same year's record reads that Lanzer had a satisfactory knowledge of French and special aptitudes in swimming and stenography. On September 30, 1900, Lanzer was promoted to corporal (*Oberjäger*) and transferred to the reserves. The only other noteworthy events at the turn of the century were his return to the university and Gisela's memorable rejection of him.

The narrative thickens. In 1901, Ernst was overtaken "for good" by obsessions. They were occasioned by a visit of condolence to his uncle in January, upon the death of his aunt. The visit had originally promised to be a customary one: in his family Ernst had won the name of "carrion crow" for his habit of going to funerals and manifesting the deepest sympathies to bereaved relatives. Alas, things were to be lastingly different after this call. At one point the widowed uncle lamented, "I lived for this woman alone, whereas other men amuse themselves elsewhere." Reflecting on his uncle's words a few days later, Ernst thought that they were hinting at his own father's conjugal infidelity. This plunged him into a whirlwind of reactions: self-reproach for having criminally overslept, so that he was not at his father's deathbed during the last moments; hostility toward his unfaithful father; and obsessive attempts to undo the fact of his father's death. When summer came, the beleaguered Ernst went on the first of the triennial maneuvers required by his new reserve status. Unlike the previous year, this time he shot "less well" (*minder gut*) and was found on examination to be shortsighted, a detail with powerful implications later in our story.

When Ernst finished his eighth and final semester in the spring of 1902, he could not relax. On one hand, he had to prepare for the third state examination, which would finally qualify him to be a civil servant; on the other hand, he was plunged into fearful jealousy by the arrival of Richard, Gisela's uncle from New York. Meanwhile Ernst developed a most unusual ritual. Between midnight and one in the morning he would interrupt his studies, open the front door for his father's ghost, return inside, turn on a great deal of light, strip, and look at his penis in the mirror for the reassurance of some degree of erection. He sometimes put an extra mirror between his legs.

He left Vienna for the more relaxed yet spectacular landscape around Gmunden in Upper Austria. In some purported connection with his abiding jealousy there arose a compulsion to take the examination in July, but upon the advice of his confidant, Dr. Palatzer, Ernst postponed taking it until October. Eventually Gisela joined him in the country, only to be called away to care for her ailing nonagenarian grandmother. Left alone, Ernst lost several weeks of study;[4] on one occasion, thinking of the command to take the examination in October, he suddenly thought to him-

---

4. In Strachey's translation we read that Lanzer "once lost several weeks owing to the absence of the lady" (p. 259). The "once" is not only an unnecessary insertion (H, p. 90) but also gives the impression that Gisela's absence occurred at some time other than the summer at Gmunden alluded to in the context.

self, "But if you received a command to cut your throat, what then?" He felt at once that the command was already given, and as he hastened to fetch a straight-edged razor, he reflected, "No, it's not so simple as that. You must go and kill the old woman." Thereupon, beside himself with horror, he fell to the ground. As surprising as it may sound, when October came, Ernst did pass, completing the three state examinations relatively rapidly. The year, however, ended badly, with Ernst again seeking out his confidant and telling his self-reproaches.

Continuing his quick pace, in January Ernst successfully took the first of the three Rigorosa, which were requisites for the doctorate in law.[5] But in February the death of an uncle, to whom he was actually indifferent, precipitated him into despair, suicidal wishes, and fresh self-reproach for having slept through his father's final moments. His ability to concentrate declined in the spring: for periods of eight to ten days he would be overtaken by an acute obsession to perform a self-inculpating act; the obsession then went away for a short while until its next abrupt appearance. The evening prior to his departure in June for the Mondsee-Unterach region, Gisela, accompanied by Richard, paid him a visit. That happenstance plus something Gisela said made Ernst feel disowned.

The summer of 1903 proved disastrous, marked by compulsions to cut his throat, jump over a precipice, and run recklessly in the hot sun. One day, as he was crossing the Mondsee, he began asking himself what he could do for his father; he then thought of jumping into the water so that no harm could come to the dead parent. On another occasion the memory of having called Gisela a whore drove him into the charming St. Bartholomew's Church in Unterach. At the sight, in the nave, of three impressive stained-glass windows, dedicated in 1900 for a three-hundredth jubilee,

---

5. Hawelka mistakenly confuses the state examination and the Rigorosa. The Rigorosa are strictly of an academic nature, being steps on the way toward obtaining a doctoral degree.

he fell to his knees and summoned up pious feelings and resolutions about immortality. In the company of her attentive uncle Richard, Gisela went to Unterach;[6] she took the opportunity to tell Ernst that he had misunderstood her words in June to mean she was disowning him, whereas her words had been intended to prevent him from behaving like a fool in public. Ernst was satisfied with her explanation, but not for long. On the day of Gisela's departure from Unterach, he found a stone on the road over which her carriage was destined to pass. He removed the stone but later, judging his action as absurd, replaced the dangerous object. That is not all. After she left, he fell victim to a compulsion to understand, as if every syllable were an invaluable treasure, and he kept asking, "What was it just said?" But every repetition sounded different to him and left him discontented. The summer past, we are hardly astonished to learn that he failed his second Rigorosum in October.

The next few years saw a considerable slackening in Ernst's studies; his promotion to lieutenant in the reserves; his first coitus, at age twenty-six; his mother's plan that he marry another woman; and two isolated employments (according to available records). He also went to Munich for hydrotherapy, although its only benefit, he opined, was that it led to regular sexual intercourse with a waitress; subsequent to one of those experiences, he pertinently reflected, "This is a glorious feeling! One might do anything for this—murder one's own father, for instance." Ernst was also immersed in long prayers which, subjected to the influence of his stenographic practice, were anagrammatically reduced to *Glejisamen*, a neologism referring to Gisela and *Samen* (sperm). In other words, while ostensibly rattling off his anagrammatic prayer, Ernst was masturbating with Gisela's image in his mind. Two other events merit mention, although they can-

---

6. That Richard accompanied her is clearer in the original German than in Strachey's translation (188/411).

not be placed in a definite sequence. To add to Ernst's amatory anguish, Gisela took off with Richard on a trip to the United States. And second, among the various doctors whom Ernst consulted was none other than the future Nobelist Wagner-Jauregg. When the distinguished doctor heard about Ernst's compulsion to take an examination at an early date but without sufficient preparation, he exclaimed approvingly, "What a salutary obsession!" In critically reporting this interview to Freud, Ernst maintained that any compulsion of whatever cast was detestable and unhealthy.

Finally we arrive at the climax of our narrative, 1907. Upon passing the third Rigorosum in July, our hero won his long-sought doctorate degree, an academic success offset by another period of coolness with Gisela. Then, starting on August 11, Lieutenant Lanzer went on the ill-fated maneuvers that attended the outbreak of his most irrational behavior. The matter described in the upcoming pages is all the more bizarre in light of Lanzer's contemporary military records, which contain this evaluation of his private conduct: "Companionable; very sensible and modest toward his superiors; tactful and helpful to his inferiors."

During military exercises in Galicia (currently part of Poland), the obsessions of Lieutenant Lanzer broke out in their brightest flare and lasted for the better part of a week. It all began one afternoon during a halt in maneuvers when Captain Nemeczek, a fellow officer with a manifest fondness for cruelty, described a horrible Oriental punishment entailing the use of rats. In Lanzer's mind, the captain was linked with Lieutenant D. of the same regiment, who was Gisela's stepfather; the latter liked to say "I will shoot you," and it was in his presence that Lanzer saw a rat. In all likelihood, Captain Nemeczek got his cruel story from a pornographic best-seller of the day, Octave Mirbeau's *The Garden of Tortures*. Since Lanzer was ultimately branded with the name "Rat Man" because of his account of that torture, we might listen to part of it.

A Chinese professional torturer tells of his preferred device in a way that tauntingly increases the excitement in one of his listeners (within two months, the Rat Man will show both horror and pleasure in trying to describe the dreadful scene to Freud):

> You take a man, as young and strong as possible, whose muscles are very resistant. . . . you strip him. . . . you make him kneel down on the ground and bend over his back, and secure him in chains which are fixed onto iron collars that fit tightly on his wrists, ankles, and the back of his neck and knees. . . . Then in a big pot you put a very big rat that's been deprived of food for a couple of days in order to stimulate its ferocity. And this pot with this rat inside you apply hermetically like an enormous cupping glass onto the prisoner's buttocks, with the help of strong straps attached to a leather belt going around his loins. . . . You introduce into the hole of the pot an iron rod, reddened at the fire of a forge. The rat wants to flee the burning of the rod and its dazzling light. . . . It panics, scrambles about, jumps and leaps, circles the walls of the pot, crawls and gallops on the man's buttocks, which it first tickles and then tears with its feet and bites with its sharp teeth . . . looking for an exit through the rummaged bleeding skin. . . . The great merit in this is that one must know how to prolong this initial operation as long as possible. . . . It can even happen that the sufferer becomes crazy. . . . The rat penetrates . . . and it dies, suffocated, at the same time as the victim who, after a half-hour of unutterable incomparable tortures, ends, he too, by succumbing to a hemorrhage. . . . it's extremely beautiful![7]

The story gnawed into our subject, deciding his fate: to be caged in a name horrifying to Homo sapiens. The Rat Man be-

---

7. It was Shengold (1971) who traced the torture narrative to Mirbeau's novel; the translation is mine.

lieved that this torture was happening to his beloved father and "revered lady," and then resorted to his usual apotropaic device, a "but" accompanied by a repudiating gesture followed by the phrase "whatever are you thinking of?" He also had the illusion that the ground was heaving in front of him, as if there were a rat under it—an illusion bound up with an early visit to his father's grave, when he imagined that a nearby rat had just fed off his father. There was more. In the course of his recital, the captain said the rectal punishment should be applied to some members of Parliament. Then, immediately after the Rat Man privately feared that Gisela's name might be mentioned, the captain referred to the political figure Dr. Adler (Gisela's surname!). The Rat Man felt destiny closing in, but he would have felt it even more had he known that the political leader and Freud were former friends and also that the prior tenant of Freud's apartment on Berggasse was the same Dr. Adler!

The other story beginning with the afternoon halt is more difficult to follow because of its tortuosity. Lanzer's dazed state along with the craziness of his actions obliged the alert Freud to listen to the recital three times before he could make any clear sense of it. The start of the story is simple enough: Lieutenant Lanzer had lost his pince-nez and wired his optician in Vienna to forward another pair by the next post. A day and a half later, the "cruel" captain transmitted the glasses to Ernst, saying in good faith that the postal charges had to be reimbursed to Lieutenant David, the military supervisor of the post office. The name triggered in Lanzer various associations about his own family.

(At this point we should be aware of the following intricacy. The "cruel" captain was actually ignorant of the fact that Lieutenant David had recently been transferred to another village and accordingly had handed over his billet near the post office to his successor, Lieutenant B. On the other hand, several hours before he heard the captain's mistaken report, Lanzer had learned that it was the trusting lady at the post office who had paid the postage required on the glasses' delivery. But Lanzer had suppressed this all-important episode to himself as he did also to Freud for a while; hence, instead of the post office lady, Lieutenant B. became his creditor.)

Immediately Lanzer thought that he must not pay back the money or else rats would anally penetrate his father and Gisela, and he uttered to himself: "You must pay back the 3.80 kronen to Lieutenant David." Eventually Lanzer met Lieutenant David, who promptly said that the financial matter should rather be settled with Lieutenant B., the present supervisor of the post office. Thrown into perplexity, Lanzer took an afternoon nap, during which he conjured up a way of carrying out his now obsolete vow: he would go to the post office with both lieutenants, David would give the post office lady the money, she in turn would give it to B., and Lanzer himself would then pay another 3.80 kronen to David. Later Lanzer drummed up a new and maddening plan, which enlisted his familiarity with train service (did he serve in the military as a *Fahrdienstleiter*, or stationmaster?): with the maneuvers ended, he had some time available before the departure of the night train for Vienna. He would use the time to take an hour's trip from the train station at Przemyśl to go and persuade David to return with him to Przemyśl and from there take a six-hour trip to the post office in order that the haunting oath might be fulfilled. Returning to a poor, interested servant girl at a local inn was also part of the bargain. Instead of executing that intention, however, Lanzer took the train to Vienna—but not without anguish, for he was tempted at the first several stops to go back and execute his mad plan. Dizzied by the rat race of his obsessions, he finally resolved to continue on to Vienna, discuss the whole affair with his confidant Dr. Palatzer for a half hour, and then catch the night train back to Przemyśl and continue the maze.

But that plan too was abandoned, for the meeting with his confidant occurred later than anticipated. As chance would have it, when the desired meeting did materialize, Palatzer was not alone but in the company of an acquaintance whom he introduced as "Dr. *Ratz*enstein"! Afterward Palatzer calmed Lanzer down, so that he had a good night's sleep, and together the next morning they sent off the 3.80 kronen to the post office near the maneuver site. In view of the fact that Lanzer still possessed 50,000 kronen out of the 59,000 he had inherited in 1901, he could have bought some thirteen thousand pairs of glasses. Yet losing perspective, as is the obsessional's wont, he anguishingly made a mountain out of a molecular sum.

The story gathers momentum. Lanzer left his friend to return to his family in Brühl on the outskirts of Vienna; there the excruciating doubts came back. First he thought of seeing a doctor who would formally certify that the patient's mental recovery necessitated repayment of the sum to Lieutenant David; surely the officer would submit to such a medical request. Then Lanzer's eyes fell upon one of a series of books lent him by a neighbor—Freud's *Psychopathology of Everyday Life,* a book whose title and contents prompted Lanzer in labyrinthine ways; among other things, Lanzer believed that its author was the brother of a murderer named Freud. Neither was it accidental that the patient (whose first name, Ernst, means "serious" in German) was driven to consult someone whose cognomen signifies "joy" in German. Let us picture the unfortunate as he entered the waiting room of Berggasse 19 on October 1, 1907: a serious young man, aged twenty-nine, five foot five (nearly three inches shorter than Freud), knock-kneed (*Kniebohrer*), with black hair, brown eyes, a sharp nose, and an oval chin.

Freud had various reasons to be well disposed toward the obsessive reserve officer and doctor of law who, in spite of his inner confusion and torment, gave the impression during consultation of being a "clear-headed and shrewd person." In the previous year Freud himself had written the first psychoanalytic treatise on the establishment of guilt in law (in the course of his exposition he drew on Jung's theory of complexes, which was also to figure as an explanation in the future case history of the Rat Man). We can be sure that Freud perked up his ears when the prospective patient remarked that his obsessional ideas affected his professional work only in the area of criminal law. Our own attention is further caught by a pair of omissions from the public record of that first hour. When Freud announced his fee, the Rat Man thought to himself, "So many florins, so many rats"—hence silently associating to psychoanalysis a multiplicity of rats far exceeding the number torturing his father and his lady. In another thought, this time voiced aloud, the Rat Man decided first of all to consult his mother, a fact that Freud in his turn suppressed in his case history.

The analysis, described by Freud as lasting nearly a year, seemingly bore fruit. Starting in April 1908, Dr. Lanzer was in almost continuous employment; part of this professional experience included approximately two years in the prestigious office of Dr. August Libitsky, an authority in international private law. In 1909 Lanzer finally became engaged to his revered Gisela, whom he married the following year. In 1913, having acquired the stipulated six years of apprenticeship, he became a formally qualified attorney—a laurel not to be long enjoyed, for the rest of the history is unremittingly sad. In August 1914, Dr. Lanzer was activated into the army and on November 21 was taken prisoner by the Russians. His death date four days later was officially established and proclaimed only in September 1919. With good cause we may speculate whether the proclamation contributed to the death of Lanzer's mother two months later. A government pension hardly alleviated the fate of sickly Gisela, who never remarried and, in 1933 at the age of fifty-four, died of chronic inflammation of the joints, progressive polyarthritis, and bronchopneumonia.

It is time for us to stop and consider how Dr. Ernst Lanzer

under his alias has figured so exceptionally in the history of psychoanalysis. The instances of exceptionality are many. The Rat Man case stands by general agreement as the single successful therapy that was directly treated and then written up by Freud. It was also Freud's major exposition of obsessional neurosis, the first of the major case histories to have an adult male as subject, and the only one for which we have process notes showing the form and timing of Freud's interpretations. Of all Freud's published cases, it was the Rat Man who had the best, perhaps the only genuine, therapeutic alliance. This positive element certainly had a bearing on the fact that Freud lectured on this patient more than on any other, thereby making him the subject of the prototypical continuous case history. The Rat Man was also the subject of Freud's most spellbinding oral performance, which itself had the double inaugural distinction of being the opening presentation of the First International Psychoanalytic Congress. Jones, one of the earwitnesses, voiced this remembrance:

> [Freud] described the analysis of an obsessional case, one which afterwards we used to refer to as that of "The Man with the Rats." He sat at the end of a long table along the sides of which we were gathered and spoke in his usual low but distinct conversational tone. He began at the Continental hour of eight in the morning and we listened with rapt attention. At eleven he broke off, suggesting we had had enough. But we were so absorbed that we insisted on his continuing, which he did until nearly one o'clock. Someone who can hold an audience engrossed for five hours must have something very worthwhile to say. What riveted us, however, was not only the novelty of what he had to tell us, but also his extraordinary gift for orderly presentation. (Jones, 1955, p. 42)

What they gathered around Freud to hear we today have the privilege of reading: a masterpiece unsurpassed for its delineation of the complex phenomenology of obsessional processes.

Erratic Design 19

There is yet another story to be told, one that reverberated throughout Freud's analysis of the Rat Man and then lapsed into obscurity until this day. In some ways, Freud's encountering the Rat Man is a Viennese version of Sophocles' drama pitting Oedipus against the Sphinx. To trace this filiation, we may start with a letter in which Freud uses the Sophoclean drama in describing an obsessional patient to Jung: "He is a highly gifted individual, an Oedipus type, loves his mother, hates his father (the original Oedipus was himself a case of obsessional neurosis—the riddle of the Sphinx)" (Freud, 1974a, p. 33). Elsewhere Freud spells out that the riddle of the Sphinx concerns that fundamental question exercising the child's mind, the origin of babies. The question

> is usually started by the unwelcome arrival of a small brother or sister. It is the oldest and most burning question that confronts immature humanity. Those who understand how to interpret myths and legends can detect it in the riddle which the Theban Sphinx set to Oedipus. The customary answers given to the child in the nursery damage his genuine instinct of research and as a rule deal the first blow, too, at his confidence in his parents. (Freud, 1907b, pp. 135–36; see also 1905d, p. 195; 1909a, p. 133; and 1916–17, p. 318)

In the light of the foregoing, we are led to think of Freud as Oedipus, who sought to explain to mankind the psychological riddles concerning the birth of children. Lest this titular identification seem too forced or glib, we may heed how Freud, in a unique moment of bewildered and uncanny feeling, avowed his fantasy of fame in being a victor over the Sphinx. To honor Freud's fiftieth birthday, some of his followers presented him with a medallion with his engraved portrait on one side and on the reverse a design of Oedipus surrounded by the words closing Sophocles' immortal play: "Who knew the famous riddles and was a man most mighty." We follow Jones for the rest of the eerie story:

> At the presentation of the medallion there was a curious incident. When Freud read the inscription he became pale and agitated and in a strangled voice demanded to know who had thought of it. He behaved as if he had encountered a *revenant*, and so he had. After Federn told him it was he who had chosen the inscription Freud disclosed that as a young student at the University of Vienna he used to stroll around the great arcaded court inspecting the busts of former famous professors of the institution. He then had the phantasy, not merely of seeing his own bust there in the future, which would not have been anything remarkable in an ambitious student, but of its actually being inscribed with the *identical* words[8] he now saw on the medallion. (Jones, 1955, p. 14)

Freud, the compulsive Oedipus, on center stage. Did he not characterize himself as being of the obsessional type (Freud, 1974a, p. 82)? It undoubtedly was a self-knowing Freud who stated, "Obsessional neurosis is unquestionably the most interesting and repaying subject of analytic research" (1926, p. 113). Did he not, from the beginning to the end of his career, discuss obsessional neurosis more than any other pathology?

Enter the Rat Man, the Sphinx-like bearer of riddles, yet puzzled by his own anxiety, which was greatly associated with the phase of the anal sphincter. Sphinx, sphincter, anxiety—all these words in their Greek etymology are united in their respective meanings: strangler, that which constricts, pressing tightly. We see both Freud and his patient tightly drawn into a contest of

---

8. The verse merits quoting in the original, for it is the only statement on record that Freud read with unprecedented shock: ὃς τὰ κλείν' αἰνίγματ' ᾔδει καὶ κράτιστος ἦν ἀνήρ.

Rätsel, riddles[9] (the translation of the elided αἰνίγματα on the commemorative medallion!): a fated uncanniness at cultural and linguistic crossroads. In a later chapter we shall eavesdrop on a series of exchanges: Dr. Lanzer's proliferation of rats to entice guessing (*Erraten*); his disclosure of an anagrammatic riddle as an ambivalent attempt to ward off rats; and, finally, the engagement of Drs. Freud and Lanzer in *Rätselraten,* the guessing or doing of riddles—and, we might also say, turning the riddles outside in.

Our preliminary overview would be unsatisfactory without some remarks about the textuality of the Rat Man case, which indeed has had riddles of its own. Although the case history was published in 1909, Freud's private day-to-day notes (found among his posthumous papers) were published for the first time in 1955 in Strachey's *Standard Edition.* When one studies Strachey's annotated edition of these notes, the term *Standard* becomes more and more a glaring misnomer. Here, for example, is Strachey's rationale for his abridgement of the notes:

> Approximately the first third of the original record was reproduced by Freud almost *verbatim* in the published version. This covers the preliminary interview on October 1st, 1907, and the first seven sessions—that is, up to and including October 9th. . . . The alterations made by Freud were almost exclusively verbal or stylistic. . . . On the whole, the differences between the two versions do not seem to be of sufficient importance to justify the publication of this first part of the record. (10:254)

But the fact is that in his final rendition of the first seven sessions,

9. *Rätsel* and the adjective *rätselhaft* recur in different forms in the English translation: problem(s) (176/400, 210/430); puzzling (187/409, 240/456); unaccountable (193n/415n). Cf., for example, Freud's procedural declaration on page 210: "Obviously the first problem to be solved was why the two speeches of the Czech captain—his rat story and his request to the patient that he should pay back the money to Lieutenant A. [David]—should have had such an agitating effect."

Freud left out some 140 lines, or about five printed pages. It took another nineteen years after Strachey's edition for a complete text of the notes to be established by Elza Hawelka, a Continental psychoanalyst. Unfortunately for the English reader, the new text is a bilingual German-French edition. Editorially it is a classic, and it stands, apart from some correspondence, as *the only bibliographically competent publication that we have of Freud's writings at large and the case histories in particular.*

Another question concerns Strachey's translation, about which I shall say much more later on. Strachey laconically tells us that his translation for the *Standard Edition* in 1955 reprints "with considerable alterations" his original English version of the *Collected Papers of Sigmund Freud* in 1925. My thorough comparative examination of the two translations uncovered a slight shift to a more familiar language (*coitus* becomes *intercourse*, for example, and *osphresiolagnia* changes to *pleasure in smell*); several minor errors were also corrected, including the change from *Christian* name to the sociologically more appropriate *first* name (p. 160n.). Much more seriously and in keeping with his repeated tendency to crystallize Freud's ideas and mute their dynamic quality, Strachey departed from his previous rendering of *Bildungen* by *formations* and instead opted for the more static *structures* (see p. 221 and *n* and pp. 222–23).[10] This crystallization on the theoretical level is one with Strachey's formality of language and his distancing rhetorical posture, all of which have influenced the history of psychoanalysis and constitute a reading experience that differs from what we have when we read Freud in the original. In many contexts Strachey neutralized Freud's present tense by the more distanced past tense, replaced living idiom by scientific terms drawn from dead languages, and substituted the closeness in Freud's use of the first personal pronoun by the use of the

---

10. For my alertness to this feature, I am indebted to my friend Darius Ornston (1985), who has underlined it as Strachey's addition in his translation.

removed third person (cf. Freud's "our patient" and Strachey's "the patient": 162/388; 164–65/390; 200/421; 210/430).

I cannot forgo the opportunity to mention one instance, highly suggestive in itself, where Strachey strikingly belies the original text and makes Freud appear inconsistent when he was not. After describing how both the patient and his sickness pluck up their courage to "speak more plainly" during treatment, Freud resolves "to drop the metaphor" and express himself more plainly—a beautiful parallel between the resolution of the Rat Man's animal symptom and a localized evolution of Freud's scriptive exposition. Nonetheless, Strachey has Freud inconsistently continue in a visual metaphor that is not justified in the original German (I have placed the metaphorical addition in italics): "To drop the metaphor, what happens is that the patient, who has hitherto *turned his eyes* away in terror from his own pathological productions, begins to attend to them and obtains a clear and more detailed *view* of them (p. 223).[11] In contrast, the original German merely says "turned away" (*abgewendet*) and "in a more detailed way" (*ausführlicher*).

To draw a timely conclusion from all this: we would also profit from a psychoanalysis of Strachey's translations. In effect, we are confronted with the problem of not only how to read Freud but also how to read Strachey. Obviously there are issues at stake in Strachey's translation and in the Anglo-American receptivity to it that exist outside the "nonconflictual and scientific."

As I write these paragraphs one after another, I am increasingly aware that the detailed subject matter risks accumulating at an uncomfortable pace. To forestall that eventuality, I shall now lay out for convenient reference the tentative story of the Rat Man in tabular fashion. Even a brief pause at the chronologically ordered

---

11. The German text (p. 441) reads that the patient who "had turned away" (*abgewendet hatte*) from the perception of his pathological productions now begins to experience them "in a clearer and more detailed way" (*deutlicher und ausführlicher*).

24 Important Events in the Life of the Rat Man

table will lighten our burden as we journey through the mass of deeper material set forth in the chapters that follow.

Important Events in the Life of the Rat Man

Year	Age	Event
1878	—	Birth of Ernst on January 22. His parents are Heinrich Lanzer (born in Silesia on May 18, 1825) and Rosa Herlinger (born in Silesia on December 31, 1844). In the household there are already three other children: Hedwig (born December 10, 1870); Camilla (born April 15, 1872), and Rosalie (born February 17, 1874).
1879	1	Birth of Robert on June 14.
1880	2	Birth of Olga on November 26.
1881	3	Death of Camilla on August 24. (Strachey, p. 256, mistakenly dates the event as occurring some time between Ernst's fourth and fifth years). Rage against father (p. 265).
1882	4	Scene with Fräulein Rudolf (p. 160). Wets parents' bed and is beaten by father (p. 284). The stuffed-bird episode (p. 309).
1883	5	
1884	6	Erections around the age of six or seven (cf. pp. 161–62, 178). Obsessions about his father's death and feelings that his parents know his thoughts.
1886	8	Birth of Gertrud on January 11. Begins school (p. 184). Scene with Fräulein Paula around the age of eight or nine (p. 161). (Strachey's contention [p. 256] that Ernst got to know Gisela at this time is unjustifiable.)

Important Events in the Life of the Rat Man

1880	10	Sees worm in cousin's stool (p. 309).
1889	11	Saved by mother from father's severest chastisement; still a "dirty pig" (p. 286). Sexual enlightenment (p. 277).
1890	12	Mother's eructations (p. 296). In love with a young girl. Masturbation and obsessive wishes for his father's death (pp. 178, 181).
1891	13	Exhibits himself to Fräulein Paula (p. 279). Father's beating of Olga (p. 307).
1892	14	Homosexual scenes of looking (p. 315). Up to fourteen or fifteen, devoutly religious (p. 169). At fourteen or fifteen, deceived by friend who is interested only in sister (p. 159).
1893	15	Occasional masturbation (p. 158; but cf. his later
1894	16	denial about adolescent masturbation, p. 309).
1897	19	Enrolls in Law Faculty, University of Vienna.
1898	20	Suicide of rejected dressmaker (pp. 300, 317). Meets and falls in love with cousin Gisela Adler (p. 317; confirmation of the year occurs in a passage, omitted by Strachey, from the session of October 9, 1907—cf. H, p. 89). Gisela, a native Viennese, was born October 15, 1879. Hostile wishes about father's death (pp. 179, 181)—miscalculated by Freud (p. 179n1) as happening "ten years ago."
1899		Father's death on July 20. Ernst's enlistment in military service for one year, starting October 1. Resumption of masturbation (pp. 203, 261). Operation on Gisela (p. 317). Passes first state examination on September 29.
1900	21	Returns to university. Oath against masturbation (p. 302). Rejection of first proposal by Gisela (p. 274)—miscalculated by Freud (p. 194) as happening "ten years earlier."

26 Important Events in the Life of the Rat Man

1901   22   Death of aunt in January and extension of obsessions to include the afterlife (pp. 175, 235, 274–75; dated erroneously by Strachey [p. 257]). Permanent obsessions (p. 181).

1902   23   In spring, the eighth and final semester in Law Faculty. Disturbing arrival of Gisela's uncle Richard from New York (pp. 275–76). Fantasies of father's ghost (pp. 204, 222, 275). Summer in Gmunden—compulsions of running and counting (p. 259). Illness of Gisela's grandmother (pp. 187, 259; the previous year posited by Strachey [p. 255] is not justified). Passes the third state examination in October (p. 259; cf. the wrong date of 1903 on p. 269). Self-reproaches in December (pp. 300–01).

1903   24   Takes the first Rigorosum on January 22. Death of uncle to whom he is indifferent in February and fresh onset of self-reproaches (p. 300). Slack in his studies during spring (p. 302). Intensification of neurosis (p. 158; cf. also a passage from the session of October 5 omitted from Strachey's edition and cited in H, p. 72). Scene of jealousy in June toward Richard (p. 303). Summer in the Mondsee-Unterach region—suicidal ideation (p. 301). Gisela's second rejection (pp. 301, 305). Laying of stone to injure Gisela on her departure from Unterach (pp. 190, 307). Failure of the second Rigorosum on October 19.

1904   26   First coitus, in Trieste (p. 158).

1905   27   Passes the second Rigorosum on July 19. From July 27 to October 4 works in the office of Dr. Jacob Freundlich; marriage of the latter to Ernst's sister Olga on October 15. Mother's marriage plan.

Important Events in the Life of the Rat Man 27

1906	28	Works in government office in Salzburg from April 27 to October 4. Replacement of prayers by anagrammatic apotropaics (p. 260). In Munich, hydrotherapy and, during coitus, death thoughts against father (pp. 263–64).
1907	29	Passes the third Rigorosum and receives Doctor juris on July 17. Maneuvers in Galicia from August 11 to September 7. Consultation with Freud on October 1.
1908	30	Works in office of Dr. Alois Schick from April 4 to September 9; then returns to office of his brother-in-law, Dr. Freundlich, from October 1 to February 22 of the next year.
1909	31	Engaged to Gisela in October. From February 22 to January 27, 1911, works in office of Dr. August Libitzky.
1910	31	Marriage on November 8 in Tempelgasse Synagogue.
1911	32	In the central Austrian city of Leoben, works in office of Dr. Hermann Obermayer from February 4 to September 30 of the following year.
1912	33	Works in office of Dr. Ernst Ulmann from October 3 to January 27, 1913.
1913	34	Formally becomes *Rechtsanwalt* (attorney). Works in office of Dr. Heller.
1914	35	Activated in the military in August; taken prisoner by the Russians on November 21.
1919		Death date of November 25, 1914, officially proclaimed on September 9, 1919. Death of Lanzer's mother on November 25.
1933		Death of Gisela.

2

Taking Apart the Psychic Apparatus

I think we are in rats' alley
Where the dead men lost their bones.
—*T. S. Eliot,* The Waste Land, *II: A Game of*
Chess

Recently analysts have supplemented Freud's psychodynamic explanation in his case history in various ways. To name a few: analysts have made a nonselective use of the process notes; they have turned to the wider implications of the Rat Man's psychopathology; and they have accorded a greater place in his life to the role of women, especially his mother and his deceased sister, Camilla. To be sure, Freud was guided by his main design and hence tended to eliminate in his final version observations that were not pertinent, even though they bore on the patient's impaired development and inclusive pathology. Occasionally in the filtered text of the case history we come across an indulgence in a conceptual throwaway whose value, nonetheless, might exceed the rest of the page (the stray insight is a stimulating feature throughout Freud's writing).

As a matter of procedure, we shall first attend to Freud's general and specific comprehension of the Rat Man's obsessional neurosis in the case history where Freud, let us remember, was groping toward the satisfactory theoretical explanation still four years away. Here, then, was the oedipal framework in which Freud etiologically understood his patient:

Infantile masturbation reaches a kind of climax, as a rule, between the ages of three and four or five; and it is the clearest expression of a child's sexual constitution, in which the aetiology of subsequent neuroses must be sought. . . . The content of the sexual life of infancy consists in auto-erotic activity on the part of the dominant sexual components, in traces of object-love, and in the formation of that complex which deserves to be called *the nuclear complex of the neuroses*. . . . It is entirely characteristic of the nuclear complex of infancy that the child's father should be assigned the part of a sexual opponent and of an interferer with auto-erotic sexual activities. (pp. 202, 208n)

In the light of this general conception of infantile sexuality, Freud posited a reconstruction that combined a constitutional factor with a trauma restricted to one event. Prior to a general amnesia before the age of six, the hypothesis goes, the sexually awakened (p. 201) Ernst made "some one" (*irgend eine,* 205/426) misdemeanor connected with masturbation; the subsequent punishment by his father not only stopped the masturbation but also left behind "an ineradicable grudge."

Let us immediately note that this one traumatic event was never anamnestically ratified in the treatment, for the most Dr. Lanzer could do was to report a tale that was repeated in the family but the events of which he had forgotten. In particular, during the time of Camilla's fatal illness, Ernst had bitten someone, perhaps his nurse. While being punished for this naughtiness by his father, Ernst furiously berated him, a piece of bravado that made the "young libertine" ever afterward react in a cowardly and fearful way both to his own violence and others'; in addition, the strongly developed sadistic components of Ernst's love were subjected to "a premature and all too thorough suppression" (p. 240). As to the fact that the mother's account contained no explicitly sexual element, Freud offered two explanations: either

her censorship effaced the sexual material or there was no erotic meaning in the misdeed at all (p. 206 and *n*).

Curiously, however, and without bringing forth concrete evidence, Freud tells us that a deeper interpretation of his patient's dreams reveals that his sister's death as well as his sexual desires for her and his mother were intimately linked with his childhood misdemeanor and his father's chastisement (pp. 207*n*, 235)—the whole, moreover, showing the clearest traces of "a poetry which deserves to be called epic."[1] Although Freud had originally suggested that this constellation of experiences chronologically related to Ernst's infantile amnesia ending at six (pp. 160, 164–65, 183, 263), he later realized that Camilla's death occurred when the little boy was three and a half—yet the consequential prolongation of the amnesic period was left unexplained. A greater lack—though understandable for the early state of psychoanalysis at the time—is that Freud did not yet see the essential relationship between anality and obsessional neurosis.[2] In the case at hand, he simply acknowledged the importance of anal eroticism in Ernst's childhood, manifest in his early coprophilia and olfactory hypersensitivity (p. 247 and *n*) as well as in the stimulation caused by rectal worms over a period of years (p. 213). It is equally noteworthy that Freud made only sparing use of the concept of regression (pp. 199*n*, 244, 292) and did not express any understanding of the patient's anal eroticism in that sense.[3]

---

1. This is my translation of the German *eine episch zu nennende Dichtung* (p. 428*n*). Cf. Strachey's translation, which tones down the note of literary fiction present in the original German: "a positively epical character" (p. 207*n*).

2. The plethora of anal material might make the modern reader erroneously assume that Freud at the time saw anality as an essential feature of obsessional neurosis. For such an error, see Gedo and Goldberg (1973, p. 30): "Freud explained the neurosis as a whole on the basis of repression of Oedipal hatred of the father as well as of the rejecting woman, followed by a dual regression: that of the libido from phallic aims to anal sadistic ones, and that of action to the sphere of eroticized thought."

3. Freud pointed out the unusual fact that Lanzer remembered his governess not by her first name but by her last, masculine-sounding name (Rudolf), an early indication of the part played by a homosexual object-sexual choice in the

In Freud's understanding, once the Rat Man entered latency, his obsessional neurosis had already passed out of its beginning stage and was fully developed, hence "wanting in no essential element, at once the nucleus and the prototype of the later disorder" (p. 162). The disorder was marked by Ernst's fear that his forbidden thoughts would cause his father's death; the repression of this infantile hostility to his father subjected the patient's whole subsequent life to neurosis (p. 238). Overall, the sensuality of Ernst's childhood considerably diminished through puberty (p. 182), and limited tactile eroticism (p. 161) gave way to voyeurism as the main source of sexual pleasure (cf. pp. 279, 309).

In his dynamic analysis of the Rat Man's adulthood, Freud repeatedly explains Ernst's major conflict as being torn between his father and the "revered lady," with his father being ultimately the preferred one (pp. 182, 218). Heinrich's opposition to the financially disfavored Gisela once more confirmed his role as "interferer" in his son's choice of sexual object (p. 237). In response to this interference, which dated from his remote childhood, Ernst's hostility to his father was repressed, and it continued in that unconscious state into adulthood (p. 238). Accordingly Ernst thought that his obsessions about his father's death were not wishes, but fears (p. 180). Ernst's deadly hatred of his father and his consequent guilt-laden denial of Heinrich's death were the chief areas of Freud's attention during the analysis.

In contrast, Ernst's hostility to Gisela was to a great degree conscious, although the depth of these negative feelings toward her escaped him (pp. 194, 237). Ernst maintained that he loved his lady but had no sensual desire for her, a defensive maneuver

---

patient's life (p. 160*n*). Freud's comments to the Vienna Psychoanalytic Society indicate that he may have considered the Rat Man's homosexuality as fully emerging only in the latency period: "The basic conflict in this case lies, roughly speaking, in the patient's struggle between his drive toward man and that toward woman (his drive toward man is stronger). . . . The patient already at such an early age clearly showed heterosexual inclinations and . . . his later homosexuality is in sharp contrast with these" (Nunberg & Federn, 1962, 1:232, 236).

further subjected to doubt and alternate periods of his loving her intensely and being indifferent to her (pp. 182, 194). Not exploring the oedipal significance of the relationship, Freud kept Mrs. Lanzer and Gisela apart. Of the two textual references to Ernst's sexual love for his mother (pp. 207n, 238), only the latter links the two women, and in a most restrained way at that. The footnote on page 207, moreover, contains the only specific reference to Mrs. Lanzer as a forbidden object: In Ernst's dreams "his sexual desires for his mother and sister and his sister's premature death were linked up with the young hero's chastisement at his father's hand." Apart from this passage, Freud was content to subsume his patient's mother into a few oedipal statements. Nor did Freud aver any oedipal conclusions from back-to-back associations that at the age of six the little Ernst complained about erections to his mother and felt that his desires to see girls naked were liable to cause his father's death (pp. 161–62).

On the other hand, Freud does expatiate on the generic issue that if the Rat Man could doubt the reality of his love, he could also put into question the reality of every lesser thing in his life. His compulsions were ways of eluding inhibition and of compensating for crippling doubt. Other compensatory measures were his omnipotent wishes, which were ultimately based on hostile impulses (pp. 234–35). In a larger sense, his preconscious superstitions and ascetic personality were mainly a reaction formation against his repressed hostile wishes (pp. 248–49).

Finally we come to Freud's interpretation of Mrs. Lanzer's plan that her son should marry a daughter of one of her wealthy Saborsky relatives. Freud's muddled story about the marriage plan and its effects needs to be straightened out, even though we must do so with some tentativeness. The central point is that Freud assigns the same dates and the identical effects to different events, Ernst's aunt's death and his mother's marriage scheme. Freud dates the latter as occurring "some six years previously"— that is, in 1901 (p. 195; cf. Strachey's assigned date of 1903 [p. 257]). The aunt also died in 1901.

According to Freud, one of the consequences of the aunt's death was that his patient "became seriously incapacitated from working" (p. 175), hence the outbreak of his illness (cf. pp. 274, 289). But Freud also construes the precipitating cause of the illness to be the mother's plan:

> This family plan stirred up in him a conflict as to whether he should remain faithful to the lady he loved in spite of her poverty, or whether he should follow in his father's footsteps and marry the lovely, rich and well-connected girl who had been assigned to him. And he solved this conflict, which was in fact one between his love and the persisting influence of his father's wishes, by falling ill; or, to put it more correctly, by falling ill he avoided the task of resolving it in real life.
>
> The proof that this view was correct lies in the fact that the chief result of his illness was an obstinate incapacity for work, which allowed him to postpone the completion of his education for years. (pp. 198–99; see also p. 237)

Along with the above, Gisela's infertility, though having nothing explicitly to do with Ernst's incapacity to work, was another reason for his hesitating to marry her (pp. 216–17).

Available documentation permits us to approximate the date of that marriage plan.[4] In response to an appeal from Mrs. Lanzer, one of the rich Saborskys was willing to offer his daughter when Ernst's "education was completed" (p. 198).[5] The source texts in

---

4. Mrs. Lanzer's marriage scheme was of long duration (p. 292) and had its termination (*Ausgang*—H, p. 206) rather than its "inception" (p. 302) in the proposal by the rich Saborsky. I have checked my photocopy of Freud's holograph and found Hawelka's reading of *Ausgang*, not Strachey's reading of *Anfang* (inception), as clearly the correct one. True enough, *Ausgang* has also the antithetical meaning of outset, albeit an alternative excluded insofar as the marriage plan had been long-standing.

5. Cf. Marcus's date of the Saborsky proposal as "probably in 1902 or 1903" (1984, p. 137). To Marcus goes the credit for having been the first to have written (p. 135) about Freud's attribution of the precipitating cause of illness to two different events. But, as my analysis shows, the matter is much more complicated in Freud's text: first, not only did Freud switch from one cause to the other, but

the process notes are more specific: the rich father of the prospective bride offered to set up a business for Ernst "as soon as he had got his doctor's degree—which was at the time only a few months off" (p. 292); in that business Ernst was to serve as clerk for his own future brother-in-law, husband to Olga, Dr. Jacob Freundlich (p. 302). Ernst was nowhere near finishing his doctorate in 1901 (Freud's proposed date) or in 1903 (Strachey's date), but 1905 is a different matter. To repeat: in that year, he finished his third state examination (July 13) and second Rigorosum (July 19); he worked for Dr. Jacob Freundlich from July 27 to October 4; and on October 15 Ernst's superior became his brother-in-law. I speculate that the rich relative changed his plans slightly and, in anticipation of Ernst's obtaining his doctorate that fall, established him in business beforehand. Another weighty factor was that in 1905 the prospective bride was fifteen (p. 292) compared with Gisela's twenty-six.

Freud's gross oversight in assigning the identical results to diverse causes is far different from favoring the possibility that one event reinforces the results of a prior event. That alternative is too simple to explain a multiplicity of issues. I propose the following account. At the beginning of 1901, some eighteen months after Heinrich Lanzer's death, the Rat Man's illness broke out following the death of an aunt. Then, in 1903, with the death of an uncle, Gisela's supposed second rejection, and the appearance of an amatory rival, the Rat Man's obsessional neurosis and incapacity for work were *further* aggravated.[6] The aggravation underwent another intensification in 1905 with the incipient ac-

---

he later quietly slipped back to his former interpretation; second, there was a series of three staggered events, not two, which effected major aggravations of the patient's illness; and third, there was the matter of Gisela's infertility; Freud's failure to integrate this outstanding factor with the rest of his interpretation is glaring.

6. Whereas Freud said there was a "flight into illness" (p. 199n), I deem it more accurate to say a "further flight into illness." Let us note, too, that Ernst's avoidance of work habitually annoyed his father; on the other hand, we have also previously seen how Ernst pursued some of his studies with exceptional rapidity.

tualization of the mother's marriage plan. But our satisfaction with this triple-tiered construction is short-lived when we become aware of Freud's single citation of the patient's "chief reason" for his reluctance to marry: being very fond of children, he was hesitant before his lady's physical incapacity to bear children (pp. 216–17). In short, Freud's dynamic description of the Rat Man's adult life is incoherent.

The previous analysis laid down by Freud in his case history variously prepares us now to consider the wider and often contrasting pictures found in the process notes and in other documentation. Most appropriately, we may first attend to the patient's mother, who appears in only a handful of remarks in the published case (pp. 161, 174, 198, 205–07, 231).[7] In the process notes, however, both she and her husband receive some forty references each, although those dealing with her are comparatively less ample. These textual differences serve to highlight the preponderant role preferentially examined by Freud in collusion with his patient's resistances. One may want to argue that Freud had to be discreet and consequently filtered out many allusions to Mrs. Lanzer, who functioned as a controller of the purse strings and thus as a participant in the analysis. Yet as sound as that objection may be, it is surely not sufficient in itself. But if we seek elsewhere, a supplementary reason comes quickly into view to resolve our puzzlement. The relatively pallid picture of the Rat Man's mother and the full-bodied picture of his father fit the lopsided pattern in Freud's descriptions of both Dora's and little Hans's parents. Reworded in a Sophoclean context, "the 'oedipal' mother in Freud's early works is a static figure who unknowingly plays out her destiny while Laius springs back into life."[8] Re-

---

7. Cf. Zetzel (1966, p. 125) and Blacker and Abraham (1982, p. 706). The latter article contains egregious factual distortions.
8. Erlich (1977, p. 284). Cf. Marcus's incisive comment: the relative exclusion of the mother in Freud's case histories "was characteristic of his culture as

worded in a contemporary context, the woman in Freud's great cases appears somewhat as a caricature, as "odd woman out."

Already on the basis of the first several weeks of clinical material presented by Freud to the Vienna Psychoanalytic Society, Rank opined that "all factors clearly point to the patient's love for his mother, even though there has not yet been any direct reference to this in the analytic material" (Nunberg & Federn, 1962, 1:233; one may guess even then how much Freud had winnowed out of his oral presentation). At any rate, Freud replied that "Rank will probably prove to be right in his assumption that incestuous wishes for the mother play *a* role [my italics], though the relationship is complicated by the presence of four sisters."

The extant evidence allows us to draw a mixed picture of the interaction between Ernst and his mother. Her controlling nature, entrenched miserliness, ambivalent attitude toward neatness, and lack of the outbursts so characteristic of her husband and son indicate an obsessional personality with restrictive traits. If she was family-conscious, concerned about the comfort of her house, and even protective of her son against her violent husband (p. 286), she could yet be critical, controlling, and dangerously seductive and phallic. If she criticized Ernst for being unkempt, she herself oscillated ambivalently between restrictive behavior on the one hand and both anal and genital exhibitionism on the other.

From the earliest times a series of events in Ernst's life occasioned developmental strain and disrupted his confidence in his preoccupied mother: at the age of eighteen months, when he was

---

well, and one of the more strongly marked features of both the major novels and major autobiographies of nineteenth-century culture is the consistency with which they place the relation of father and child (particularly, of course, father and son) at the center of the human universe of development, passion and choice, and how relatively infrequently the relation of mother and child (with a few notable exceptions) occupies that paramount position. One can say that one of the themes of nineteenth-century literary culture has to do with the conflict surrounding this tendency to a suppression of the mother" (1984, p. 113).

living through the phase of gender consolidation and rapprochement, his privileged position as the only son in a family of daughters was undermined by the birth of a rival brother; when Ernst neared three, another sister was born; and nine months later, Camilla died. In general, Mrs. Lanzer hardly appears to be a preoedipal or oedipal mother who functioned as a consistent developmental stabilizer or as one who maintained an open dialogue with her son that would have constantly promoted and solidified ego functioning. She did not suffice for her son to deal with his unresolved distress, frustration, and rage; he turned then to other family members for gratifying solace and sustenance. We attain a clear idea of the oedipal constellation if we understand that Ernst's sisters became substitute objects more approachable than his mother.

In her highly dominating role over her adult son, Mrs. Lanzer did not fail to criticize Gisela's family as "futile persons" and even forbade Ernst from going to the funeral of Gisela's grandmother. If it is only probable that Mrs. Lanzer controlled her family's financial affairs, it is certain that she was the strict administrator of Ernst's inheritance (he abandoned to her the anal penis). As the distributor of the analytic fees, did she force the precipitate ending of the treatment? Other implications of that question will be examined later in our study; here we may focus on another striking indication of Mrs. Lanzer's inhibitory force, as evidenced in the following passage (I have replaced Strachey's "came into the picture" by "moved up," to conform with Freud's use of the military verb *anrücken*):[9]

> Even in recent years, when his youngest sister was sleeping in his room, he took off her bed-clothes in the morning so that he could see the whole of her. Then his mother moved up as

9. It was Hawelka (p. 145*n*) who first brought attention to this military verb. This is one of countless instances throughout his writings where Freud lets his choice of expository language blend into its subject matter. Here, so to speak, Mrs. Lanzer joins the military ranks of her husband and son.

an obstacle to his sexual activity, having taken over this role since his father's death. (p. 279)

The resentful son had a "low opinion" of his mother, fantasized that she was a whore, and thought that everything bad in him came from her side of the family (p. 297); she was the object of a primitive splitting.

Given her son's strengths, however, chances are that Mrs. Lanzer must have been quite motherly at times. In his omniscience Ernst identified with her prophetic magic, which in reality was an autosuggestiveness bringing out psychosomatic illness (p. 231); he could also masochistically identify with his mother and be made pregnant by his father or could anally introject his father's penis and in that way castrate him. But generally Mrs. Lanzer remained a threatening, archaic phallic mother whom Ernst unconsciously wanted to castrate in his oedipal phase marked by an anal fixation. His mother was significantly absent from all his conscious hostile compulsions, which characteristically were directed against his father and Gisela. By partially replacing his mother, who robbed him of his father's love, Gisela also served to disguise matricidal wishes. It was presumably within this context and its attendant problems that Freud was moved, albeit exaggeratedly, to ask his patient, "Hasn't it ever occurred to you that if your mother died you would be freed from all your conflicts, since you would be able to marry?" (p. 283).[10]

Of the five daughters in the Lanzer family, the deceased Camilla has received the most extensive psychoanalytic attention, perhaps in part because some of the bases for her undeniable importance are still shrouded in mystery. Freud's pertinent official comments are teasingly brief: Camilla's death figured prominently in her brother's fantasies and bore upon his childish biting

---

10. For various ideas in this paragraph, see Myerson (1966, p. 141), Grunberger (1966, pp. 166–62), Veszy-Wagner (1967, pp. 595, 599), and Chasseguet-Smirgel (1967, p. 609).

and other misbehavior (pp. 205, 235). The greater detail scattered throughout the process notes can be summarized as follows: Ernst's first perception of sexual difference dating from his observation of Camilla on the pot; her declaration to him, "If you die I shall kill myself"; remembered scenes of her illness and death and the distressed reactions of himself and his parents; his fear that his own masturbation might have caused her death; and last, his experience of her death as a relief over a rival being eliminated, as an admonitory sign of what might happen to him if he continued to masturbate, and as the origin of his omnipotent belief that by giving or retaining love he could control life (pp. 264, 276, 284, 299–300, 309).

Being a focus of Camilla's oedipal strivings obviously intensified Ernst's choice of her as his incestuous heterosexual object. If the one reported event of Ernst's early biting is seen phasically, we might understand that to ward off the painful affects of anxiety and helplessness connected with Camilla's impending loss, he regressed to the conflicts of the anal stage and the oral-sadistic rage he had brought into it. Occurring during the height of his oedipal phase, the catastrophic loss of the mother surrogate traumatically shaped his infantile neurosis and left lifelong sequelae in his development. While hostilely gratifying the demands of his ideal ego, he was buffeted by mortal fears of erotic satisfaction and weakened in his ability to cope with ambivalence. A guilt of the survivor shot through his psychic world of self and object representations where vulnerability was ever more confirmed by cryptorchism and death.

Another drastic sequel to Camilla's death was Ernst's putative denial of it, a pathological reaction which we should see as underlying the psychical event assigned by Freud as the cause of his patient's neurosis—namely, his denial of his father's death. We might also say that some developmental failure, overdetermined by Camilla's illness, and an abiding pathological attraction to mourning help explain Ernst's eventual inability to accept the death of his father. Other available perspectives fill out this picture: with his synthetic function being disrupted at a critical time in its formation, Ernst resorted to the solution of denying death, which consequently caused a chronic split in his ego; and the tragic event in its turn further impaired his very synthetic function that ordinarily resolves the problems posed by bisexuality. On another score, did the Lanzer parents make things worse by conferring some of Camilla's role onto Ernst and thus increasing his bisexual turmoil and castration anxiety? Another consideration is that the demise of the older sister impaired Ernst's evolving identification with his father, whom he unconsciously blamed for the tragedy; if so, Ernst consequently regressed to reestablish the earlier passive relationship, which then conflicted with unconscious active wishes to recover the lost heterosexual object.[11]

Ernst's remaining four sisters are not specifically mentioned in the official history. Even the process notes give but the slightest reference to Gertrud (p. 272) and Rosalie (pp. 306, 308). (Possibly Ernst was distanced from the latter because she was named after her mother and perhaps preferred by her.) Olga, the sister born after Ernst, best qualifies as the triggering figure in Freud's generalization that a child's nuclear complex is set in motion "usually by the arrival of a new baby brother or sister" (p. 208n). When Camilla died, the nine-month-old Olga might have been the object of Ernst's deflected libido. We are on surer grounds when we postulate that at least during adulthood, Olga was his incestuously preferred sister and a choice object of sadistic-anal fantasies. The finicky brother brought himself to tell her, "Nothing about you would be disgusting to me" (p. 287), a total acceptance no other woman in the case history receives. After the death of their father (the "interferer"), Ernst repeatedly attacked Olga and once "assaulted" her; he even had to make a vow to

---

11. In this paragraph I am indebted to Zetzel (1965, p. 45; 1966, p. 127), A. Freud (1966, p. 117), and Gedo and Goldberg (1973, p. 113).

keep away from her. Once he dreamed of copulating with her and of then being fearful for having broken his vow; upon waking and recognizing that he had only been dreaming, he was so delighted that he "went into her bedroom and smacked her bottom under the bedclothes" (p. 278; cf. pp. 279, 282). Servants thought that Ernst and Olga kissed not like siblings but like lovers. Even her eventual husband became jealous to the point that Ernst said to him, "If Olga has a baby in 9 months' time, you needn't think I am its father; I am innocent" (p. 314).

The little we know of Hedwig, Ernst's oldest sister, is suggestive. She appeared in his dental dreams symbolizing masturbation and castration (pp. 269, 315ff.); that he had his first coitus in Trieste, the city where she lived, might have been not at all accidental; and her beautiful body was admittedly the possible "root of his love" for Gisela (p. 317). In sum, Hedwig, Camilla, and Olga figured prominently in Ernst's shifting relationship between younger and older sisters. Overdetermined by the impact of the preoedipal and oedipal mother, this shifting relationship, Freud twice remarks, formed the basis of Ernst's later conflictual choice between Gisela and another woman (pp. 287, 292).[12]

It is only in the process notes that we can fully grasp Gisela's identity and significance. At the age of six she suffered the death of her father and afterward was apparently sexually assaulted by her stepfather, factors contributing to her hostility and erotic inhibition with regard to Ernst (p. 279). It is open to question as to how long-standing were the physical ailments that caused her death. At any rate, her illnesses preoccupied Ernst and he became depressed over them (pp. 277, 308, 317). In reparation for Camilla's death, which he had omnipotently caused, he had kept Gi-

---

12. However meager the evidence may be, it sufficiently undercuts the contention of Veszy-Wagner that the "Rat Man had three sisters who, apart from the possible occasional sexual games in early childhood, later played no role in his life" (1967, p. 602).

sela alive, so he told Freud, on two occasions by his omnipotent wishes:

> One of these was last year, when she suffered from sleeplessness and he stayed up all night and she in fact slept better for the first time that night. The other time was when she was suffering from her attacks; whenever she was verging on a state of insensibility, he was able to keep her awake by saying something that would interest her. (p. 299)

Relevantly, Gisela, a blood relative, was sterile like a prepubertal girl. Her illness unconsciously stirred up his conflicts over Camilla's death: he wanted to resuscitate Camilla; he wanted Gisela alive; he wanted her dead; he was unconsciously afraid that she would die. At the same time, he externalized his own sense of defectiveness in her.[13]

Not having attained a mature capacity for mourning and for a tender genital love, Ernst resorted to a devaluation and idealization of women, both of which were equally foreign to empathy, and he was led to exclude copulation from any relationship of love (pp. 263, 267–68, 271). Massive denial, idealization, and devaluation accompanied his splitting and ambivalence: he felt no sensual desires toward Gisela, and he was especially attracted by her buttocks, which he fantasized as the site of the rat punishment (pp. 182, 277); she was a "whore" or the esteemed "pearl," the condemnable villain or the "revered lady."[14]

Any reader of Freud's case history is impressed by the impact

---

13. Cf. Zetzel (1966, p. 127) and Kestenberg (1980, p. 166). Hawelka (p. 267) made the astute observation that the patient never alluded to a pregnant woman in spite of his having seen his mother in three pregnancies.

14. Both components of the epithet merit examination. First, Strachey's translation of "admired" for *verehre* tones down the force of Ernst's distancing veneration (158/384). Second, no doubt Ernst's appellation of Gisela as his "lady" was partly in compensation for his mother's objections to her poverty, but in a deeper and contrary sense it can be traced to his devaluation of his mother as the primary object of dependency (Kernberg, 1976, p. 195; see also esp. pp. 211–13, 217–23).

of the father who appears on every other page and stands as practically the sole parental presence. Again and again we come across references to the patient's love, hostility, and self-reproaches concerning the father not only as "best friend" but also as sexual "interferer." Not recognizing the *full* importance of early object relations[15] at the time, Freud put predominant weight on the father's role as interferer of instinctual gratification, especially autoerotic masturbation—hence, the content of Freud's principal reconstruction. The *Minutes of the Vienna Psychoanalytic Society* show Freud explaining a further basis for his position: "Hatred for the father as strong as in this case can arise only if the father has disturbed the child in his sexuality" (Nunberg & Federn, 1962, 1:236).

Let us look at the relationship of the father and son within a wider perspective. Nineteen years older than his wife, Heinrich Lanzer must have been something like a patriarchal figure; he was fifty-three, moreover, when Ernst was born. Although reportedly an essentially kind person, he could fly into a passionate temper such that he did not know what he was doing (p. 284; see also pp. 206, 286, 290, 307). Revelatory of this terrifying part of his character, he often spoke of the "Nuremberg funnel" (now a museum exhibit) through which water was poured down the victim's throat; in connection with that he used to say to his son, "You'll get things into your head some day" (p. 272). Libidinal factors also undercut the father's role as empathic caretaker and sustainer—Ernst often suspected that his nervous troubles were due to syphilis contracted by his father during his military escapades (p. 289). Was not the father—impulsively unpredictable—suddenly moved to have his wife swear on her children's

---

15. I use the word *full* designedly so that my statement must be constructed in a relative, not exclusive, sense. Here is an atypical yet extraordinary example of Freud's awareness of internalized object relations: "It seems likely that he [the patient] is also identifying himself with his mother in his criticisms of his father and is thus continuing the differences between his parents within himself" (p. 298).

lives that she had never been unfaithful (pp. 291–92)? And where was the father's reliability as an introjectable ego ideal and superego if he could risk his welfare by gambling and, to Ernst's horror, had married for money rather than for love? Perhaps a historically earlier consideration is appropriate and enlightening. During the critical event of Camilla's fatal malady, it was to his paternal parent that Ernst turned "to find out what was happening" (Nunberg & Federn, 1962, 1:235)—was this to win assurance, to accuse, or both?

Still in all, Ernst could not fully identify with the father, let alone freely attempt to surpass him. If the powerful oedipal father had seven children, Ernst would choose a woman who could not give him any (marrying an infertile woman was, secondarily, a vengeful way of preventing the father from having descendants and thus perpetuating his name). And not only did Ernst postpone finishing his doctorate for years but when he finally attained it, we should observe, his obsessional neurosis reached its crippling climax just a month later. Before the castrating risk of competing with his father, then, Ernst masochistically identified with his mother, a maneuver that permitted him unconsciously to introject his father's penis anally; anal regression stood as a faltering attempt to contend with identificatory conflicts.[16] Concomitantly his deeply rooted desires to kill his father served as a reaction formation of latent positive homosexual strivings.

Ernst's castration anxiety was increased in the interaction with his brother, Robert, who, though younger, certainly represented the dominant father. Robert was even delegated by the father to mete out physical punishment to his older brother (p. 313). Being the stronger and the more handsome, Robert became the favorite, was considered sexually more adept by one of the governesses (p. 161), and conveniently served as the displaced object of

---

16. Cf. Grunberger (1966, p. 161; 1967, p. 609), Meyerson (1966, p. 141), Chasseguet-Smirgel (1967, pp. 617, 619), and Kestenberg (1980, p. 169).

Ernst's jealousy and murderous hostility toward his father (p. 184).[17] It is instructive to follow Ernst's dynamic reactions when his father did die. Instead of occasioning a developmental opportunity for Ernst to successfully overcome his pathological mourning, unresolved since childhood, the father's death prompted Ernst into primitive denial and stimulated desires of omnipotently resurrecting his father in the next world. In a peculiar move "to undo" (p. 235) his father's death, as we have seen, he would interrupt his studies during the night to open the door for his father's ghost and then look at his penis before a mirror. If Ernst wanted to defy his father sexually and to please him by studying (p. 204), he also strove for mirror magic, which functioned as a febrile attempt to shore up his threatened ego and optically incorporate the envied paternal penis.[18]

We may pause here to examine the temporal phenomenon in Ernst's mourning for his father, which took place eighteen months later and was brought about by the death of an aunt. I suggest that the delayed period of eighteen months was an anniversary reaction to the birth intervals between the Lanzer children. Hedwig and Camilla were born within sixteen months of each other;

---

17. In his later compartment as an adult, Robert seems to have been a source of worry for the Lanzer family (pp. 184, 298). In her will Mrs. Lanzer specified that her fortune was to be divided equally among her six children or their survivors (the total fortune, before the governmental claim of 10 percent, was 22,000 kronen); she further exacted that Robert should liquidate his debt to his two immediately older siblings, Ernst and Rosalie.

18. See Meyerson (1966, p. 141) and Bradlow and Cohen (1984, pp. 281–82). I should say a word about "undoing," which Freud will distinguish as *ungeschehenmachen,* or to make (an action) unhappened (Freud, 1926, p. 119n). Cf. the Rat Man case: "Compulsive acts . . . , in two successive stages, of which the second *neutralizes* the first, are a typical occurrence in obsessional neuroses" (192/414); "The strange extension of his obsessional fears to the 'next world' was nothing else than . . . to *undo* the fact of his father's death" (235–36/452). The words I have italicized are Strachey's translation of the single term *aufheben,* which Freud applies to both material and psychical acts (obsessional fears). A beautiful pun enriching Freud's text in a way that Hegel would have been proud of, the word embraces the meanings of ceasing or annulling and conservation (see also 243/458).

there were eighteen months between Ernst and Robert, and seventeen between Robert and Olga. What does this all mean? Given the volubility of the Lanzer family, presumably its members often referred to the similar birth intervals, which may have been rounded off to a year and a half. The coincidence of the same interval separated the death of Heinrich Lanzer and that of the aunt (pp. 174–75, 235–36), thereby furthering the imbrication of death and life in the Rat Man's fantasies. But there is more than just coincidence here. The remorse-provoking period when the Rat Man slept throughout his father's last breaths lasted an hour and a half; during his revived piety, he said prayers that eventually continued for an hour and a half (p. 193). He erroneously reported that he had wired his Viennese optician for glasses and received them the same evening, whereas in reality he received them a day and a half later (p. 271n). If we cannot discard in these examples the telescoping of anniversary reactions into hours and days, neither can we overlook the significance of the Rat Man's stopping his magical prayers eighteen months before his analysis (p. 260)—as if beginning his analysis took on the supplementary meanings of mourning and rebirth. Those anniversary meanings acquired a new depth when Ernst finally became engaged to Gisela in October 1909, some eighteen months after termination of his regular analysis.

The basis of the last assertion needs further commentary. There is a variety of possible interrelationships among what I call "the ultimate scenes"—those fantasies dealing with the unique ontogenetic experiences of conception, birth, and death. For example, Lady Macbeth's rejection of a maternal identification becomes understandable when seen within the more comprehensive picture of an enraging destructiveness dominating her imbricated ultimate scenes, thereby keeping at bay a life of creation and reparation.

The Rat Man, like other obsessional neurotics, had a "death complex" (p. 236), whereby he wished the solution of his amatory conflicts to be brought about by the death of his loved ones. Elements of the death complex appear in the Rat Man's mirror masturbation, embedding a combination of the ultimate scenes. And to cure or revive himself, did not the Rat Man seek out an analyst whose brother he supposed had murdered and then was executed for it (p. 285)? It is significant, too, that during his analysis the identification of children and deadly rats emerged with specific reference to Ibsen's play *Little Eyolf*. In this play the Rat-Wife, a latter-day version of the Pied Piper of Hamelin, is a figure embracing the roles of savior and bringer of death: she can rid a town of fatal rats and also of its survivability. The clinical material becomes more comprehensible when we see the coherent pattern of the Rat Man's ultimate scenes as tending to be dominated by the anal phase: as a youth he thought that people make babies by exposing their bottoms; babies were born through the anus (pp. 219–20); and the very rat punishment, a lethal anal rape, was the oneiric reversal of anal birth. Briefly, the anus was the way station to both cradle and cemetery.

One of the curious aspects of the Rat Man's case history is that although as a child he had slept mostly with his parents (p. 161), Freud completely avoided any direct analysis of the potential over-stimulation deriving from this habit. Although he had referred to the primal scene as far back as *The Interpretation of Dreams* (1900, p. 585), Freud explored its traumatic impact only in the case of the Wolf Man, where, indeed, he placed it at the very core of the treatment. One easily gets the impression that if the Rat Man had been in analysis longer or came after the Wolf Man, Freud would have written a very different case history. The Russian child, we recall, regularly slept in his nurse's room. There is greater suggestive evidence, moreover, for the Rat Man than for the Wolf Man to have witnessed coitus *a tergo*. All this raises the consideration that the Wolf Man case may have been derivative of the Rat Man case, as a clinical and scriptive return of what Freud repressed.

The likelihood of primal-scene exposure bears on young Ernst's disquieting belief that his thoughts were known by his parents—his way of understanding was that he said things aloud without hearing them himself, which contrasted with Freud's explanation of the phenomenon as Ernst's perception of his unconscious processes. I propose that Freud's explanation should be supplemented: during exposure to primal scenes, our little hero, who had the ability to recognize everyone by his or her smell (pp. 247, 295), smelled and heard his parents and perhaps tried to see them peripherally (thus the beginning of his uncanny use of peripheral vision—p. 231). Consequently, in more senses than one, he could "guess" their thoughts. Perhaps also at that time he believed that his parents did not hear themselves and were unaware of his listening. More assuredly, a reproachful rage directed inward and outward informed the boy's conflictual understanding of his perceptions and those of his parents. Was not one of his later disturbing obsessions to cut his throat, the very locus of the organ of speech? More important in this connection, after mentioning his parents' mind reading, the patient immediately brought in oedipal associations about his early desire to see naked girls and his ensuing fear about his father's death (p. 162).[19]

However primal-scene overstimulation might have, among other effects, injured the Rat Man's phallic narcissism, we must not neglect the far-reaching consequences of cryptorchism on his body image. More precisely, his undescended testicle impaired sexual development and self-esteem and brought about confusion between front and back, masculine and feminine, active and passive; he felt that he was a *Miessnick* (ugly creature) and was tor-

---

19. Lanzer referred these memories back to his sixth or seventh year of age. In that light, cf. H. Lewis (1958, pp. 19, 29, 31): the patient's amnesia ending in the sixth year coincides with the shedding of the first tooth; psychoanalytic literature amply testifies to the first deciduous tooth effecting a secondary repression of oedipal strivings.

mented by the idea that his penis was cut off (pp. 264, 284). His putting the mirror between his legs was done not only to check if his penis was too small (p. 302) but also to find his lost testicle. His castration complex extended to what frightful death meant to him: "not to see or hear or feel anything" (pp. 300–01)—that is, to be like a stool or a hidden testicle.

Did his mother have something hidden like his testicle? The question is worth pursuing, for although Freud noted the identification of rat as baby, he did not connect it with Ernst's wish to deliver his undescended testicle. The available data allow us to surmise that Ernst entered the phallic phase under the burden of an ambivalent feminine-anal identification and a desperate desire to recover his lost testicle. With the taboo of touching being at the core of his subsequent obsessional neurosis, erotic activity was displaced onto the eye, which acted like a sphincter on the anal-sadistic level. Collaterally, Ernst's constant desire to see naked girls was a quest for the mother's anal genitalia. We may also trace the much later doubt about the father's death to the voyeurism and persistent question of the young cryptorchid, "Is the hidden testicle dead, and where exactly is it?"[20]

Lanzer's testicular defect also left derivatives in his uncertain reportage of Gisela's operation concerning single and double entities and of the rat story. Thus, when he broached the topic of Gisela's ovariectomy, he claimed at first not to know whether it was unilateral or bilateral (the latter being the reality). On the other hand, the single torturing rat in Mirbeau's novel became "some" in the first account of the Rat Man (p. 166), who subsequently said there were two, of which one, he fantasied, possessed a name and behaved like a domestic animal (pp. 290–91).

---

20. Cf. A. Bell (1961, pp. 280–81), B. Grunberger (1966, p. 160), and J. Kestenberg (1980, pp. 151, 165–68). Kestenberg's developmental approach to cryptorchism complements Holland's (1975) stressing of an identity theme throughout the Rat Man's life: his need to control benevolent goings out and catastrophic comings in (such as mental invasion and sexual penetration).

Pertinently, the Rat Man was brought to fantasize and dream about his undescended right testicle in various ways: meeting a captain who had his badge of rank only on the right side, with one of the three stars hanging down (p. 295); visiting a dentist who mistakenly pulled the tooth adjacent to the defective one (pp. 315–18);[21] his father's being in a sack (*im Sacke*) which a workman was beating against the ground (p. 290). This last fantasy graphically depicts the Rat Man's rage over his impaired bodily development for which his father is held accountable and is vengefully punished in a "sack" (I suspect this to be a condensation of *Hodensack*, the German for *scrotum*). I further surmise that underlying the Rat Man's fear of sexual penetration were unconscious fantasies that the descended testicle would ascend into the body much as the other testicle was imagined to have done. Accordingly, his fear about the retractability of the descended testicle was defensively hidden in the rage about the rat-penis dentatus eating its way into his father's and Gisela's bodies.

The last sentence signals that the appropriate time has come for us to explore the psychic relevance of the rat for Freud's patient. Because of its extraordinary teeth and intraspecific destructiveness, the rat lends itself to being one of the main cannibalistic imagos. As such it has figured prominently in the enraged fantasy life of many people who were beaten and seduced as children. In terms of libidinal regression, their experience is often a canni-

21. Strachey (p. 316*n*) thinks it "probable" that this tooth dream was "to some extent" the basis of a passage added in 1909 to *The Interpretation of Dreams* (pp. 387–88). I adduce more evidence to confirm Strachey's statement about the two dreams interpolated on these pages. First of all, their allusions to pulled teeth, single and double entities, fastidiousness, and strongly repressed homosexuality are recognizable themes in the Rat Man's analysis. Furthermore, the dreamer's being bound by four silken cloths might refer to the Rat Man's sexual attachments being determined by his four surviving sisters (pp. 273, 276, 278). Finally, the statement in the dream book that the university-educated young man never had intercourse might be based either on Freud's effort to conceal his patient's identity or on the possibility that the dental dreams came from an earlier phase of the Rat Man's life (for this plausible connection, see p. 269).

balistic one in which, ratlike, they may be victim or tormentor. Counting among these patients, the Rat Man regressed from oedipal conflicts to an anal phase invaded by oral sadism. Concomitantly, with a disruption occurring between their cognitive and experiencing ego, autohypnotic states act to repeat past trauma in controlled attenuation and to stave off ego regression from ending in ego dissolution. With the functioning of his ego severely afflicted in certain areas, he was brought to feel profoundly that he did and did not commit criminal acts and that he consciously did not believe in the very premonitory powers of dreams he unconsciously believed in. Then again, a certain lack of closure in his body ego undermined healthy self-representation and threatened to undo the sphincter control of primitive destructive effect—hence, his terror of psychic disintegration owing to the rat imago's cannibalistically destroying the powerful seat of control.[22]

Uncontrollable throughout world history, pestilently ravaging Vienna in the seventeenth century, and greatly alarming it at the turn of the twentieth century, the rat found a new home in Lanzer's mind, where it thrived in infectious symbolism of good and bad, whole and part objects and their identifying features. Accordingly, in resuming Freud's exploration of meanings for the rat, we see that it could be the Rat Man himself, his mother, father, Gisela, babies,[23] anuses, genitalia, dirt, feces, money, syphilis, gamblers (*Spielratten*), the acts of guessing (*raten*),[24] marrying (*heiraten*), devouring and penetrating, the states of

---

22. For the matter in this paragraph, I am especially indebted to Shengold (1965, 1967, 1971, 1980, 1982, 1985).
23. In Viennese dialect, *Ratz* designates a rat as well as a young child; and in Austria at large, *Rätsche* means a child's rattle.
24. This is particularly true of numbers (*Minutes of the Vienna Psychoanalytic Society*, 1:370)—in this context, rats are "countable" rather than "payable" as Strachey would have it (p. 297). Strachey obviously read *zahlbar* (payable) in Freud's manuscript, whereas Hawelka (p. 191n) contends that the word is *zählbar*. According to my photocopy of Freud's manuscript, Hawelka's reading of the umlaut is incontestable.

containing or being contained, and so on contagiously. Feeding on both semantic and phonetic similarities, the symbolism had a self-generating momentum. Lanzer even shortened the *a* of *Raten* (installments) so that the word was pronounced like *Ratten* (rats). Equally notable was his memory of his gambling father who was financially rescued by a comrade—the final *d* in the German term *Kamerad* is pronounced like a *t* (210/430).

The completion of our rat survey beckons us to return to the maneuver site and there examine the birth and spread of Lieutenant Lanzer's rat obsession. On the verge of listening to the tale of torture, the imminent Rat Man was in a state of acute conflict. Not unusually for him, he was somewhat estranged from Gisela; his stimulability, increased by a long period of sexual abstinence, stirred up superego conflicts with its threats of the internalized father. Attendantly, he was identifying with the father not only in military matters but also in his hesitation about whether he should marry a rich or a poor woman (pp. 199*n*, 210). There was also the fact that in having recently acquired a doctorate, he had surpassed his father. Since it had been particularly during times of study that Ernst anguished about his penis being cut off (p. 264), he was now beleaguered all the more by castration anxiety and fear of success. There was also the homosexual atmosphere of military life, a context he would soon leave to live out his day-to-day conflicts in the activating presence of his mother and Gisela.

The breech birth of the rat obsession took place upon the narration of the cruel captain, a father figure toward whom the Rat Man had repressed homosexual fantasies. A complex primal-scene derivative, the furious rat fantasy was especially disturbing in that it included the active homosexual component of anally penetrating the father as well as the passive component of being similarly treated by him. Added to the various active and passive positions in the primal scene, the Rat Man also assumed in the guise of the rodent the identity of a third-party punitive partic-

Taking Apart the Psychic Apparatus 53

ipant. If the rat was tormented, it was also fired into a mindless fury much like Heinrich Lanzer's. In effect, the cruel captain's story about a holed pot applied to the anus was speaking about two juxtaposed anal containers for the rat-penis; the ensuing simultaneous death of the rat and its victim indicates the primitive masochism underlying the Rat Man's aggressive strivings and his archaic fears about their phallic expression. Another germane point is that the cruelly biting rats were in a pot (*Topf*, 166/392), the very object upon which Camilla sat when Ernst first noticed their sexual differences (p. 276); it was as if the mnemic image of the pot became a seething cauldron of negative affect tied to the Rat Man's anxiogenic discovery of sexual difference and his subsequent conflicts over object choice.

Rapidly propagating, the id-saturated rat fantasy had counterparts with higher organization—superego-colored compromise formations—when the cruel captain transmitted the postal package and mentioned the outstanding debt. The Rat Man's internal monologue at that point is unwieldily reconstructed by Freud in two different passages (pp. 168, 218–19), which themselves need our further reconstruction.[25] Accordingly, upon interiorly re-

25. We can get a further glimpse of Freud's confusion when we turn to his elucidation of the spatial and temporal details of the case. Fourteen years after publication of the case history, Freud added a map drawn up by Strachey and his wife to clarify the location of the post office, railway station, and so on. Sixteen years later, taking account of Freud's original notes, Strachey emended his previous, radically erroneous map (pp. 212–13*n*); but even the emendations leave matters cloudy. Chronologically, Freud brought forward a rectification to the Rat Man's original contention that he had wired to Vienna and received the pince-nez on the same evening—it was rather a day and a half later, Freud explained (p. 217 and *n*). We know from the Österreichisches Kriegsarchiv that the Rat Man's maneuvers ended on Monday, September 7, 1907; hence that infamous halt in maneuvers took place two days earlier, on Saturday afternoon (p. 168). Freud would have us believe that the glasses arrived from Vienna one and a half days later—therefore on Sunday, approximately at midnight. According to the general chronological framework proposed by Freud, the following events, noted in the process notes, took place between Sunday midnight and Monday morning: the Rat Man dispatched another officer to the town post office to pay the debt, the officer returned without paying, the Rat Man met Lieutenant David, and so on; somewhere in that time there was also the officers' final banquet (p. 170). I have omitted a number of other improbabilities.

fusing the reimbursement request, Freud's Rat Man in a first reaction gave himself the sanction that he must repay or else his father and lady would be anally tortured. In a second step, the Rat Man derisively rejected the sanction by postulating that he would defray the expenses if a doubly impossible condition could be fulfilled: when his dead father and infertile Gisela would have children. In a third step,[26] feeling that he had insulted both Gisela and his father, the Rat Man repressed his knowledge of the true state of affairs and reissued himself the command of reimbursement.

We readily notice that with his introduction of rat currency, the Rat Man made an abortive effort to succeed, to surpass his father morally ("I will be more promptly responsible in financial matters than he"). But in the fraternal maze of reimbursement plans, the kind though underrated post office lady remained unjustly unpaid. Put differently, the homosexually motivated transactions excluded the woman as a place of deposit for the anal penis. Another point: it is not certain exactly when during the maneuvers the Rat Man lost his pince-nez; yet we may compensate for our ignorance of the associative sequence if we attend to the two German renderings for pince-nez, namely, *Zwicker* and *Kneifer*.[27] Along with the other meaning of *Zwicker* as whiplash, we should bear in mind that *zwicken* and *kneifen* both mean to pinch; and Freud perspicaciously brought up another sense of *kneifen*, to retreat or back down. In this light, the symptomatic act of losing glasses was presumably the Rat Man's self-castration which accorded with the psychic economy of his sadomasochistic fantasies.

26. In his initial version (p. 168), Freud says that this "immediately" follows the first reaction.
27. For the sole mention of *Kneifer*, see p. 318 and also the *Minutes of the Vienna Psychoanalytic Society*, 1:287 (January 22, 1908). Before January, the Rat Man always referred to the pince-nez as *Zwicker*: 165/391; 172/396–97; 217n/436n; 212n/431n; 168/393; 217/435. Apparently, the belated use of *Kneifer* was a compromise return of the repressed.

For the sake of completion, I might briefly refer to an interpretive outlook on the reimbursement fantasy peculiar to French psychoanalysis. Lacan (1979) makes a great to-do about what he calls the Rat Man's "mythic network," especially as it surfaced in the last phase of his military obsession: in the payment scenario the Rat Man tried to negotiate between the rich post office lady and the poor servant girl of the nearby inn. This scenario, Lacan flies on, arises from the Rat Man's identification with his father who contracted an unpaid debt to a military companion and forsook a poor girl to marry someone from the wealthy Saborsky family; following suit, the Rat Man in his analysis switched his financial preoccupation onto the "rich" daughter of his simultaneously protective and malevolent analyst.[28]

Somewhat influenced by Lacan, another noted French psychoanalyst looks at the Rat Man's history in terms of circuits: the circuit of the Rat Man's reimbursement as a *modified* sequel to his father's past; the circuit of the rats in all their symbolism, and chiefly as objects of a sadomasochistic exchange; and the circuit of treatment whereby the Rat Man did not, as he himself claimed, consult Freud so much for a psychoanalysis as for a medical certificate countenancing the resumption of the fiscal rigmarole.[29] We might immediately add two other circuits: the Rat Man's unusual lifetime scurrying about from one professional employment to another and the endogamous circulation within

---

28. While purposely leaving aside Lacan's elaborate theoretics, I want to concentrate on his own "mythic" distortion of Freud's case history. To Lacan's triple insistence that the father's military debt was never paid (1979, pp. 414–15, 424), compare Freud's notation: "After ending his military service, his father tried to find the man, but failed. (Did he ever pay him back?)" (p. 290). Another objection may be drawn against Lacan's sheerly gratuitous assumption that the post office lady was rich and the servant girl at the inn was poor; we know that the latter's father was the owner of the inn. Finally, Lacan mistakenly states that the Rat Man's reimbursement of the post office lady happened after his analysis began (cf. p. 172).

29. Cf. Laplanche (1980, pp. 271–89). As far as the circuit of treatment is concerned, we might relevantly say that since the Rat Man did not consult further than Berggasse 19, the buck stopped at Freud.

the Lanzer family at large. The proclamation "After all, the Lanzers are the only nice people" (p. 286) summed up familial exclusiveness: Mr. and Mrs. Lanzer were cousins, as were Ernst and Gisela; Ernst was urged to follow his father and marry into the Saborskys; Olga married a cousin, whereas another of Ernst's sisters by her amatory refusal provoked her first cousin's suicide (pp. 302, 306). The various incestuous and other meanings of the foregoing circuits lead us back to the centrality of the Rat Man's primal scene and the confusing archaic fantasy about a fixed or circular ownership of the anal penis.

Having journeyed through selected domains in the Rat Man's psychological world, his object relations, body image, and rat symbolism, we pick up the pace to arrive at his language, our last stopping place. We join Freud as he spells out elements of style in the obsessional's associations: the use of distortion, generalization, indefinite and ambiguous wording, and ellipsis. Concurrent with the expressive mode may be a defensive manner of articulation—for example, the Rat Man's pronouncing indistinctly and talking with great rapidity. Yet as pertinent as these observations are about the obsessional's discourse, Freud made another series of scattered remarks which, if pursued, lead to surprising conclusions. It is in this direction that we now turn.

Similarity and contiguity are the two well-known principles governing the laws of free association and of magic. In magic by similarity, for example, one may injure an enemy by damaging an effigy of him, whereas in magic by contiguity, one obtains possession of the enemy's clothes or hair and treats them in a hostile way (Freud, 1913c, pp. 79–95). Although Freud cursorily analyzed obsessionality in terms of the principle of similarity and contrast (the displacement of the impressive onto something small or trivial [p. 241; 1913, p. 87]), overall he says much more about obsessionality and contiguity. In fact, one may find ample justification at hand to call obsessionality predominantly a neurosis of contiguity.

We have seen that in the Rat Man's sexual life, there was little contact, that is, contiguity. Indeed, "looking took the place of touching for him" (p. 309), hence his overdetermined and defensive use of the eye, which is "perhaps the zone most remote from the sexual object" (1905, p. 209). Relatedly, it was through his idiosyncratic use of peripheral vision that the Rat Man managed to introduce contiguity into the visual function and then lay claim to magically prophetic powers (p. 231). But the Rat Man is like other obsessionals in disrupting contiguity between causal connections, a disruption brought about in affective and temporal ways:

> Repression is effected not by means of amnesia but by a severance of causal connections brought about by a withdrawal of affect. (p. 231)
>
> *An interval of time* is inserted between the pathogenic situation and the obsession that arises from it so as to lead astray any conscious investigation of its causal connections. (p. 246; see also p. 303)

One of the dynamic features assigned by Freud to hysteria is clarificatory here. It is simultaneity rather than sequentiality that characterizes hysterical compromise in which conflicting tendencies find satisfaction at the same time—two birds are killed with one stone (p. 192). In contrast, a contiguity marks the diphasic obsessional acts where a first activity is undone by the second (p. 190). We might even add that the terminally stressed contiguity of some undoing is anally overdetermined.

Keeping the notion of terminality in mind, let us examine some of the Rat Man's verbalizations to see what we may find. In view of the fact that the nature of verbal discourse is that of a linear or verbal string, the frequent designation of the anus as the rear end, backside, or behind makes it mimetically appropriate that the ending of sentences be a choice site of decisive utterances of obsessionality. Since the Rat Man was obsessed with anal penetration, we might expect that the terminal parts of his utterances would be hyperinvested; and in reality, such was the case. It is as if his utterances at times were symbolic extensions of his corporeal schema where an investment was defensively displaced from the front to the anal region. The oath "May God protect him/her" demonstrates what I mean (pp. 193, 242). A *not* would suddenly emerge from the Rat Man's unconscious and turn the sentence into its opposite. As opposed to English, however, in German the negative *nicht* is appended to the end of the sentence so that it penetrates the formula just as the rats did the anus.[30]

Closely associated with the *nicht* specimen is the protective formula *aber*. According to Freud's report, the Rat Man was given to rapidly pronouncing *aber* (but), accompanied with a repudiating gesture. After a while, he changed from correctly pronouncing *aber* to accenting the last syllable, for he felt that the unaccented *e* (which the Rat Man erringly called a mute or silent *e*) of the second syllable afforded no defense against the intrusion of a foreign element. For Freud, the accentual shift was motivated by the approximation of *aber* to the psychoanalytic term *Abwehr* (defense), the *e* of which has a marked secondary accent. In that way, Freud explains, the Rat Man inducted psychoanalytic treatment into a neurotic formation (pp. 224–25, 294–95). Fair enough, but several supplementary remarks are called for. First, the Rat Man's argument about the "mute" *e* pertained not to the beginning of the word but only to its multivalent termination—its ending had to be stressed, fortified. Second, besides signifying *but*, *aber* when used as an adverb can mean *again*; hence, the very

---

30. See R. Fliess's explanation of "anal reversal" (1956, pp. 126–27); cf. also Kestenberg (1980, p. 167): motivated by his testicular defect, the Rat Man "turned his attention away from the front of his body and, progressively, hoped to create a dental-fecal-testicular baby." Chasseguet-Smirgel (1967, p. 618): the obsessional is often compulsively driven to confirm what has happened behind (therefore a going back in space and time) in order to verify whether anal penetration has taken place.

repetition of *aber* with its ambiguous meanings of disjunction (*but*) and conjunction (*again*) beautifully demonstrates how in time drive contaminates defense. Third, there is a narcissistically phonetic feature in *aber*; that is, the *e* of the Rat Man's monosyllabic first name (Ernst) partakes in the stress, whereas the final *e* of his family name (Lanzer) is unstressed; his full name begins and ends with *er*, significantly repeated in the overdetermined pronunciation of the terminal syllable in *aber*.[31]

The Rat Man's most remarkable apotropaic formula is, of course, *Glej(i)samen*.[32] Fearing that his masturbation injured his revered lady, he then rattled off the anagrammatic prayer that was supposed to protect her as he carried through masturbating with her image before him. Freud decoded the formula this way to the Vienna Psychoanalytic Society:

gl = glückliche, that is, may G(isela) and L(anzer) be happy.
e = alle [all], that is, may all be happy.
j(i) = jetzt, immer [now, forever].
Samen = Samen [semen].
     = s + amen. (Nunberg & Federn, 1962, 1:246)[33]

As Freud points out, the first part of the verbal conundrum contains the letters in the name of the Rat Man's revered lady, Gisela. It is also noteworthy that the Rat Man affixes, finalizes his semen with an amen and then puts it partly behind Gisela—hence, an

---

31. Cf. Viderman (1970, p. 120): "It's the *front* which he first defends (a defense against castration by the father and captain); the displacement of the tonic accent prevents that something (rats) penetrates from *behind*."

32. Cf. the variant spellings: *Glejisamen* (p. 280), *Gleijsamen* (p. 291), *Glejsamen* (p. 294). Actually the second of these is a misspelling by Strachey, as he avowed in a letter to Sherwood (Sherwood, 1969, pp. 200–01n). I suspect that the alternates recorded by Rank in the *Minutes of the Vienna Psychoanalytic Society* were carefully dictated by Freud and are the definitive ones (see November 20, 1907, 1:246).

33. According to Kestenberg (1980, p. 168) the *e* and the faintly present *i* refer to *Ei*, the German word meaning both egg and testicle.

anal penetration carried out in the guise of an articulated prayer.[34] If any of my readers find my interpretation too fanciful, I beg them to consider that the patient eventually followed the formula with the supplement "without rats" (p. 291): here we have an extraordinarily ambivalent attempt to conjure away the rats with a back-up formula.

We might remark that the initial parts[35] of the Rat Man's utterances were not anxiogenic as were the medial and terminal parts. In fact, the Rat Man's projection of his corporeal schema into his utterances took on two forms: both the terminal part as well as the medial part of the entire utterance figured as a rectum dangerously liable to penetration. Thus he resorted to abbreviation and rapid pronunciation (pp. 243, 260) as means to prevent words from intruding (pp. 225, 294), making an insertion (p. 242), creeping (p. 193), or slipping (pp. 193, 260) into his speech. True to his ambivalence, however, in describing the rat torture to Freud, Lanzer both feared and invited anal penetration on the symbolic level of articulation per se. He thereby hesitated between phrases for the purpose of both isolating and creating gaps to be penetrated;[36] his very indistinct pronunciation of separate words also enticed Freud to guess (raten) them. Clearly the Rat Man's manipulation of Freud and his engineered reconstruction of the torture in the acoustical sphere were among the high points of the creative genius of his psychopathology, whereby cavities were ubiquitously created, both between enunciated words

---

34. For other examples of the subtle presence of anality in language, see Mahony (1979, 1980, and 1984).

35. Cf. Nunberg and Federn (1962, 1:246): "In order to prevent their being disturbed or nullified by his obsessional contradictions, he [the Rat Man] makes the prayers as brief as possible (often only one word, the first one), and then he isolates them (to prevent the next thought from attaching itself to them)."

36. See, on one hand, Shengold's description of the Rat Man's "peristaltic language" (1980, p. 181) and, on the other hand, Kestenberg's postulate (1980, p. 167): "The disequilibrium that ushers in the inner-genital phase reveals itself also through the invasion of pregenital components into language and thought. To the oro-anal play with sounds is added the fluidity of urethral modes of expression, with words running together, making speech unintelligible or dysfluent."

and within the words themselves. To be sure, along with a symbolic manner of articulation, Lanzer's rat dialect was semantically distinguished by idioms that found their way into his retrospections: he used to creep away (*verkroch*) when one of his brothers or sisters was beaten (206/427); he begged Fräulein Rudolf to let him creep under (*kriechen*) her skirt (160/386); and the rat punishment itself was one of creeping into (*Hineinkriechen*) the rectum (220/438). Memories together with obsessions went on all fours.

Our account of the Rat Man's id-laden language would be scarcely satisfactory if we did not address the role of names in his life. The determining value of names, let us remark, is a widespread cultural phenomenon. In many primitive nations the neonates did not acquire life until a name-giving ceremony was held, and the Biblical Jews themselves would say, "Like him, like his name"; germanely, the very word *Semitic* hearkens back to Noah's eldest son Shem, the meaning of which is "name" (Roback, 1954, p. 59). But as Freud insisted, apart from this historical interest the general topic of names demands our clinical attention:

> Even a civilized adult may be able to infer from certain peculiarities in his own behaviour that he is not so far removed as he may have thought from attributing importance to proper names, and that his own name has become to a very remarkable extent bound up with his personality. So, too, psycho-analytic practice comes upon frequent confirmations of this in unconscious mental activities. . . . Like other neurotics, they [obsessionals] show a high degree of "complexive sensitiveness" in regard to uttering or hearing particular words and names; and their attitude towards their own names imposes numerous, and often serious, inhibitions upon them. (Freud, 1913c, p. 56)

Nevertheless, Freud contended that names are not so frequently used in obsessional neurosis as in hysteria for the purpose of establishing a link between "unconscious thoughts" and symptoms (p. 189*n*), and he detected but two instances of that phenomenon in the Rat Man (pp. 160*n*, 189*n*, 318). Besides the symptomatic significance of calling a governess by her last name, Freud noted the verbal translations in the Rat Man's physical stringencies over one summer. The patient was suddenly given to taking exaggerated weight-reducing measures because he felt too "fat" (the German word is *dick*). He would also get up from the table and without a hat sprint in the blazing sun or try to dash up a mountain. The underlying motivation of these otherwise senseless activities was that he was jealous of Gisela's uncle Richard, called Dick for short. Not only did the Rat Man try to be attractively slim like Dick but also, internalizing him, engagingly subjected him to killing exercises.

Let us go beyond where Freud stopped. The patient was recurrently tempted to cut his throat with a razor (pp. 158, 187–88, 255, 260) or, more precisely, as the German text would have it, with a straight-razor (*Rasiermesser*). The word *Messer* (knife) itself is in the same generic class as *Lanze*, lance, the origin of the Rat Man's family name of Lanzer; as a consequence, the Rat Man pronouncedly showed the paternal roots of his masochistically affected narcissism.[37] In addition, a phonetic association to *rat* appears in the first two letters of *Rasiermesser*, therefore contributing to the overdetermination of the selected suicidal instrument. The Rat Man's first name, Ernst, also came into play. He said that the German word *sterben* (to die) sounded like death to him (p. 300), an association that Hawelka (p. 203) tries to explain in alluding to the German *Scherben* (pieces of a broken object). There is more. With the exception of *b*, the word *Ernst*

---

37. Cf. Weiss (1980, pp. 205–06): the Rat Man's castration anxiety for years "appears to have revolved around swords. . . . Such swords were very popular as decorative wall hangings with young men at the time." Apart from this military perspective, the Rat Man would have been concerned about names within the religious context of Catholic Vienna. That the first names of the Lanzer children were not Jewish is quite to the point.

contains all the letters of *sterben*. The Rat Man, moreover, reproached himself for not being at the deathbed of his father, who cried out, "Is that Ernst?" (p. 174).[38]

That the Rat Man's beloved bore the surname *Adler* (eagle) is not entirely accidental, even though, apart from designating a national symbol, it is a widespread family name in Austria. Was not the Rat Man's greatest fright due to a stuffed bird in his mother's hat? Was he not nicknamed in his family carrion crow (*Leichenvogel*, literally, corpse bird)? Did he not fear Freud to be a beast of prey (p. 285)? We allow ourselves to surmise that these references might have unconsciously constituted ancillary reasons for the Rat Man's refusal to divulge his lady's name in the analysis.

The Rat Man's deterministic world of names contains other specimens for us. In his romantic life was a woman who had the same name as his preferred sister and whom he also "revered" (*verehrte* [H, p. 128], a word Strachey again tones down to *admired* [p. 274]). In a pertinent dream the Rat Man wanted to present Freud with a card of condolence on the death of his mother, but instead of writing "p.c." (*pour condoler*) on it, the patient wrote "p.f." (*pour féliciter*). I suggest that the *p.c.* refers also to the deceased Camilla and that *p.f.* is also Professor Freud, thus constituting a transferential hostility that was overlooked in the treatment. In another instance, Freud judged the name of Lieutenant David in the reimbursement episode to be "of little consequence"

---

38. The phonetic strings *sterben* and *Ernst* were echoed in Freud's pivotal clinical emphasis on Heinrich Lanzer's deadly threat toward his son in terms of sexually *interfering* (*stören*: 182/405, 406; 183/406; 205n/426n; 208n/428n). Since the menacing father might have explicitly linked masturbation with death or threatened to cut off the penis (p. 263), Ernst might well have associated *Schere* (scissors) with *sterben* (die) and with *Scherberl*, which in Viennese dialect means chamberpot. Perhaps Ernst might have even said that he first noticed sexual differences when he saw Camilla sitting on the *Scherberl*, which Freud synonymously recorded as *Topf* (we recall the pot with the deadly rats). Seemingly there was a phonemic cluster with a pervasive, unconscious meaning in the Rat Man's life, comparable to the *tr* and *tor* in the Wolf Man's (cf. Mahony, 1984, pp. 38–39).

(p. 168n). Yet elsewhere he related that his patient had seen Wagner's *Meistersinger*, in which the name David is called out and that the Rat Man used this episode as an exclamatory motif in his family. Undoubtedly he identified with the operatic character, who was notably versed in the rules of his craft, provoking laughter at his own expense. As a matter of fact, the name seemed so significant to Freud that he believed for a long time that it was the name of his patient's father (p. 276). Language most conclusively did not exist as a mere instrument of effective communication for the Rat Man; rather, it was inscribed by his death complex, wounded narcissism, and conflictual body schema. Yet whatever misapprehension (p. 190) and doubt clouded over the Rat Man's world of sound and its oral-aural termini, his distinguishing sense of smell seemed to remain unaffected.

Summing up: Freud diagnosed the Rat Man as a "moderately severe" (p. 155) case of obsessional neurosis, the Wolf Man as a severe one, and Frau C. as a "very severe" obsessional neurotic[39] (Freud, 1974a, p. 175; cf. also pp. 183–84, 423, 473–74, 479). Upgrading those diagnoses, most analysts today would see the first patient as a severe obsessional, the second as a borderline, and the third perhaps as a psychotic. Severe as the Rat Man's condition was, we should not let it distort our evaluation of his whole personality. While referring to the "intactness" (p. 178) of the Rat Man's personality, Freud was also careful to point out that "in his normal state he was kind, cheerful, and sensible—an enlightened and superior kind of person" (p. 248). The extant evidence also indicates that the Rat Man enjoyed beneficial relationships with significant figures—his father, sisters, and confidant; it is safe too to say that during her son's early years Mrs. Lanzer provided some necessary sustenance that guaranteed a certain amount of sound structuralization and internalization.

---

39. Actually the gravity of the patient's illness is somewhat intensified in German: *ein furchtbar ernster Fall* (literally, a terribly serious case).

Just as positive is the variety of his intense emotions (love, shame, disgust, and so on), which sets him off as an obsessional neurotic in contrast to the obsessive-compulsive personalities, whose emotional spectrum is quite limited. In addition, changing defensive organization and dramatic symptomatology differentiate the Rat Man as a neurotic from obsessive character personalities, in whom symptomatology tends to be even and undramatic, whose defenses are rigid, whose openness to a psychoanalytic vantage point is negligible, and whose capacity to associate is severely restrained (Eissler, 1959, pp. 39–40). Insight, self-awareness, and intelligence also testified to the Rat Man's developmental achievement. Although obsessional at a young age, he suffered crippling symptoms only much later in life, a very good prognosis in itself, and he never showed any physiological regression. Then again, he experienced his symptomatology as ego-alien in a much more definite way than did, say, the Wolf Man.

Now the less positive side. Cryptorchism, primal-scene exposure, an early history of sibling birth and death, unresolved mourning, overstimulation, seduction, some deficient parenting—these were stresses that entailed developmental deficit and conflict in varying measure. That Mr. and Mrs. Lanzer had children at less than two-year intervals until the relatively long childless aftermath of Camilla's death might be taken as an index of a parental depressive reaction bearing on their son, who reported hardly any happy memories of his childhood.

Not achieving oedipal resolution,[40] the Rat Man all the more easily regressed to an anal fixation, which itself was modified by an oral-sadistic libido. In his homosexuality the Rat Man identified masochistically with his mother and submitted passively to his father, thereby attempting to ward off the dangers of oedipal rivalry and of an intimidating preoedipal mother; another defen-

---

40. Cf. Zetzel (1966, p. 45): "a major impediment to the resolution of his oedipal conflict . . . was his reaction to the death of his sister;" and Gedo and Goldberg (1973, p. 112): the Rat Man "achieved full Oedipal resolution."

sive tactic was to displace precarious negative and positive affects onto his brother and sisters. Considerable castration anxiety showed up in the Rat Man's impaired masculine identity, fear of success, and marked hesitation toward marital and professional commitments; relatedly, humiliation and defeat at the hands of male figures moved him into masochistic subjugation (pp. 265, 318). In his representational world the female imago was split into the idealized and the debased, while gratitude, tenderness, and mature concern were lacking in his object relationships with women.

The Rat Man's optimal ego functioning was thwarted by a series of factors, among which numbered distorted self and object representations, massive reliance on obsessional defenses, taxing ego states that ranged from daze to listlessness to agitation, and the relentless self-reproaches of a sadistic superego. The externalization of critical and self-observations of his superego were manifest in his excessive dependence on reassuring confidants and his lifelong belief that his parents could read his thoughts (see Morgenthaler [1966]; Kanzer [1980, pp. 242–44, 420]; Shengold [1980, pp. 189–90]). The undermined regulatory functions of his ego and superego fostered an instability whereby he could not master the middle range of feelings—hence the correspondence in extremeness between his affective states and his self-representations as either "a great man or a great criminal" (Kestenberg, 1980, p. 149; for examples of the Rat Man's histrionic behavior, see pp. 187, 203, 261, 271, 278). In the rat fantasy, the affective extreme reached that of primitive destructiveness, accompanying a disruption of the closed body-ego representation that is fundamental to self-identity; in a more specific sense, the rat fantasy as one of anal cannibalistic rape invoked a primal terror toward the destruction of the sphincteral source of control (Shengold, 1985, esp. p. 70).

In his disrupted narcissism, the Rat Man tried desperately to shore up his crumbling world. To fend off developmental anxieties, depression over object loss, and the regressive emergence of unconscious conflicts, he turned to vigorous sexual activity and obsessional symptom formation; and doubt feebly staved off repressed hatred and death wishes. Attempts at reparation and restitution militated against healthy self-esteem: he relinquished his money to his mother and in that way gave her the anal penis; as a carrion crow he identified with others who, unlike himself, could mourn and he tried to revive them; and he resuscitated his dead sister by choosing an unhealthy, nonprocreative woman as love object. Another means of compensating for his wounded narcissism was a heightened reliance on omnipotent wishes. Two capsule instances of this, overlooked by previous commentators on the Rat Man, are found in the *Minutes of the Vienna Psychoanalytic Society,* vol. 1, pp. 345–46. There, although not naming his subject, Freud explained away the Rat Man's telepathic knowledge about a certain lady's death and demystified his prophetic vision about the wages to be earned by his seamstress-mistress (the story of kronen is back in circulation!).

I want to offer a final suggestion about the psychodynamics of contiguity in the Rat Man's life. To start off, four kinds of contiguity may be semiotically distinguished: existential or materially real contiguity (the park abuts the mountain); imputed contiguity (a sound image or signifier combines with the signified to produce a word); rhetorical contiguity proper to metonymic figures of speech ("I read Virgil," instead of "I read the *Aeneid*"); and syntactical contiguity (the juxtaposition of words in discourse). In terms of the last of these, the Rat Man used isolation in the sense of temporal intervals to disrupt syntactical contiguity. The notion of imputed contiguity needs a slightly expanded explanation: alongside the dyadic conception of imputed contiguity in language, psychoanalysis considers a third factor, affect, especially in cases where words constitute some measure of discourse; when engaged in the communication of imputed contiguities, the Rat Man also resorted to isolation, though this time in the sense of removal of affect. Relative to the syntactical and imputed contiguities, the impact of existential contiguity in the Rat Man's obsessional neurosis is far more complicated and forces me to further clarify my evolving hypothesis. Whatever the eventual interaction between precocious repression and anal regression, the result is a reactivation of preoedipal and oedipal conflicts directed toward the anal zone. Putatively, the existential proximity of the anal and genital zones becomes an organizing feature in the body schema with a role peculiar to obsessional neurosis. And following that, it is as if a taboo against touching asserts itself not only in external but also in endopsychic reality. By their linkage with anal body parts, products, and sensations, the drives are somewhat defused, and a severance is imposed between negative and positive affects and feelings. The coherence of this theoretical schema may become more cogent if we remind ourselves that the narcissistic investment of mental processes as a substitute for anal derivatives testifies to obsessional control and the sublimating aesthetic and moral imperatives of the ego and superego.

Aided by our foregoing diagnoses of the Rat Man's earlier history, we are prepared to examine his psychoanalytic treatment. In the course of doing so, we shall again and again be surprised by gaping differences between Freud's clinical and subsequent expository techniques.

3

The Rat Man's Treatment:
General Facts and Questions

We continue now with Ernst Lanzer on October 1, 1907, the date he presented himself for psychoanalysis with Freud. But immediate questions about the length, evolution, and results of the treatment will involve us in a scrutiny of what has been traditionally received as fact. First of all, how long did the treatment last? The two germane statements by Freud are congruent: it "lasted for about a year" (p. 155); it "lasted in all for more than eleven months" (p. 186).[1] From these remarks critics have unanimously and confidently concluded that the case lasted from October 1, 1907, to some time in September 1908. Available documents, however, modify this assumption and lead us to the provisional conclusion that the treatment did not extend beyond July 15—that is, nine and a half months. Indeed, a pair of letters have survived in which Freud expressed his intention to leave Vienna on July 15, 1908, for his summer holidays.[2] The intention was carried through as planned, for on July 18 Freud wrote to Jung from Berchtesgaden, saying that he had already been there for a few days.[3] Freud left Berchtesgaden on September 1 for the

---

1. Strictly speaking, the words *in all* in Strachey's translation are not justified: cf. *G.W.*, 10:409: *der über 11 Monate verlaufenden Behandlung*. The nuance is important because Strachey's formulation favors the possibility that Freud might have been referring to an intermittent analysis.
2. See letter of 7/11/08, *A Psycho-Analytic Dialogue*, p. 43, and letter of 6/30/08 in *Freud/Jung Letters*, p. 161.
3. Ibid., p. 164.

second trip in his life to England. From England he went to Berlin, then to Zurich for a visit with Jung, and then on to Lago di Garda, where he vacationed with his sister-in-law Minna; he returned to Vienna early on September 29.[4]

Freud's declarations about time are even more problematic when he broached the story of the Rat Man's evolving treatment. In fact, portions of Freud's case history, when cross-checked with the process notes, show that he was wont to lengthen (never to shorten) the period of the treatment in the public account, thereby giving the reader the impression that the narrated material embraced a much longer span of analytic work. In this connection we should bear in mind that Freud's overall analytic stress on memory retrieval and reconstruction rather than on transferential working through in the here-and-now, which is clearly reflected in his case history, guided his daily note taking; the resulting abundance of restrictive temporal markers permits us to trace the emergence of associative material that would have been otherwise impossible.

Freud's fictive manipulation of time is especially prominent in the case history's section concerning the precipitating cause of the patient's illness (pp. 195–200). Here Freud aimed to create the belief that the narration was drawing on a very prolonged clinical period, whereas in actuality he was relying on process notes recorded only on December 8. They elliptically begin: "Much change in the course of one week," suggesting that the previously recorded session dates from November 30. The process notes of December 8, however, can hardly refer to a week of continued sessions without note taking, for some time during that period Freud was prompted to send a postcard to his patient (p. 293).

What follow are excerpts from Freud's case history which are

---

4. See Jones, 2:52–53; *Freud/Jung Letters*, editorial note on p. 171.

based solely on his notes of December 8. (The words in capitals in this and subsequent citations are my own emphasis.)

> ONE DAY the patient mentioned quite casually an event which I could not fail to recognize as the precipitating cause of his illness. ... As was to be expected, the patient did not, TO BEGIN WITH, accept my elucidation of the matter. ... But in the FURTHER COURSE OF TREATMENT he was forcibly brought to believe in the truth of my suspicion, and in a most singular manner. With the help of a transference phantasy, he experienced, as though it were new and belonged to the present, the very episode from the past which he had forgotten, or which had only passed through his mind unconsciously. THERE CAME AN OBSCURE AND DIFFICULT PERIOD IN THE TREATMENT; EVENTUALLY IT TURNED OUT that he had once met a young girl on the stairs in my house and had on the spot promoted her into being my daughter. She had pleased him, and he pictured to himself that the only reason I was so kind and incredibly patient with him was that I wanted to have him for a son-in-law. ... I will repeat one of the dreams which he had AT THIS PERIOD so as to give an example of his manner of treating the subject. He dreamt that *he saw my daughter in front of him; she had two patches of dung instead of eyes*. No one who understands the language of dreams will find much difficulty in translating this one: it declared that *he was marrying my daughter not for her "beaux yeux" but for her money*. (pp. 195, 199–200)

Comparing the above to its source passage in the process notes for December 8, the reader can appreciate for himself Freud's fictional methods of extending time:

Our pursuit of the treatment-transference led along many devious paths. He described a temptation whose significance he seemed to be unaware of. A relative of Rubensky had offered to fit up an office for him in the neighbourhood of the Cattle

Market as soon as he had got his doctor's degree—which was at the time only a few months off—and to find him clients there. This fitted in with his mother's old scheme for him to marry one of R.'s daughters, a charming girl who is now seventeen. He had no notion that he took flight into illness. . . . He was clearly struggling against phantasies of being tempted to marry my daughter instead of his cousin, and against insults to my wife and daughter. One of his transferences was straight out that Frau Prof. F. should lick his arse—a revolt against a grander family. Another time he saw my daughter with two patches of dung in the place of eyes. This means that he has not fallen in love with her eyes, but with her money. (pp. 292–93)[5]

The most remarkable chronological discrepancies figuring in Freud's case history, though, come from the section entitled "The Father Complex and the Solution of the Rat Idea" (pp. 200–20). In the course of his exposition, Freud gives a picture of the Rat Man's masturbatory behavior and then terminates with the related spectacular episodes of his patient's "crazy" (*tolle,* 204/425) phallic exhibition before a mirror. Those episodes, jotted down by Freud on October 27 (p. 275) and December 27 (pp. 302–03), are described this way in the case history:

[The Rat Man] used to arrange that his working hours should be as late as possible in the night. Between twelve and one

---

5. See Kanzer (1952, p. 234): "When the Rat Man dreamed, after a real encounter with Freud's daughter, that he saw her before him with two patches of dung instead of eyes, Freud translated this to mean thoughts of a marriage for money rather than beauty. Now, he insisted, the Rat Man must accept an earlier interpretation to which he had been resistant—namely, that at one time he reacted neurotically to his father's demand that he wed for money (as father had done with mother) rather than love. In the official text, Freud leaves the matter with the rather unrevealing comment that the patient 'could no longer remain blind to the overwhelming effect of the perfect analogy between the transference phantasy and the actual state of affairs in the past.' In the supplementary notes, however, we find no evidence that the patient was really overwhelmed or even influenced by the interpretation."

The Rat Man's Treatment: Facts and Questions 73

o'clock at night he would interrupt his work, and open the front door of the flat as though his father were standing outside it; then, coming back into the hall, he would take out his penis and look at it in the looking-glass. This crazy conduct becomes intelligible if we suppose that he was acting as though he expected a visit from his father at the hour when ghosts are abroad. . . . in a single unintelligible obsessional act, he gave expression to the two sides of his relation with his father, just as he did subsequently with regard to his lady by means of his obsessional act with the stone. (p. 204)

As soon as Freud tells us about these exhibitions in the mirror, he proceeds chronologically to situate his first construction in the treatment:

STARTING FROM THESE INDICATIONS and from other data of a similar kind, I ventured to put forward a construction to the effect that when he was a child of under six he had been guilty of some sexual misdemeanour connected with masturbation and had been soundly castigated for it by his father. This punishment, according to my hypothesis, had, it was true, put an end to his masturbating, but on the other hand it had left behind it an ineradicable grudge against his father and had established him for all time in his role of an interferer with the patient's sexual enjoyment. (p. 205)

It is important to realize that Freud offered the preceding construction on October 12. Contrary to what Freud would like us to believe, therefore, the construction could not have started from the indication of the mirror episodes, which he recorded hearing for the first time on October 27. The resemblance of the construction in the case history to the one in the process notes dated October 12 eliminates the possibility of there being another construction under consideration, but for purposes of my readers' independent verification, I cite from the process notes of October 12:

> I could not restrain myself here from constructing the material at our disposal into an event: how before the age of six he had been in the habit of masturbating and how his father had forbidden it, using as a threat the phrase "it would be the death of you" and perhaps also threatening to cut off his penis. This would account for his masturbating in connection with the release from the curse, for the commands and prohibitions in his unconscious and for the threat of death which was now thrown back onto his father. (p. 263)

From all this a conclusion relentlessly follows: through the altering of temporal sequence, Freud's construction given to the Rat Man becomes in turn a fictionalized reconstruction shown to the reader. Obviously Freud thought that to have his construction refer to an episode he heard only later made for a better story.

According to our next focal point in the case history, the Rat Man subsequently brought up the beating incident with his mother, who confirmed it and added that his punishment had been due to his biting someone (pp. 206–09); most strangely, however, the process notes do not register the emergence of that episode in the treatment. At any rate, we read in the case history that "only along the painful road of transference" (p. 209) was the Rat Man able to be convinced of the evidential worth of the story. The "painful road" naturally makes us think of a long time, an impression reinforced by Freud's expatiation on the transference:

> Things SOON reached a point at which, in his dreams, his waking phantasies, and his associations, he began heaping the grossest and filthiest abuse upon me and my family, though in his deliberate actions he never treated me with anything but the greatest respect. His demeanour as he repeated these in-

sults to me was that of a man in despair. "How can a gentleman like you, sir," he used to ask, "let yourself be abused in this way by a low, good-for-nothing fellow like me? You ought to turn me out: that's all I deserve." While he talked like this, he would get up from the sofa and roam about the room,—a habit which he explained at first as being due to delicacy of feeling; he could not bring himself, he said, to utter such horrible things while he was lying there so comfortably. BUT SOON he himself found a more cogent explanation, namely, that he was avoiding my proximity for fear of my giving him a beating. If he stayed on the sofa he behaved like someone in desperate terror trying to save himself from castigations of terrific violence; he would bury his head in his hands, cover his face with his arm, jump up suddenly and rush away, his features distorted with pain, and so on. He recalled that his father had had a passionate temper, and sometimes in his violence had not known where to stop. Thus, LITTLE BY LITTLE, IN THIS SCHOOL OF SUFFERING, the patient won the sense of conviction which he had lacked. (p. 209)

As I said, Freud's chronicle of this agonizing transference, the "turning point" in the treatment, leads us to conjure up a lengthy period of duration. In reality, however, he draws his descriptive material from a phase lasting in the process notes from November 21 to December 8. Thus Freud's seemingly unending "school of suffering little by little" turns out to be just a sixteen-day crash course.

Let us return to the case history. After elaborating on the period of painful transference, Freud promptly announces, "And now the path was clear to the solution of the rat idea" (p. 209)—and he devotes the rest of the clinical section of his case history to tracing and recounting that solution which, by textual implication, seems to have taken up the rest of the treatment. Before we resume our journey with Freud, however, we may want to ask ourselves, how long did that solution really take? And of Freud's statement that a quantity of previously withheld information now became available and permitted a construction and solution of the rat idea we may further ask, how much of that solution is contained within the process notes, which, let me stress, date only from October 1907 to January 1908? Some replies are available.

In beginning to unfold the rat solution, Freud brings in the following series of new findings about rats (I use parentheses to date the emergence of the associations in the process notes):
- The father as gambler, *Spielratte* (November 30)
- Worms as rats in Ernst's anus (January 2)
- Rats as money, installments, and carriers of syphilis (November 29)
- Rats as similar to penises, and the Slavic curse about anal intercourse (January 3)

After mentioning the Slavic curse of anal intercourse, Freud made a link, found only in the original record, between "all of this material, and more besides," with the screen-association *heiraten* (to marry). The next paragraph permits us roughly to locate the screen-association's emergence in the treatment (bracketed dates refer the material back to the process notes):

> The story of the rat punishment, as was shown by the patient's own account of the matter and by his facial expression as he repeated the story to me, had fanned into a flame all his prematurely suppressed impulses of cruelty, egoistic and sexual alike. Yet, in spite of all this wealth of material, no light was thrown upon the meaning of his obsessional idea UNTIL ONE DAY the Rat-Wife in Ibsen's *Little Eyolf* came up in the analysis, and it became impossible to escape the inference that in many of the shapes assumed by his obsessional deliria rats had another meaning still—namely, that of *children* [possibly from the session of November 29 or near to it]. ENQUIRY INTO THE ORIGIN OF THIS NEW MEANING AT ONCE BROUGHT me up against

some of the earliest and most important roots. Once when the patient was visiting his father's grave he had seen a big beast, which he had taken to be a rat, gliding along over the grave. He assumed that it had actually come out of his father's grave, and had just been having a meal off his corpse [December 16]. . . . But he himself had been just such a nasty, dirty little wretch, who was apt to bite people when he was in a rage. . . . According, then, to his earliest and most momentous experiences, rats were children. AND AT THIS POINT HE BROUGHT OUT A PIECE OF INFORMATION which he kept away from its context long enough, but which NOW fully explained the interest he was bound to feel in children. The lady, whose admirer he had been for so many years, but whom he had nevertheless not been able to make up his mind to marry, was condemned to childlessness [December 10 and January 7].[6] . . . It was ONLY THEN that it became possible to understand the inexplicable process by which his obsessional idea had been formed. (pp. 215–17)

I could not specifically locate the crucial reference to Ibsen's *Little Eyolf* in the process notes; the entry for November 29 speaks of a purposive but not an identificatory relationship between rats and children. Yet this obstacle is short-lived when we recall that for Freud this new meaning led to more material, whose emergence in the treatment we have been able to date as not long afterward. The session of November 29 carries even more importance for our investigation in its revelation that from the very start of analysis the Rat Man secretly associated Freud's fees with rats. Yet Freud, consistent with his narrative aim of making phases in the treatment appear longer than they were,

---

6. Freud does add with utmost brevity that the lady's sterility was the Rat Man's chief reason for hesitating to marry her (p. 216). Since Freud does not expatiate on this as he did on other reasons for the Rat Man's not marrying, it is possible that the childlessness, perhaps first brought up during the months of December and January in connection with Gisela's operation, did not receive particular attention then from Freud.

states in the case history that he learned of the Rat Man's secret association of fees and rats only six months into the treatment (p. 213), whereas the association emerged in half that time (p. 313)! Another thing: employing the process notes as a guide, we can estimate that the solution seems to have taken place in the period between November 6 and January 7. In other words, the rat solution occurred a little more than three months into a treatment that reportedly lasted nearly a year.

At this juncture one may object that the stuff of psychoanalytic treatment is not the mere mentioning of material but rather its working through, that the use of the term *solution* might be vague, and that it would be clinically absurd to postulate that the historical reconstruction of a symptom automatically entails its immediate disappearance. Of course, I would be in general agreement with such reasonable statements, and I would even join to them my observation that Freud often used the term *Lösung* (solution) ambiguously, hence not letting one know whether he means solution as an answer to something or solution as a resolution or dissolution of a symptom, neurosis, and so on (cf. Freud, 1900, p. 108). These reservations, however, do not apply to the issue at stake. Freud's case history of the Rat Man permits no doubt that the mere solution or reconstruction of the rat delirium caused its disappearance:

> We should not be justified in expecting such severe obsessional ideas as were present in this case to be cleared up in any simpler manner or by any other means. When we reached the solution that has been described above, the patient's rat delirium disappeared. (p. 220)

How are we to explain the implications of the mounting evidence up to now? Perhaps a slip of attention or a lapse of memory might occur here and there, but surely that cannot account for Freud's recurrent narrative attempts in his case history to create the impression that clinical events took a much longer time in the treatment than they actually did.⁷ And in particular, in contrast to Freud's implication that the solution of the rat idea happened near the end of a year's analysis, we have shown through the time sequences in the case history and process notes that they allot the phase of the solution to a time roughly coordinate with the sudden discontinuation of the process notes in January.

The comfort of our logical procedure would be superficial if we avoided asking ourselves still another question: if there are serious discrepancies between the case history and the process notes, is any adjusted synthesis of their chronological indications reliable? How are we to understand that the rat solution took place by the month of January? Since our quest for assured answers seems to be increasingly frustrated, let us look for other documents containing Freud's comments on the Rat Man. The *Minutes of the Vienna Psychoanalytic Society* is one such document, but are its revelations reliable? How can they fit into our chronological synthesis? Let us see.

At the meeting of the society on November 20, 1907, Freud said that the name of the Rat Man's lady could be guessed from his magic, anagrammatic prayers, even though her name had not yet been disclosed in treatment.⁸ In truth, however, Freud had learned her name on October 27; and it is baffling that he could have forgotten this, for he felt that without the knowledge of her

---

7. There remain a few details in the entire case history that cannot be directly found in their substance in the process notes: Mrs. Lanzer's predictions about her getting sick (p. 231); the Rat Man's attraction to a woman living near the post office (p. 211); his childhood coprophiliac tendencies (p. 247n); an obsessional idea concerning a little niece (p. 226); a second temptation to travel back to the maneuvers area and begin all over again the farcical attempts to pay back the money for his glasses. Relative to the Rat Man's first month of treatment in October, his second temptation to return to the area occurred "many months later, when his resistance was at its height" (p. 173). However, there are indications elsewhere in the text that this second temptation did not take place "many" months later but some time around the period from November 21 to December 8, when the transference was reportedly agonizing and the Rat Man had the "severest resistances" (p. 200).

8. *Minutes of the Vienna Psychoanalytic Society*, 1:246.

name much of the clinical material would have been incomprehensible during the treatment. Here, then, are Freud's germane process notes from October 27:

> So long as he makes difficulties over giving me the lady's name his account must be incoherent. . . . After I had persuaded him to reveal the name . . . and all the details about her, his account became clear and systematic. (pp. 272–73)

After October 27, Freud spoke four times about the Rat Man to the Vienna Psychoanalytic Society: whereas the subject matter of November 20, 1907, and January 22, 1908 (the anagrammatic prayer and the two modal words, *pince-nez* and *Dick*), can be found in Freud's day-to-day notes on the Rat Man, that does not hold for the two revelations of March 4 (taken up in chapter 2)— the seamstress's wages and the report of a lady's death. The fourth and last occasion before the Vienna Psychoanalytic Society was on April 8, 1908, when Freud once more announced the rat solution, but this time with some new material. Those *Minutes* read:

> PROF. FREUD reports on the solution of the rat idea in the obsessional neurotic; it means:
> 1. Guess (numbers). He admits that he does not distinguish between *Ratten* [rats] and *raten* [to guess].
> 2. The identification with his father, who also was in the army and contracted a gambling debt there; a friend loaned his father money to settle this debt; his father probably never paid this debt since he was a *"Spielratte"* ["gambling rat"].
> 3. A very special type of *"Ratten"*: *Heiraten* [getting married].[9]

Of the three items, only the *Ratten-raten* (rat-guess) association is new; we are able to locate the emergence of the gambler (*"Spielratte"*) association, and Freud has told us that the *Ratten-heiraten*

---

9. Ibid., 1:370–71.

(rats-marriage) connection had appeared before other material, which we could date from the process notes.

This fresh information plunges us into still more queries. Was Freud declaring on April 8 a solution that was previously arrived at? Or does Freud's declaration generally situate the phase of the real solution whose chronological coordinates were distorted in the case history? Perhaps an overview of our findings will help us out of the uncertainty that now seems to face us in every direction. When verified against the day-to-day notes, the case history gives evidence of some unreliability of its own; in addition, the two texts when seen together suggest that the rat solution arose by the month of January. The process notes themselves record sessions more or less regularly from October 1 to January 7; then there is a long interruption until the final entry for January 20, 1908 (incidentally, the process notes last essentially for a little over three months, hence approximating the period of eleven weeks in which Dora was analyzed by Freud). My suspicion is that after January 20, Freud saw the Rat Man irregularly until April, and after that most irregularly, hence accounting for the absence of any more reference to the patient at meetings of the Vienna Psychoanalytic Society.[10]

My assumption about the brevity of an intense, regularly scheduled analysis receives unexpected support from a single isolated statement by James Strachey. In his editorial introduction to "Character and Anal Eroticism," first published in March 1908, he disclosed that the essay "was no doubt partly stimulated by the analysis of the 'Rat Man,' which had been concluded

---

10. After writing this chapter, I received a copy of Dr. Lanzer's professional dossier from the Österreichischer Rechtsanwaltskammertag. Under the rubric of "Praxis" (practical experience) the first entry shows Lanzer in the employ of Dr. Freundlich for a little over two months in 1905; the second entry places him in the office of Dr. Alois Schick from April 15, 1908, to September 30 of the same year. Apparently, then, the Rat Man was unemployed during his analysis until April 1908. This piece of unexpected information reinforces what I concluded strictly on the basis of textually internal evidence—namely, that the Rat Man discontinued his regular psychoanalysis early in 1908.

shortly before" (1908a, p. 168). Such an early dating confirms my conclusion that the Rat Man case, commonly regarded as Freud's only published, complete case, is nothing of the kind. Freud's published history of the Rat Man describes a symptomatic remission, not the resolution of the transference neurosis and the obsessional neurosis itself; to cure the Rat Man's severe neurosis, a considerably longer time, among other things, would have been necessary. Hence the case write-up we have shows no more resolution than Freud could have given in his five-hour oral report on April 26, 1908, at the first International Psychoanalytic Congress in Salzburg. For further valuable information about Freud's lecture and subsequent reflections on the Rat Man, we have the correspondence with Jung at our fortunate disposal.[11]

Jung took to heart his duties as organizer of the congress. On March 11, he wrote that he was planning to allot an hour or more to Freud and but a half hour to each of the other speakers. Within two days Freud replied that he was working on a case whose decisive phase and result were still missing. "If it should turn out badly," Freud mused, "I want to be free to substitute something else; who knows what may happen in six weeks?" That case (whose cure was indeed announced by Freud on May 19) was of little Hans. Just twelve days before the congress, however, Freud again expressed doubt about the subject of his address. Finally, with just a week to spare, Freud resorted to a second choice:

> And I have no case that is completed and can be viewed as a whole. I have given up the idea of the five-year-old boy because his neurosis, though resolving itself splendidly, hasn't kept the deadline. So it will probably be a potpourri of particular ob-

---

11. For the material of the next six paragraphs, see the following dated correspondence in *Freud/Jung Letters* (1974a): 3/11/08, pp. 133–34; 3/13/08, p. 136; 4/19/08, p. 141; 4/30/08, p. 144; 5/3/08, p. 145; 5/19/08, p. 152; 6/21/08, p. 159; 8/5/08, p. 166; 8/13/08, p. 169; 11/12/08, p. 178; 6/3/09, p. 227; 6/18/09, p. 235; 6/30/09, p. 239; and 7/7/09, p. 239.

servations and general remarks based on a case of obsessional neurosis.

How ironic that two years previously "rats were responsible" for Lanzer's having spent six months in Salzburg (p. 291), and now Freud was bringing his rat lecture there—the rodent version of bringing coals to Newcastle. Be it so, Freud's lecture so impressed Jung that even at the end of the month he could write: "I am still under the reverberating impact of your lecture, which seems to me perfection itself. All the rest was simply padding, sterile twaddle in the darkness of inanity." Were Jung's judgment taken literally, the trivial speeches would include his own on dementia praecox along with Jones's on rationalization and Abraham's on the psychosexual differences between hysteria and dementia praecox.

After the Salzburg congress, uppermost in Freud's mind was the publication of the first psychoanalytic review, *Jahrbuch für psychoanalytische und psychopathologische Forschungen,* under Jung's editorship. For the inaugural number Freud proposed on May 3 a choice between two possible case histories, one on little Hans and the other, more significant to our purposes, entitled "Aphorisms Relating to Obsessional Neurosis" (the date of Freud's proposition, some eight months after the Rat Man's treatment began, cannot have escaped our attention). Toward the end of June Freud resolved to wait until the summer vacation to write up the little boy's phobia and the freshly titled "Aphorisms on Obsessional Neurosis." Once installed in his summer residence at Berchtesgaden, Freud set about his proposed tasks. By August 5 he had finished the younger patient, but then was busy on other projects: reading the proofs of the second editions of the *Studies on Hysteria* and *The Interpretation of Dreams,* and writing an article on infantile sexuality and another on hysterical attacks. Before August 13, however, Ferenczi arrived to stay in the vicinity of Freud's place, and that was the end of his effort to compose the second case during the summer. The fall found Freud working on an exposition of psychoanalytic technique; meanwhile, fears about indiscretion prevented his writing on the Rat Man, who, Freud affirmed, was "getting along splendidly."

There followed months of silence about the patient, and then suddenly, on June 3, 1909, Freud announced a breakthrough:

> I suddenly feel like writing about the Salzburg rat man. . . . It will *not* be long, because in print I shall have to be much more discreet than in a lecture. But here is a case that will enable me to throw full light on certain aspects of the truly complicated phenomenon of obsessional neurosis.

It was perhaps during the period of Freud's hesitancy over his own discretion that the Rat Man gave him permission to publish the case (1905a, p. 14). In any event, toward the end of the month, Freud started to benefit from a caseload reduced by half. On June 30, he exclaimed, "I am too deep in my rats," and by July 7, he had finished the manuscript.

This part of our story ends rapidly. After having corrected the proofs of the case in October, Freud confessed, "I still didn't like it." Jung responded with assuaging reassurances of praise and of friendly envy that he himself was not the author. Nevertheless, Freud's grateful reaction to Jung's solace is for us anything but final:

> You are the first critic of the Rat Man. Because I myself was dissatisfied with it I was waiting anxiously for your opinion. I am overjoyed at your praise. Of course you will notice the obvious shortcomings. . . . Last week the newspapers carried the Rat Man's announcement of his engagement to the "lady"; he is facing life with courage and ability. The point that still gives him trouble (father-complex and transference) has shown up clearly in my conversations with this intelligent and grateful man.

This appraisal of the cure sends us back to Freud's overall contention in the case history: The patient's treatment "led to the complete restoration of the patient's personality, and to the removal of his inhibitions" (p. 155; cf. also pp. 207–08*n*, 249*n*, as well as Freud, 1913a, p. 85). However, all the findings of this chapter as well as the next converge to make the claim about the complete restoration of the Rat Man's personality a public instance of Freud's therapeutic exaggeration, an exaggeration so much the more patent in that the patient's maternal and negative transference neurosis apparently received little attention at the time.

It appears that Freud overstated in order to make the Rat Man's treatment temporally and qualitatively superior to Dora's—hers, the only other previously published case that Freud himself conducted after his discovery of the Oedipus complex, ended as a failure in less than three months. Seemingly, therefore, Freud desperately wanted the appearance of a complete case to impress his recently won international followers and to promote the cause of the psychoanalytic movement. By the same token, Freud's private acknowledgment, seemingly alluding to postanalytic interviews, that the Rat Man had continuing difficulties with the "father-complex and transference," prepares us to understand his public minimizing of another famous patient's posttreatment pathology. In *Cries of the Wolf Man* (1984), I marshaled sufficient evidence to controvert Freud's official contention that his second analysis of that distressed man dealt merely with "a piece of the transference" left over from an allegedly successful four-and-a-half-year analysis.

Our story would not be complete without the mention of a minor plot noteworthy in its own right—a series of intriguing events involving Freud and the Rat Man but whose evolving interconnections became known only to Freud himself. In one of his first letters to Freud, Jung briefly described the remarkable anal symptoms of his patient Sabina Spielrein. In his prompt reply Freud said that such anal individuals present the traits of neatness, stinginess, and obstinacy, an observation considerably anticipating his well-known publication on the subject in 1908. With the start of the next year a new topic emerged in the correspondence between Freud and Jung, occasioned by the latter's lecture in Amsterdam on "The Freudian Theory of Hysteria." In it Jung queried whether child hysteria should be put in the same grouping with adult hysteria. As he later explained to Freud, "Child hysteria must be outside the formula applicable to adults, for whom puberty plays a large role."

Upon receiving the revised reprint of Jung's Amsterdam lecture, Freud hinted that his analysis of little Hans would establish an opposing viewpoint; yet he doubted that he would be able to present the case within two weeks in Salzburg, as we have already seen.[12] Although Freud finally chose to lecture on the Rat Man, he might still have been addressing Jung's paper on two counts: first, Freud's case history demonstrated the commonality and continuity that existed between child and adult neuroses; and second, Freud might have been directly responding to the sole clinical vignette in Jung's paper, that of Sabina Spielrein and her impressionable history of anal eroticism.

We seemingly leave Spielrein to pass on to another subject—Freud's referral of Otto Gross for treatment with Jung. Jung's diagnosis of Gross as "a definite obsessional neurotic" drew this long response from Freud:

> I can imagine how much of your time he must be taking. I originally thought you would only take him on for the withdrawal period and that I would start analytical treatment in the autumn. . . . But seriously, the difficulty would have been that the dividing line between our respective property rights in cre-

---

12. For the sources of the next five paragraphs, consult the following correspondence in *Freud/Jung Letters*: 10/23/06, p. 7; 10/27/06, p. 8; 4/18/08, p. 139; 5/19/08, p. 152; 5/25/08, p. 153; 6/4/09, p. 229; and 6/30/09, p. 239.

ative ideas would inevitably have been effaced; we would never have been able to disentangle them with a clear conscience. Since I treated the philosopher Swoboda I have had a horror of such difficult situations.

I think your diagnosis of Gross is correct. His earliest childhood memory (communicated in Salzburg) is of his father warning a visitor: Watch out, he *bites*! He remembered this in connection with my Rat Man story.

Before our eyes, the set of entanglements now widens to enclose Gross, the Rat Man, Swoboda, and through him, Fliess, the most intimate friend Freud had ever had and whom he then painfully repudiated.

Meanwhile Jung was so countertransferentially entwined with his analysand that they would switch roles within apparently unending sessions:

> I have let everything drop and have spent all my available time, day and night, on Gross, pushing on with his analysis. . . . Whenever I got stuck, he analysed me. In this way my own psychic health has benefited.

As if that were not enough, Jung was concomitantly treating Sabina Spielrein, with whom he was amorously involved. Not without a sanctimonious cast to his proclaimed altruism and self-victimization, Jung linked the two patients in their lack of gratitude for his devoted care:

> Like Gross she is a case of fight-the-father, which in the name of all that's wonderful I was trying to cure *gratissime*. . . . Gross and Spielrein are bitter experiences. To none of my patients have I extended so much friendship and from none have I reaped so much sorrow.

In a summary letter on June 30, 1909, Freud optimistically felt that Jung's twofold clinical difficulties had the positive effect of reconciling him with genuine psychoanalysis once more. Glossing over Jung's imbroglio with Spielrein as a "happy fault," Freud exclaimed:

> When I think that I owe your ultimate conversion and profound conviction to the same experience with Gross, I cannot possibly be angry and can only marvel at the profound coherence of all things in this world.

"The profound coherence of all things in this world"—the extended list of dramatis personae now comprises Gross, the Rat Man, Swoboda, Fliess, Spielrein, Freud, and Jung. "The profound coherence of all things in this world"—both event and personal motive appeared in that month of June 1909, to form a weave patterned on both its top and its underside. But Freud's curtained coherence would not last for long.

4

Freud's Technique:
Tracing Its Historical and Clinical Features

It is the Wisdom of Rats, that will be sure to leave a House, somewhat before it fall.
—Francis Bacon, "Of Wisdom for a Man's Self," Essays

The rats are leaving the sinking ship.
—The Rat Man, "Notes upon a Case of Obsessional Neurosis," p. 299

In order to fathom Freud's technique, we must keep in mind the obstacle presented by three rhetorical scenes, each with its different aims and audiences: the clinical scene, where Freud and the Rat Man as mutual audiences were engaged in a therapeutic aim; the writing of the process notes, whose isolated setting shows Freud making daily memoranda for himself, though with the purpose of eventual publication; and the writing of the public version, throughout whose overall structure Freud addressed his readers and endeavored to instruct them. Since Freud did not compose his case history primarily to demonstrate technique, however, our study at some points is tentative, the more so because numerous textual passages are open to various interpretations about what Freud actually did and said. In addition, the very absence of detailed transferential interpretations, both as to what Freud specifically represented and as to what was the Rat Man's immediate reaction, fuels the doubt that Freud persistently focused on clarification and dissolution of the transference neurosis. Yet in spite of those restrictions, the case, when judiciously used in combination with the day-to-day notes, affords a reliable picture of Freud as frequently intrusive, reassuring, and seemingly more drawn to genetic interpretations and to reconstruction of past events than to the current interplay in the clinical situation.

In attempting to portray Freud's technique, we shall investigate some of his key conceptions and his clinical application of them. In pursuit of these far-flung goals we shall cover the following topics: general historical issues about free association, transference, and countertransference; the opening sessions of the Rat Man's analysis; and three of Freud's questionable gestures during the treatment.

Historical Issues about Freud's Technique

Freud's statements about free association do not invariably clarify the chronology of his technical development. Referring to his former advocacy of directed associations, Freud wrote that with Dora he was introducing a liberating procedure: "I now let the patient himself choose the subject of the day's work, and in that way I start out from whatever surface his unconscious happens to be presenting to his notice at the moment" (1905a, p. 12). We know only too well from Dora's case history, however, that in practice Freud seriously limited free association. Eight years after her treatment, while lecturing on the Rat Man to the Vienna Psychoanalytic Society, Freud once more alluded to a general modification in his clinical practice: "The technique of analysis has changed to the extent that the psychoanalyst no longer seeks to elicit material in which he is interested, but permits the patient to follow his natural and spontaneous trains of thought" (*Minutes*, 1:227). Seizing on Freud's remark, Nunberg and Federn, the editors of the *Minutes*, conclude: "Here, for the first time, we have a report of an analysis which was carried out with the help of *free associations"* (1:227n). But Freud said no such thing. He pointed out a change in psychoanalytic technique but did not name 1907 as the starting date for that change. As we shall see from the Rat Man's treatment, moreover, Freud still had not mastered the technical requirements to facilitate free association (self-evidently, theoretical and practical comprehension may be far from simultaneous).

The question as to when Freud arrived at a stable, mature understanding of transference is somewhat more complicated. We may start out with his theoretical account in three pieces of writing, the first of which is the well-known postscript to the Dora case; the other two, with lesser canonicity in their textual status, have been neglected in psychoanalytic literature. In the Dora postscript, Freud's elucidation of transference (1905a, pp. 116–17) is literally an afterthought, for he candidly admitted that he had passed over it during the treatment. Freud spelled out six pertinent ideas that speak, among other things, of a transference neurosis, even though the term was not formally used until 1914:

1. Transferences are of two types, one like a reimpression of a past text, the other more like a revised edition on account of its ingenious construction.
2. As the most recent creation of the patient's pathology, transference sets up "obstacles" to treatment.
3. Only after transference has been "resolved" (*Lösung*, 117/280) does a patient become convinced of connections constructed during analysis.
4. Psychoanalytic treatment arouses both affectionate and hostile transferences.
5. Upon being made conscious, the transference is "annihilated" (Strachey's "destroyed" does not carry the extremeness of *vernichtet* [117/281]).
6. If its presence can be pointed out and explained to the patient, transference changes from being the "greatest obstacle" to psychoanalysis to becoming its "most powerful ally."

Subsequently, in a letter sent to Jung in 1906, there is a slight shift in Freud's grasp of one transferential element. According to Freud's previous conception, a patient becomes convinced of the analyst's constructions only after transference is resolved; according to the revised conception, the patient's conviction is concurrent with a positive transference:

> Transference provides the impulse necessary for understanding and translating the language of the ucs.; where it is lacking, the patient does not make the effort or does not listen when we submit our translation to him. Essentially, one might say, the cure is effected by love. (Freud, 1974a, pp. 12–13)

Then in the following year Freud elaborated his views of transference, omitting reference to its resolution and ascribing the patient's dynamic change to positive transference as well as to the analyst's extratransferential and authoritative suggestion:

> The nature of therapy could be characterized in various ways: (1) as filling the gaps of memory (which have come about through repression); (2) as removing the resistances; (3) as replacing the unconscious by the conscious. All of this is really the same. There is only one power which can remove the resistances, the transference. The patient is compelled to give up his resistances *to please us*. Our cures are cures of love. There would thus remain for us only the task of removing the *personal* resistances (those against the transference). To the extent that transference exists—to that extent can we bring about cures. . . . the vicissitudes of the transference decide the success of treatment. *The only thing the method still lacks is authority; the element of suggestion must be added from without.* (*Minutes*, 1:101–02; italics in last sentence mine)

In brief, Freud never added any substantial improvement to his theoretical grasp of transference as outlined in the case history of Dora. After some wavering, he firmly reasserted in "Remembering, Repeating and Working Through" (1914) his insight about the resolution of the patient's reedited pathology in the transference. Although Freud's theorization about the transference and, much more, his application of it varied in the interval between Dora's psychoanalysis and 1914, it is pertinent that we do not see in the Rat Man case any persistent evidence of transferential liquidation as a preeminent goal; instead, Freud seemed chiefly to use the transference in a retrospective way, reconstructing the great rat idea and convincing the patient of his rage toward his father (pp. 209–20).[1]

As can be expected, countertransference in the Rat Man case also raises complex problems, above and beyond the fact that the terms designating the phenomenon did not yet exist. To risk repeating what is rather well known, *countertransference* occurs only four times in the *Standard Edition*: twice in "The Future Prospects of Psycho-Analytic Therapy" (1910) and twice in "Observations on Transference-Love" (1915a). Hardly known, however, are two earlier texts in which Freud astutely shows a fine technical awareness of the still nameless dynamic:

> It has often been my experience that just those cases in which I took an excessively personal interest failed, perhaps just be-

---

1. My remarks find their place in the current debate concerning the time when Freud arrived at his definitive technique with transference, that is, whether it did not essentially alter after 1900 (Gill, 1982, p. 156) or after the Rat Man case (Lipton, 1977), or whether it did not mature until 1914 (Kanzer, 1952, pp. 233–34). More or less in agreement with Kanzer, Muslin (1979, pp. 561–64, 574) describes Freud's evolution from seeing transference as an "obstruction" (1905) to seeing it as the central "battlefield" of analysis (1917); but the six items I have singled out in the Dora postscript convergently demonstrate that at that time Freud theoretically conceived of transference as the "central battlefield" in the clinical setting. Where I may sharpen my previous contention concerns the *temporal* pervasiveness of the transference per se; in the process notes to the Rat Man, Freud habitually refers to the transference in the plural, a morphological indication that he tended to think of it as an interrupted rather than a global manifestation. Putatively, the latter would not occur until a climactic point in the treatment (cf. Hawelka, p. 179*n*).

cause of the intensity of feeling. (Letter of 12/26/08 to Abraham; Freud, 1965, p. 63)

While I am analysing and am waiting for the patient's reply, I often cast a quick glance at the picture of my parents. I know now that I always do this when I am following up the patient's infantile transference. The glance is always accompanied by a certain guilt feeling: what will they think of me? This is of course connected with my breaking away from them, which was not too easy. Since explaining this symptomatic action to myself, I have not caught myself at it any more. (Letter of 4/7/09 to Abraham; Freud, 1965, p. 77)

As suggestive as Freud's two self-observations are, they cannot of course illuminate all the effects of his unconscious and conscious awareness of countertransference in the previous treatment of the Rat Man.

But concerning what is known about the historical particulars of Freud's countertransference, can anyone claim it to be solely coincidental that the subjects of his most famous and reportedly his only successful published cases were dramatically anal from the outset of treatment? A story of anal torture with rats helped drive Ernst Lanzer into psychoanalysis, and the Wolf Man in his very first session said that he would like to "use" Freud from behind and defecate on his head. Freud himself was an "obsessional type" according to his self-description and that of Jones (1955, p. 423), and his anality, both constitutionally and experientially, surely conditioned his clinical interest. Our considerations here are given further direction when we turn to Schur's comments about Freud's later intestinal symptoms seen in the light of his self-analysis at the end of 1897:

With regard to Freud's gastrointestinal symptoms, there was later evidence that Freud had an "irritable colon," which is frequently the functional expression of a psychic conflict. In later years Freud maintained that the appearance of "anal" material in analysis is frequently preceded or accompanied by functional or even structural gastrointestinal pathology. It is therefore possible (although such a hypothesis must remain purely speculative) that Freud's discovery of this very phase, about which he reported in the following two months [letters to Fliess in November and December 1897], had something to do with the type of somatic symptoms he had during that period. (Schur, 1972, p. 133)

To add weight to Schur's hypothesis, we might point out that Freud's father died in October 1896; that for Freud "the most important event, the most poignant loss" in his life was his father's death (1900, p. xxvi); that the tragic cause of the death was "an intestinal carcinoma . . . intractable constipation alternating with explosive stools" (Hartman, 1983, p. 582); that, in an anniversary reaction, Freud discovered the Oedipus complex in October 1897; and that in the two months following his promulgation of the Oedipus complex, Freud announced his discoveries of anality.[2]

In a comparison of Freud's countertransference with his major patients, one feels that he was more sympathetic and empathic with the Rat Man than with Dora and the Wolf Man. If Freud was a prosecutor with Dora, he was a befriending educator to Lanzer. And if Freud appraised his contact with the Wolf Man as a "therapeutic experiment" (1918, p. 10), he banished the experimental in psychoanalyzing Lanzer's core oedipal fantasy: "It was impossible to unravel this tissue of phantasy thread by thread; the therapeutic success of the treatment was precisely what stood in the way of this" (p. 207n).

Matters of kinship contributed to Freud's empathy. Like the Rat Man's parents, Freud's parents came from the outer Slavic

---

2. See Freud's letter of 11/14/97 to Fliess: "To put it crudely, the memory actually stinks."

regions of the Austro-Hungarian Empire and eventually settled in Vienna. When the Rat Man narrated his recent maneuvers in Galicia, particularly in Spas (H, p. 40), Freud must have perked up his ears, not only because his parents were Galician, but also because his mother was born in Brody, about forty kilometers from Spas. In his immediate family, Freud had one surviving younger brother, five sisters, and a powerful mother; the Rat Man had a younger brother, four surviving sisters, and a similarly powerful mother. Both analyst and patient suffered the early loss of a sibling, an experience offering itself as a screen for the son's deep antagonism toward the father; and in oedipal rebellion against their quite elderly patriarchlike fathers, both the young Freud and the Rat Man urinated in the parental bedroom (Kanzer, 1980, pp. 237, 246, 416). Moreover, like the Rat Man, Freud had to overcome the difficulties of being Jewish in a severely anti-Semitic Catholic atmosphere. But even though Freud was the omniscient Jewish father–God in the treatment, he significantly underplayed the ambivalent use of Jewish words and allusions in the Rat Man's associations. Nor did Freud address himself to the implications of the patient's relating rats to installments in view of the fact that Jews were particularly linked with the introduction of installment buying into the Viennese commercial world; otherwise, Freud might have interpreted the projected meaning onto him as a revived omnipotent father presiding over a new scene of mockable religious rituals and hushed utterances (Weiss, 1980; Kanzer, 1980, pp. 244–45). Another factor has to do with what I learned from the archives in the Israelitische Kultusgemeinde in Vienna: Ernst Lanzer's Jewish name was יעקב, Jacob, the same name as Freud's father; but there is no evidence that the name was brought up in analysis.

From such a countertransferential complex we might expect some disruption in Freud's note taking, and this is what happened. At the end of the October 12 entry in the process notes, Freud himself remarked on the curious phenomenon that he forgot the Rat Man's second reason for not committing suicide and that he was not sure whether the memories he had just recorded belonged to the Rat Man (cf. the entries for October 12 and 14, both on p. 264). More significantly, Freud misdated as December 2 a session that initially announced the death of Dr. Pr., Henrich Lanzer's physician, toward whom the Rat Man had a highly ambivalent filial attitude. There is no indication that Freud analyzed the transference here, yet he did leave the private trace of misdating the session of January 2 one month earlier, thereby keeping the paternal physician alive!

There is more. The Rat Man's first name was the same as that of Brücke, whom Freud acknowledged as having had the greatest influence on him and after whom he named his oldest son. Besides that, the Rat Man's beloved Gisela bore the same name as Freud's sole adolescent love, Gisela Fluss. Yet the matter does not stop even there. The Rat Man asseverated his magical desire to prevent any contact between his lady and a woman identified by the cruel captain as none other than Gisela Fluss, whose name, as we know from chapter 1, Freud recorded in his private notes and then followed it with a triad of exclamation marks!

Along with the foregoing contextual information, which throws light on the countertransference in the Rat Man's treatment, we have at our disposition a pair of appraisals about Freud as a clinician. The fact that they date from the 1920s, when Freud was more experienced, permits their adjusted applicability to his practice nearly two decades earlier. The first appraisal is actually a self-critique, which Freud gratifyingly gave in response to a direct request by his analysand Abram Kardiner during an analytic hour:

> In the first place, I get tired of people. Secondly . . . I am not basically interested in therapy, and I usually find that I am engaged—in any particular case—with the theoretical problems with which I happen to be interested at the time. . . . I

am also too patriarchal to be a good analyst. (A. Kardiner, 1957, p. 52; for a slightly different version, see Kardiner, 1977, pp. 68–69)

The second appraisal comes from another analysand, Raymond de Saussure, the son of the founder of modern linguistics:

> Freud was not a good psychoanalytic clinician. Since he had not been analyzed himself, he tended to commit two kinds of errors. First, he had practiced suggestion too long not to have been materially affected by it. When he was persuaded of the truth of something, he had considerable difficulty in waiting until this verity became clear to his patient. Freud wanted to convince him immediately. Because of that, he talked too much. Second, one rapidly sensed what special theoretical question preoccupied him, for often during the analytic hour he developed at length new points of view he was clarifying in his own mind. This was a gain for the discipline, but not always for the patient's treatment. (Saussure, 1956, p. 359)

With noticeable compatibility the two accounts disclose a Freud whose clinical practice was affected by his impatience, his theoretical preoccupations,[3] his use of suggestion, and his patriarchal attitudes—personal traits that also left their mark on the Rat Man's psychoanalysis.

Those distracting personal traits should be factored into a triple set of assertions that add up to one conclusion: Freud avowedly had little of the clinical experience he judged desirable in order to analyze the Rat Man. The first assertion was made in 1904, when Freud estimated that a period of six months to three years was necessary for effective psychoanalytic treatment and that "for the most part" he had had the opportunity of managing such

---

3. After I had finished writing this section, Helene Deutsch's estimate was published: "Freud may have been a holy figure to Helene, but she had her reservations about him as a therapist; he sought to teach more than to cure" (Roazen, 1985, p. 193).

treatment only in severe cases (Freud, 1904, p. 254). Just a year later, Freud claimed to have even less clinical experience: "Actually, I have been able to elaborate and to test my therapeutic method only on severe, indeed on the severest cases" (1905c, p. 263). We arrive now at 1907, the year when Freud first saw the Rat Man and when he "successfully" treated a female hysteric in nine months; subsequently she became irrecoverably ill, with the possibility that her ailment was due to "the same repressed impulses, which the analysis had only incompletely resolved" (Freud, 1937, p. 222). Continuing in the same spirit of calm retrospection, Freud admitted: "The successful analytic treatment took place so long ago that we cannot expect too much from it; it was in the earliest years of my work as an analyst. . . . since then we have acquired deeper insight and wider knowledge, and . . . our technique has changed in accordance with our new discoveries" (Freud, 1937, pp. 222–23). How that earlier Freud dealt with the Rat Man is our next preoccupation.

The Start of the Analysis

The first seven analytic sessions with the Rat Man constitute a series that supposedly "coincides roughly with the expository portion of the treatment," the critical account of which (pp. 159–86) comprises more than one-fourth of the total case history. On Wednesday, October 2, what Freud considered to be the first analytic session proper occurred (pp. 159–65).[4] After pledging to follow Freud's fundamental condition about freely associating, the Rat Man immediately referred to a current male friend (Dr. Palatzer) who, when he was in distress, reassured him about his moral worth; next he mentioned a former acquaintance whose

4. For other commentary on the first session, see Kanzer (1952, p. 138), Langs (1976, pp. 216–17), Muslin (1979, pp. 564–65), and Marcus (1984, pp. 114–15).

reassurances were actually deceitful and were given for utilitarian reasons; then, "without any apparent transition," the Rat Man drew a sketch of his infantile sexuality, starting with his first governess whom he remembered only by her surname, a common male first name (Rudolf). He went on to say how at six he had already suffered from erections and how once, in a spirit of complaint and misgiving, he had showed his erect penis to his mother; at the time, he had also believed that he spoke out his thoughts without hearing them and that his parents knew his mind thereby.

Mindful of Adler's observation about the particular importance of a patient's first communications, Freud noticed that the Rat Man was initially uncovering the part played in his life by a homosexual object-choice and subsequently by the opposition and conflict between man and woman. Freud's curiosity at this point is best seen in a portion of the process notes not included in the *Standard Edition*:

> I stick to Miss Rudolf and want to know her first name. He does not know it. Isn't he surprised to forget the first name which so exclusively designates a house-woman, and to have noticed her family name? He is not surprised about it, but according to his introducing the compromise "Rudolf," I identify him as a homosexual. (H, p. 38; my translation and insertion of the governess's last name)

Freud also gave us a specimen of his early handling and comprehension of the obsessional's characteristic generality and indeterminateness. Thus when the Rat Man said that around the age of six his wish to see women naked was accompanied by an uncanny fear, Freud was brought to ask for an example. The Rat Man's reply, "that my father might die," was thereupon thought by Freud to be "the original and actual thing which has tried to hide itself behind the generalization." In contrast to his confident ease in this assumption, Freud was understandably taken aback to learn that the adult patient still had the uncanny fear although his father had died some years previously. Another point is that Freud from the very outset pursued his genetic interest, which led to this conclusion: the patient's sexual wish and reactive fear about his father's death referred to the time of infantile amnesia, prior to the age of six, when his conflicts were overtaken by repression.

As readers we may be struck by Freud's omission of transferential comment even when he addresses us. The Rat Man's true and false friends have obvious transferential implications, particularly since the false one was identified with a nongratuitous detail—he was a medical student. Once during a walk this student incited another student to tell a tall story to the gullible Ernst, who was thereupon mocked for his stupidity (H, pp. 32, 34; details not in the *Standard Edition*). Accordingly, forebodings were already present about how the Rat Man might receive reconstructions from his medical analyst. On the other hand, there was a positive gesture to placate Freud: having dipped into *Psychopathology and Everyday Life*,[5] the Rat Man knew what interested Freud and consequently carried out his "pledge" to free-associate by narrating his history of infantile sexuality. Freud was already the object of an activated ambivalence—was he to be trusted, and, if so, at what price of homosexual submission? Not fully comforted by a trustworthy confidant in his current everyday life, the Rat Man was now seeking in the analytic setting an even greater moral reassurance to overcome his self-torment about being a criminal, and his preliminary supine confession was colored by transferential implications of long-standing fantasies of parental omniscience and wishes for his father to die.

I approach the second session (pp. 165–70) with the obligation of sounding a preliminary note of caution, for a textual imbroglio makes commentary tentative. Not only is the account of the ses-

---

5. We learn this from a passage taken in the third session but not contained in the *Standard Edition* (H, p. 62).

sion twice as long in the private record as in the case history; but there are also some differences in the sequence of material. Discrepancies of another sort unexpectedly exist: only in the case history do we read that upon Freud's urging, the reimbursement story was told three times, upon which the Rat Man finally owned up to its obscurities; according to the contrasting private version, the Rat Man told the story in three, mostly nonrepetitive segments, interrupted by two digressions, and he did not utter any avowal about the story's obscurities. Of equal interest, during the second session Freud was told of the Rat Man's pivotal prior knowledge that Lieutenant David was no longer in charge of the post office; for that and other restrospective self-corrections (H, pp. 55, 57) Freud relied on the private version of the third session, which he then silently incorporated into his public account of the second session. One of the effects of this historical manipulation is that, with some of the obfuscation being shifted from analyst to patient, Freud presents himself as a storyteller in better command of his story about a character correspondingly more confused.

The Rat Man opened the second session[6] by saying that he would have to overcome much within himself in order to relate a certain experience. Freud's educative response, one of many to punctuate the analysis, was to explain the concept of resistance. Momentarily pacified, the Rat Man went so far as to mention the cruel captain's tale of an Oriental torture and then rose from the couch and pleaded to be spared the misery of going into details. To Freud's reassuring claim that he had no desire to torment him, the Rat Man replied by calling him "Captain" (H, p. 52).[7] Freud

---

6. For the second session, cf. Kanzer (1952, pp. 138–40; 1980, pp. 235, 419), Major (1971, pp. 540–41; 1974, pp. 430–31), Weiss (1980, p. 205), and Marcus (1984, pp. 119–21).

7. Hence the process notes confirm Kanzer's opinion (1952, pp. 139–40) as against Gill and Muslin's (1976, p. 790) that the Rat Man first addressed Freud as "Captain" after the latter's pacifying gesture. A thornier issue concerns the

added that to ask to be excused from overcoming resistance was tantamount to asking for a gift of "two comets."[8] On the other hand, Freud ventured, he would "guess" the full meaning from any proffered hints. There followed a mutually recomposed story of the rat torture, during which the Rat Man rose from the couch for the second time (was this resistance a motoric association to Freud's two comets?).

Freud apparently did not understand that the Rat Man's peculiar way of describing the rat torture was like an acting-in. That is to say, the very mimetic manner of the Rat Man's expression turned it from being a discourse that simply narrates to one that enacts, performs; its very style and delivery *in* and *through* themselves constituted an enactive meaning. To be more specific: after initially voicing his resistance, the Rat Man went on, for one long uninterrupted paragraph in Freud's text, to introduce the narrative setting of the rat torture. With that accomplished, his gaping delivery elicited Freud's narrative participation in a complementary movement of thrust and counterthrust. The crucial passage concerning the Rat Man's allusion to the torture and his sudden self-interruption is worth quoting. Because Strachey

---

interpretive status of Freud's saying in the session that unlike the captain he was not fond of cruelty; questions still remain even if one agrees that very early transferential interpretations may be necessary to prevent disruptions of the analysis (cf. Gill & Muslin, 1976, esp. pp. 783, 792). Was Freud forsaking interpretation for a nontransferential reassurance (Langs, 1976, p. 217)? Alternatively, was he making an indirect interpretation of a transference resistance in stating that he was not the captain (Gill & Muslin, 1976, p. 789; cf. Kanzer, 1952, p. 246; 1980, p. 419)? Incidentally, the detail about the Rat Man's "repeatedly" calling Freud "Captain" contrasts with the single occurrence listed in the process notes (H, p. 52).

8. Opting for a figurative translation, Strachey wrote "the moon" (p. 166). Although Hawelka tried unsuccessfully to track down the literal sense of Freud's allusion, we need not be discouraged from adducing new material and tentatively offering a hypothesis. The fourth comet of the year 1907, famous in astronomy, was last sighted on September 24, and it is possible that a newspaper article covered the event. The phenomenal comet was part of a comet that in 1783 had split in two.

dismisses certain nuances in the original German, I have supplied my own translation:

> Here he breaks off, stands up and asks me to spare him the description of the details. I assure him that I myself have no inclination whatever for horror and certainly have no desire to torment him, but that naturally I cannot grant him something over which I have no ordinance. He may just as well ask me to grant him two comets. . . . I continued: but what I could do is to guess[9] fully, from something hinted by him, *about what ought to happen* [my italics]. Is he perhaps thinking of impalement?—"No, not that, but the condemned is being tied up"—(he expressed himself so indistinctly that I could not immediately guess in what position)—"over his buttocks a pot is turned upside down, into which then rats are let in, and they"—he was again standing up and gave all signs of horror and resistance—"*bored in.*"—"Into the anus," I permitted myself to complete it. (166/391–92)

This extract represents and re-presents a verbal exchange that was a verbal "happening." "What ought to happen" did happen; the gap between reference and referent, between the anus and the lexical allusion to the anus, was closed. As a matter of fact, much of the transferential and countertransferential dynamics of the

---

9. On the basis of this single occurrence of "guessing" (*erraten*) and reflecting a certain proneness among some French psychoanalysts for a figurative formulation in their preconsciously oriented interpretations, Major (1971, pp. 540–41; 1974, pp. 430–31) attempted to justify Freud's participation in the guessing game in the following manner: by using *erraten* as the primal word in the analysis, Freud "furnishes the verbal bridge which evokes the animal of the torture, and makes possible the pursuit of the narration rather than let it be blocked under the dominion of affect" (p. 540). Major then criticized Kanzer (1952) for creating a dictionary of "received" symbols by reducing Freud's exchange with the Rat Man to a mere penetration of erotogenic zones, thereby excluding all possible symbolic transformations (p. 541). Major seems unaware of the full import and omniscient claim in *erraten*; my further analysis supports Kanzer's later disapproval (1980, p. 419) that Freud's use of the nodal word "further invokes the rat as an instrument of divination by boring his way into the patient's mind."

case were already played out in the overdetermined juxtaposition of the telegraphic statements "bored in" (*einbohrten*)/"into the anus" (*in den After*). I begin with *bohr-*, which undoubtedly was a highly important signifier in the life of the Rat Man. He was, to refer again to his military dossier, a person with knock-knees (*Kniebohrer*), and he accused Freud of nasal boring (*Nasenbohren*, 293/H, 180). I suggest that *bohr-* relates not only to Ernst's fantasy of the body's danger of being sadistically penetrated but also to his rage at being replaced by his younger brother Robert, the first syllable of whose name is the phonemic palindrome (another reversal!) of *bohr*. The ultimate scenes informing Ernst's fantasy receive some unexpected confirmation from little Hans's fantasy of his stomach being pierced by a plumber's "borer." Freud's speculation is equally relevant to our purposes:

> Perhaps, too, the word "borer" [*Bohrer*] was not chosen without regard for its connection with "born" [*geboren*] and "birth" [*Geburt*]. If so, the child could have made no distinction between "bored" [*gebohrt*] and "born" [*geboren*]. (Freud, 1909a, p. 98*n*)

In light of the above, we are even more assured that boring and being born were also components of Ernst's sadomasochistic fantasies of conception and death.

We now come to Freud's guessing the words "into the anus." Although it has been pointed out that the German word for "guess" is *erraten*, we should make a paramount nuance: both *raten* and *erraten* mean "to guess," but *erraten* includes the extra meaning that the guess is correct. Consequently, Freud's guesses take on an omniscient coloring. The Rat Man multiplied holes in his sentences which Freud filled in with correct guessing—*erraten*; the substantival rats crossed over grammatical and conceptual borders to become a mind-reading verb. Not only did the Rat Man assimilate free association, the object of his previous day's pledge, into the rat torture; he also enticed Freud to act with parentlike omniscience and even to encroach ("I permitted myself") in climactically locating the torture. And although elicited, the persecutory omniscience and homosexual intrusiveness characterizing Freud's role in the duet of staccato responses further intensified the Rat Man's burgeoning ambivalence toward him. In their antiphonal reconstruction of the climax of the rat story, they seemed to be unconsciously attuned to the fired rats scuttering between the ends of a small pot. But if in the in-play Freud became a homosexually cruel protagonist, he was at the same time being stylistically manhandled.

Immediately after Freud's guess about "into the anus" came his silent reflection: "I indeed recognized the homosexual component after the utterances of the first session" (H, p. 44; my translation). These words, found only in the process notes, significantly omit any countertransferential or transferential reference to what was going on in the here and now. Our attention is next caught by the Rat Man's hesitation when it first was necessary to specify whom the rats were biting. Then the Rat Man yielded "after a little prompting"; unfortunately, however, the continuing rodentlike intrusiveness of Freud's prompting emerges distinctly only in the original German phrase, "nach kurzem *Raten*" (167/392). We may wonder, incidentally, whether the Rat Man's later link between guessing and rats was suppressed in the case history by Freud because it would not have confirmed his interventions in the second session.

The fact that the Rat Man both lost his glasses and had the tormenting anal fantasy during maneuvers comes into play at this point. Although it is not textually clear in what order these two events took place, the visual diminution and punishment of father constitute a connection to the Rat Man's voyeuristic experience and desire for his father's death he had expressed in the previous session. His rising twice in the second hour changed his visual field, but we are not told if he then looked at Freud and what impact that looking or refusal to look had on the ongoing construction of anal rape in lexical installments.

In his next story, about the reimbursement, the Rat Man still appeared quite disordered although less panicky. Undoubtedly relieved by Freud's complicity, the Rat Man gave some "discreet" praise, mentioned having read an extract from *The Interpretation of Dreams*, and complained about the incomprehension among doctors he consulted, including the previously named Wagner von Jauregg. Contrary to Jauregg, the Rat Man thought that no obsession was beneficial, and then broached the topic of free association, which Freud reported this way:

> He says that, as if by a compulsion, it is actually harder for him to tell what comes now—as if it would happen if he spoke [a hint about the mutual verbal "happening" that just occurred]; this became more accentuated when I spoke of the conditions of treatment. His idea immediately was: "How will you get over this difficulty?"—I say that it is a special refinement of sickness to protect itself in this way against the attack by his psychic forces.—"Cunning" is the right word, he thinks, but sometimes it appears as if external conditions would also be cunning. (H, pp. 48, 50; my translation)

In effect, the Rat Man voiced his fear that his obsessional disorder would take over the entire psychoanalytic process. But what he did not tell Freud until some three months later was that upon hearing the conditions of treatment, he silently thought, "So many florins, so many rats"—such was the cunningness of the external conditions. Through payments in "rats," the patient homosexually submitted to Freud and at the same time treated him like a prostitute in a brothel or *Freudenhaus* (p. 284). In short, from the very beginning the Rat Man's neurosis contaminated both the analytic process and the setting in ways of course that were to challenge and test Freud's understanding, which was drawn to the genetic point of view. This becomes evident when the Rat Man in another digression brought up the subject of religion, and Freud intervened with a genetically oriented intellectual indoctrination: "I drew his attention to the meaning of the infantile factor in his religiosity and indicated to him that one could find precisely in childhood the connections between his involuntary and consciously normal thinking" (H, p. 52; my translation).

I do not want to leave this session without introducing a topic upon which I shall have much more to say later. It is difficult to specify a certain warm atmosphere that presided over the psychoanalysis of the Rat Man, although Freud's genuine interest in him comes through the material. If we judge from observations Freud thought important enough to write down, his attentiveness on so many levels must have been felt as another empathic factor inspiring confidence. Freud noted the Rat Man's indistinct speech and then a little later regretted being unable to reproduce its peculiar quality; he noted the Rat Man's facial expression of horror toward his own unconscious pleasure, his feeling of being invaded by thoughts of extraordinary rapidity, and his daze and bewilderment at the end of the session.

We may skip by the third session (pp. 170–73), in which Freud apparently intervened strictly for purposes of getting clarification. The Rat Man went on to tell of his reimbursement antics, fantasies of scurrying from person to person, breaking his vow to pay back Lieutenant David, and finally, as the process notes disclose, reading some of *The Psychopathology of Everyday Life*, which impressed him enough that he consulted its author. The session is brimming with signs of how the Rat Man in panic might take flight from Freud—running about inside his office as a precursor to, I suspect, running away eventually from the analysis itself.

Freud's question opening Saturday's fourth session (pp. 174–76)[10] "And how do you intend to proceed to-day?" gives some indication that in those early days of psychoanalysis the analyst's

---

10. For the fourth session, see also Bessis-Rubin (1979, pp. 45, 224) and Kanzer (1952, p. 140; 1980, pp. 235–36).

permissive attitude toward free association did not extend to "free" silence. The Rat Man's "free" association to Freud's query was anamnestic data about having been absent when his dying father called him and sleeping through his father's hour of death. (Was there an underlying wish to sleep through and beyond the analytic hour and not respond to a fatally struck paternal analyst?) Freud's implicit demand for talk merits the further critical consideration that in general patients defensively resort to talking more than to silence. It is timely also to recall here that the Vienna Psychoanalytic Society was so organized that members were obliged to speak in meetings if summoned and had the option to maintain silence only after February of 1908.[11] By and large, one gets the impression that the early Freud tolerated neither the Rat Man's silence nor "unimportant" associations very long; as Freud comments on a later session, apart from a brief list of subjects, the patient "had only trivialities to report and I was able to say a great deal to him to-day" (p. 308).

Like the previous session, the fourth one contained a story involving the Rat Man's temporal protractions, either in punitively postponing the reimbursement of the post office lady or in trying to avoid painful mourning. In the latter sense, the Rat Man pursued the course of keeping his parricidal guilt at bay by fantasying his father as still living; as we know, it was only upon the subsequent death of an aunt that he accepted his father's terminal fate and self-reproach hit home. Thereafter the Rat Man was sustained only by his friend's consoling minimization of his self-reproaches.

Freud did not withhold a reaction to his patient's tale: "Hearing this, I took the opportunity of giving him a first glance at the

11. In order to prevent some members from monopolizing the discussion in the Vienna Psychoanalytic Society, all the members' names were put into an urn, and any person whose name was drawn was obliged to speak; the practice was finally abolished (see *Minutes*, February 5, 1908, pp. 299–303, and February 12, pp. 313–17).

underlying principles of psycho-analytic therapy. When there is a mésalliance, I began . . ." We as readers stop our scanning eyes on *mésalliance* and instantaneously think that Freud will finish the sentence by linking up the consolatory friend and the kind of alliance the patient was expecting in the analysis. But our eyes come upon a surprise: the *mésalliance* refers not to the interaction within the analytic setting but rather to the intrapsychic disparity between the patient's strong affect and its ideational contents; accordingly, if the contents are missing for an intense affect, we make a false connection with some substitute content, much as, Freud continued with his own imagistic association, "our police, when they cannot catch the right murderer, arrest the wrong one instead." Freud's intervention, however, is not to be completely faulted: although nearly 40 percent of the process notes for the fourth session show Freud relying solely on intellectual explanations, they nevertheless differ from Dr. Palatzer's guilt-banishing consolation in suggesting sources for the patient's self-reproaches.

Following the treatment's first weekend break, the fifth session (pp. 176–78)[12] took place on Monday, October 7. We hear a ratiocinating Freud being maneuvered into giving encouragements to the patient, who maintained his doubt right up to the end of the session; otherwise, the therapeutic couple spoke at cross-purposes, their duologue replacing dialogue. Condensable into five movements, the session opened with the Rat Man's doubting that discoveries about his self-reproach could have a therapeutic effect. Freud in turn began with a cognitive explanation about the differences between the unconscious and the conscious, the contents of the latter being subject to a process of wearing away (Freud's unconscious reference to the weekend's erosion of analytic progress?). Then Freud followed with a singularly inappropriate "illustration": he pointed to antiques in his consulting

12. For this session, cf. the commentary by Muslin (1979, p. 565), Bessis-Rubin (1979, p. 229), Kanzer (1980, pp. 236–37) and Marcus (1984, pp. 126–27).

room taken from a tomb in Pompeii; if their burial was their preservation, their disinterment meant the destruction of Pompeii. (Is there a topsy-turvy hint that Freud's consulting room houses a testimony to destruction? that an afterlife follows the tomb? How problematic is Freud's association, implying his paternal role as custodian of antiques, to the Rat Man's guilt-laden denials about his father's death?)

Understandably, the Rat Man's disquiet persisted while he inquired whether self-reproach would be increased or lessened as a result of discoveries in one's own mind. Freud's reply was one of pacifying encouragement: "It followed from the nature of the circumstances that in every case the affect would be overcome—for the most part during the progress of the work itself." Actually the Rat Man's concern was psychoanalytically more well founded than Freud's confidence, for, as we remember, it was years later before Freud fully realized that the uncovering of guilt could lead to the negative therapeutic effect of worsening a patient's condition.

In the next step the Rat Man wondered whether his personality, ruptured by infraction of his moral principles, could achieve a reintegration; if that could happen, he pursued, he would succeed "more than others who would be presented to him as models" (H, pp. 68, 70; my translation). Significantly, Freud omitted the latter statement, with its weight of negative transference, from his published account.[13] But Freud does tell how he took up the Rat Man's reference to a self-conscious splitting and reassigned it to a contrast between the evil unconscious and the moral conscious. There ensued an exchange in which Freud intellectually clarified that derivatives of the repressed infantile period were responsible for his patient's obsessions. Besides the repressed and

---

13. Compare the excerpt from the official account: "he thought he would be able to make a success of his life, perhaps more of one than most people" (p. 177). Here, Freud defensively inserts a "perhaps" and substitutes the generalizing "most people" for the more specific, transferentially critical remark of his patient.

the infantile, there remained the discovery of a third and sexual characteristic of the unconscious, which, Freud averred, he "would be glad to let him [the patient] make for himself."[14]

As a retort the Rat Man first repeated his doubt that it would be possible to undo long-standing problems. Then, in a sideswipe at Freud's theorizing procedure, he asked what could be done to combat his logically irrefutable obsessions about the next world. Freud's succeeding intervention has come down to us in two versions. Here is the intervention that Freud privately remembered: "I express my very favorable judgment of him, which openly pleases him very much" (H, p. 70; my translation). In the censored derivatives of his public write-up, Freud toned down "very favorable" to "appreciative" (*anerkennendes*) and deprived "pleases" (*erfreut*) of the adverb "very much" (*G.W.*, p. 402). Strachey followed suit and made even further modifications, so that "appreciative judgment" dwindles to "*a word or two* upon the good opinion I had formed of him" (p. 178; italics mine). Whereas the fifth session in the official history ends here, the private records show that analyst and patient had another go at it. The Rat Man once more recounted the change in his health, especially since 1903, and how in his defensive struggles he despaired of being able to surmount the thought that he had already done something criminal. Thereupon Freud flattered him again, complimenting the patient on the clarity with which he expressed his condition.

In the sixth session (pp. 178–83),[15] the Rat Man set out by stating that the fear about his parents' guessing[16] his thoughts

---

14. The process notes do not contain Freud's wish made to the patient, but on the other hand it shows the unaided patient making efforts to find the third unconscious trait: "Now there would be still a characteristic to discover, but he does not find it" (H, p. 70; my translation).

15. For this session, cf. Langs (1976, pp. 217–18), Muslin (1979, p. 565), Kanzer (1980, p. 237), and Marcus (1984, pp. 127–28).

16. In German, *erraten*. Again the patient spoke of his parents "ratting" into his thoughts.

had endured all his life. Perhaps this association was triggered by Freud's flatteries from the previous hour, anxiogenically felt as a homosexual seductiveness. Continuing his defensiveness, the Rat Man referred to his nonsensual heterosexual interest at the age of twelve and brought up an attendant "idea," rather than wish, about the amatory advantage he would derive if his father were to die. At that point, as Freud's words exhibit, argument took over the clinical situation:

> By way of objection, I asked him why, if it had not been a wish, he had repudiated it. . . . He was shaken, but did not abandon his objection. I therefore broke off the argument with the remark that I felt sure this had not been the first occurrence of his idea of his father's dying; it had evidently originated at an earlier date, and some day we should have to trace back its history. (pp. 178–79)

We remark from this passage that while the Rat Man was depicted as "shaken," Freud did not display how disturbed he himself was by the argumentation; yet he possibly was, for he forgetfully postulated as a novel consideration something he had already heard in the first session—namely, the patient's childhood obsession that his father would die (p. 162).

The continuation of the sixth session is equally revelatory. Rather than stay in the childhood period introduced by Freud, the Rat Man pointed to later, adult fantasies about profiting from his father's death and then denied that these "thoughts" could be desires on his part. To the patient's "forcible enunciation" Freud answered with more theorizing. Once more the patient denied that his lethal thoughts were wishes, and once more Freud felt it a due season for lengthy intellectual indoctrination, refurbished with an analogy from Shakespeare's play to the effect that Caesar could simultaneously be loved and murderously hated. The Rat Man's conscious love for his father, the explanation drove on, could not vanquish the intense hatred remaining in his unconscious. Upon this explanation the Rat Man tendered a retractable concession: it all sounded rather plausible, but he was not convinced.

After a brief exchange Freud expounded that the Rat Man's sensual desires were the source of his hatred's "indestructibility" (H, p. 80) and that in this connection his father was perceived as "interfering" (H, p. 82). Before moving on to the Rat Man's response, we may notice that the English translation does not reveal the echoic and semantic bonding that Freud established between the indestructible nature (*Unzerstörbarkeit*) of the Rat Man's hatred and its object, the interfering father (*störend*).

We attend now to the Rat Man's reaction, which the belabored Freud recorded with a repetitive parapraxis unique in his process notes: "He now asks. He now asks" (H, p. 82; my translation). Here Freud was trying to record the Rat Man's puzzlement about why he himself did not decide, in the period of love for his lady, that he could also love his father despite his interference (*Störung*). Freud came back with a construction: the patient's indestructible wish to get rid of the paternal interference must have originated before the age of six, when little Ernst's memory became continuous. Unfortunately, this genetic perspective culminated a session where no reference was made to the question as to who was interfering with whom in the current interplay between Freud and patient. In a concluding note to October 8 that is found only in the process notes, we hear a seemingly tired Freud resolving to change his technical strategy: "But now is the time to abandon theory and return to self-observation and memory" (H, p. 84; my translation).

The seventh and last session (pp. 183–86)[17] demonstrates that Freud's approach, frequently intellectual as it was, yet managed to lower the Rat Man's resistances. Thus, after reasserting that

---

17. See Langs (1976, p. 218), Muslin (1979, p. 566) and Kanzer (1952, pp. 141–42).

he could not wish parricide, the patient mentioned sororicidal wishes in a German novel and then remembered how he had attempted to injure his brother over twenty years previously. When Freud again urged his case that a still earlier hostility involved the father, all the Rat Man could do was to recall hostility toward Gisela. Freud thereupon assumed the role of a benevolent confessor, indicating that the patient logically should exculpate himself for the amoral impulses from childhood that survived as unconscious derivatives. Once more the Rat Man uttered his doubt, and Freud then promised that he would prove the infantile etiology throughout the course of treatment "in each particular instance" (H, p. 90; my translation). From this last remark, and especially in the quoted part omitted from the published case, one gets a glimpse of how much in the remaining analysis was determined by the imposing and insistent authoritative logic bulwarked at one end of the couch.

Freud's Technical Irregularities and Their Consequences

From looking at the first seven sessions, we pass on to another perspective on the treatment, namely, Freud's three irregular technical measures: requesting the lady's photograph, sending the Rat Man a postcard, and giving him a meal. It was in the ninth session that Freud asked for Gisela's picture as a means of overcoming the patient's reluctance to talk about her. In light of the Rat Man's erotically visual history and his substitution of looking for touching, the request risked being provocative. Rather than depend solely on interpretation, Freud made a direct, intrusive demand and then saw a resistance in his patient's following violent struggle and temptation to abandon treatment. Did he feel that in some way Freud was trying to take possession of Gisela or even attack her? Perhaps so, for shortly thereafter, in an acting out, the Rat Man was impelled, without knowing why, to kiss his servant girl and then attack her (p. 261). He might have had fears, similar to the ones divulged at the very start of his analysis, of being deceitfully befriended by someone who primarily wanted access to the Lanzer home so as to pursue his interest in one of the daughters; in any event, if the Rat Man worried that military officers might soil Gisela's name just by pronouncing it (pp. 277, 288–89), he was that much more apprehensive about someone's studying and handling her picture. The end of the ninth session is also remarkable: the Rat Man spoke about his magical prayers and then brought up the incident in the Munich sanatorium where he had death wishes against a professor who had innocently spoiled the success of his amatory plans. As it turned out, the professor died a short time later; Freud, however, leaves no evidence that he interpreted the transferential import of the patient's resulting feeling of murderous omnipotence.

A second irregularity concerns Ernst Lanzer's receiving a postcard that was sent and signed "Cordially" by Freud.[18] In the session of December 8, when the Rat Man brought up the missive, he uttered a number of ambivalent references to both his parents, which we must also understand as critical associations to Freud's technical deviation. Although Freud indicates that he did interpret the transference, it seems from the material that his interpretations were genetically weighted and directed toward the parental sources of the patient's love objects—hence, neglecting the centrifugal presence of the transferential here and now as well as of the postcard throughout the session's associations.

The Rat Man spoke of his mother as economically exacting to the point of provoking his virile defense. Her control appeared

---

18. See Langs (1976, pp. 221–23), Muslin (1979, pp. 569, 571), Kanzer (1980, p. 234), and Weiss (1980, p. 211). Mindful of the gap in the notes from October 30 to December 8, Langs suggests that Lanzer was angry about Freud's vacation during the interim. Whether Freud took a vacation is problematical, for available documentation shows that he was in Vienna on December 4 at his society's meeting (*Minutes*, 1:254) and on December 6 at the Heller Verlag, where he lectured (Freud, 1908b, p. 142).

also in her advocating a plan that Ernst set up an office near the Cattleslaughter Market (*Schlachtviehmarkt*) and marry a rich cousin. Freud, however, apparently did not interpret the Rat Man's transferential wish for good mothering; nor was there an interpretation of the Rat Man's simultaneous criticism of his analyst as a bad mother who encroached upon her son's amatory and fiscal life and believed her domineering, "nosy" attitude to be "cordial" interest.

If in the session the Rat Man's father was excoriated for his lack of education, bad manners ("breaking wind openly"), and opportunistically forsaking the butcher's daughter he loved for his economically more attractive wife, Freud was similarly reproved for being coarse and uncultivated; his card was too intimate, and he was a "filthy swine" (fit for a butcher at a slaughterhouse?). Furthermore, Freud was accused of not just nose-picking, as the *Standard Edition* would have us believe, but nose-boring (*Nasenbohren*), an allusion to the anal-boring of the cruel captain's rats. The Rat Man went on to fantasize Mrs. Freud licking his behind and brought in a dream of her daughter with dung patches for eyes (an olfactory component to looking and a displacement relating ultimately to the Rat Man's own unconscious wish for an anal eye to watch out for attacks from behind). Throughout this material there is a variety of current erotic and hostile wishes aimed at Freud, in the guise of other members of his family. Among other things, Freud was relegated to kissing the body part that breaks wind, and, fated to have dung for eyes, he was a sniffer and nose-borer who was, in an ambivalent sense, deprived of more than a pince-nez—he was deprived of sight itself. Freud's interpretive focus, by contrast, was on the Rat Man's wish to marry into a grander family and thus follow in his father's footsteps.

The meaning of Freud's postcard also embraces the Rat Man's tryst with the dressmaker, limned this way in the beginning of the session:

> His spirits rose greatly on account of his rendezvous with the dressmaker, though this ended in a premature ejaculation. Soon afterwards he became gloomy, and this came out in transferences in the treatment. During his meeting with the girl there were only slight indications of the rat-sanction. He felt inclined to refrain from using the fingers that had touched the girl when he took a cigarette from the cigarette-case given him by his cousin, but he resisted the temptation. (p. 292)

Like the ejaculation, Freud's intimate postcard was felt to be premature. And the Rat Man's temporary hesitancy to contaminate Gisela's gift with his lascivious fingers was outdistanced by his unstinting refusal to shake hands with Freud—handling the postcard was enough.

In sum, receiving Freud's postcard was experienced erotically and aggressively. The epistolary seduction and assault stirred up the Rat Man's unconscious fantasies and conflicts in the here-and-now psychoanalytic setting. But overvaluing the revival of memories, Freud did not adequately analyze how he mobilized in the Rat Man a combination of anxiogenic homosexual impulses, phobic avoidance, slaughtering rage, and a defensive displacement of erotic wishes onto the less censorable heterosexual substitute.

Freud's giving a meal to the Rat Man on December 28 was a technical deviation with far-reaching results, but in order to follow them we must first comprehend the frame of mind the Rat Man brought into that feeding hour.[19] Just a week before, he had

---

19. Lipton (1977) maintained that Freud separated his technique from his personal relationship to the Rat Man and that such a separation even furthered the analytic process. In this light, Lipton insisted, Freud's personal response to sudden contingencies, such as giving a meal to the Rat Man, did not interfere with treatment, for the patient's real object relationship and its new investiture could be duly analyzed (see also Lipton, 1971). I would side with Stone's position that Freud's early naturalness is superior to the robotlike anonymity of many American analysts in the 1950s; but rather than choose between these two extremes, Stone suggests, one would do better to "work within professional limitations—reasonable and liberal, but very strict at certain points—and thus avoid overstimulation or excessive gratification as well as irrational deprivation" (1981, p. 106; see also Gill, 1982, p. 104). For other critical opinions of the meal, cf. Zetzel (1968, p. 129), Langs (1976, pp. 223–28), Biegler (1975, pp. 273–80), Kanzer (1980, p. 245), and Rosenfeld (1980, pp. 79–80).

openly manifested an unprecedented identification with his mother, repeating her captiousness toward his siblings and dead father. Then, on December 23, the Rat Man declared how ambivalent he was about the serious illness of a paternal figure, Dr. Pr., the longtime family doctor who had treated both Camilla and Lanzer *père*. The omnipotent feelings of the Rat Man were now reactivated—he could kill the physician or keep him alive. Next, the Rat Man remembered how he had magically sustained Gisela in life on two occasions; this in turn led to tracing the origin of his omnipotence back to Camilla's traumatizing death. At this point, I opine, came the most significant emendation of memory in the analysis. Whereas previously the Rat Man had thought of his father's carrying the sick Camilla back to bed, he now recalled that it had been some time prior to her illness that, upon her father's scolding, she was carried *from* the parental bed by someone else—thus the comforting father gave way to an irately banishing one. But unfortunately Freud's record at this critical juncture does not indicate that he dealt transferentially with all this in the ongoing interaction.

In the succeeding session of December 27, the Rat Man again adverted to his mother's plan that he marry a rich relation (a hint of his wish in the maternal transference whereby Freud would favor a marriage between his own twelve-year-old daughter and his patient). The patient followed with two memories about looking: first, guiltily spying through wall cracks at a naked girl bathing; second, exhibiting his penis before a mirror in the hour between midnight and 1:00 A.M. and meanwhile waiting for his father's ghost to return. Clearly the Rat Man's fear that his penis was too small and his search for his missing testicle and the hidden female phallus were motives subtending the visual material, which suggestively make us think about the patient's mirror fantasies about Freud within the analytic hour. Once more, let it be said, there is no indication that Freud transferentially analyzed the Rat Man's reflections. There is evidence, however, of Freud's unconscious perception of the patient's visual hunger, for the final process note of December 27 reads: "This consecutive account of events *swallowed up* any reference to current happenings" (italics mine).[20] Into the following session the Rat Man brought his visual hunger.

Freud's initial description of that next hour on December 28 is biblically resonant: "He was hungry and was fed." In its proverbial brevity the description starkly contrasts with the subsequent recorded associations, whose exceptional amplitude may have been due partly to the mutual stimulation between analyst and analysand and partly to Freud's counterreaction, deferred until scriptive recording. In an explicit sense Freud completely overlooked the face-to-face gratification of the optic appetite of his guest, who shifted from the visual associations ending the previous hour to chiefly kinesthetic ones. The sizable psychoanalytic criticism has not done justice to the dynamic interplay between the session's seeing and eating, and no one has ever related Freud's meal to the fact that the Rat Man's responsive trauma to the captain's story happened during the officers' mess. Presumably during both meals there was a reactivation of archaic cannibalistic fantasies and conflicts of penetrating and being penetrated. This carries all the more purport in that the patient left the serving of herring untouched, and, as we shall better see later on, he never felt quite at home in the feeding hour. Its undigested repercussions, moreover, can be traced right up to the end of Freud's private record on January 20 and permit us to assume that they continued much beyond that.

While avoiding direct discussion of the homosexual seductiveness of the anxiety-provoking meal during the hour, the Rat Man did speak of his former obsessions in the resort region of Unterach, including his suicidal thoughts, not completing meals, and reckless feats of running to cut down weight. This memory of

---

20. The particular German verb Freud uses here, *verschlingt*, denotes a more avid swallowing than such synonyms as *schluckt* or *verschluckt*.

suicidal ideation was especially appropriate in that the ghost of the Rat Man's father did return, without the prop of a mirror, in the person of Freud—as a masturbatory substitution subject to paternal sanction, the ongoing ocular satisfaction did verily prompt memories of suicide. The Rat Man next recalled his military service, his soldierly apathy and forsaken fantasies about challenging a mean officer to a duel; then intense filial ambivalence toward the father came up. To judge from the process notes, there were no transferential interpretations of these associations, so fraught with frustrated anger about what was taking place in the current hour. Instead, we come across Freud's slender musing, "There is evidently an effort to please his father by running" (rather than by biting?). Later in the text are the Rat Man's communications about other obsessions at Unterach and his mistaking Gisela's behavior as a rejection of him. Believing that the Rat Man's suicidal impulses were self-punishments for wishing Gisela dead, Freud gave him a copy of Zola's *La joie de vivre* (Freud's unconscious reaction to the visually charged hour and his countertransferential invitation to sublimate were perhaps other motivations behind this second gift of ocular feeding).[21]

---

21. Several words deserve to be said about what the novel and its author meant to Freud. Around the turn of the century Freud lectured twice to B'Nai Brith on Zola as a prominent example of the obsessional neurotic who reached the highest moral development and was a "fanatic lover of truth" (see *Minutes of the Vienna Psychoanalytic Society*, 1:101, 2:103; and Klein, 1981, pp. 89–90). Elsewhere, Freud referred to Lazare's fear of death in Zola's *La joie de vivre* and the wish that his conflicts would be resolved through the death of Pauline, his cousin and fiancée (*Minutes*, 3:224–25). Possessed by an insatiable desire for affection, Pauline continued to be totally self-sacrificing until, at one point, she found her place taken over by a female rival (Freud, 1905d, p. 239n). Freud's gift might have been additionally motivated by the partial phonetic association between Lanzer and Lazare, the hero of *La joie de vivre*. There is also the pertinent fact that some three weeks before the Rat Man's eventual meal, Freud had given a lecture on "Creative Writers and Day-Dreaming" at the publishing house of Hugo Heller. One passage from that lecture reveals a further, heuristic motivation behind Freud's gift to his patient: "Certain novels, which might be described as 'eccentric,' seem to stand in quite special contrast to the type of the day-dream.

Thereupon the Rat Man talked of the memorable act of undoing when he took the stone away from the road and replaced it twenty minutes later—an allusion in reverse to his expressing hunger and then refusing food, the desired and repulsive herring, the fecal penis.

After misdating the session following December 28 as December 2, Freud initially referred to the short analytic interruption owing to the illness and death of the Rat Man's father figure, Dr. Pr. Through his slip, therefore, Freud copied the Rat Man's undoing with the stone by placing himself back before the feeding hour and thus restoring the paternal Dr. Pr. to his period of life. We then read about the Rat Man's identifying with his mother in criticizing Dr. Pr. for some medical inadequacy in treating Heinrich Lanzer; yet Freud did not give evidence of making any transferential interpretation based on this oedipal issue or on the Rat Man's estimate of Dr. Pr.'s consultation fees as an affair of "so many *Kreuzers*, so many rats." We might not even go far astray in thinking that Freud's parapractic dating was nourished by his countertransferential identification with the defunct Dr. Pr.

The patient went on to fantasize Dr. Pr.'s sexually assaulting Olga and to remember his own father's punishing her and commenting, "That girl has an arse like a rock." Discarding any transferential implication, Freud once more gave vent to a genetic perspective: "Strangely enough, his belief that he really nourished feelings of rage against his father has made no progress in spite of his seeing that there was every logical reason." The Rat Man then continued with a fantasy that a herring, stretched be-

---

In these, the person who is introduced as the hero plays only a very small active part; he sees the actions and sufferings of other people pass before him like a spectator. Many of Zola's later works belong to this category. But I must point out that the psychological analysis of individuals who are not creative writers, and who diverge in some respects from the so-called norm, has shown us analogous variations of the day-dream, in which the ego contents itself with the role of spectator" (Freud, 1908b, pp. 150–51).

tween the anus of Freud's mother and his wife's, was cut by Freud's daughter into two pieces, which thereupon fell away as if peeled off.

Although these fantasies were left untouched by Freud in the process notes, we would serve ourselves well to expatiate on them. In the transferential situation a precipitant of the rat deliria was the overdetermined herring (spelled *Hering* in modern German, although Freud more frequently used the older orthography *Häring*). Both in colloquial German and in Viennese dialect, *Hering* also means a thin person, as in fact the Rat Man sought to be through his fanatic reducing exercises; in this view, the herring was the Rat Man's ideal body image. From another perspective, his identifying with the manhandled Olga indicates a counter-identification with the herring, for he experienced the meal as a homosexual anal assault, leading to retaliation and returned retaliation (note that *Hering* may be broken down into *Herr*, gentleman or master, and *Ring*, which in its verbal form means struggle). Then again, his mother's maiden name was Herlinger, hence a resonating, taboo-charged source for the fish that he "disliked intensely" and that he concomitantly was one with. In a wider sense, the herring could be a maternal and paternal fecal penis which both attracted and repelled the Rat Man. Surrounding that fecal penis was a castrative taboo which itself was violated, for the fish was cut in two. Being castrated in that overdetermined way facilitated the Rat Man's identification with the female members of Freud's family circle, thus establishing other vicissitudes of the patient's fear and desire of a passive homosexual relationship to Freud.

The few recorded sessions in January show clearly that the Rat Man continued to be preoccupied with the assaulting seductiveness of the eventful meal. The ending of the session for January 3, which Strachey omitted to translate, pertinently reads: "Besides, many associations which are not to be interpreted, and also some hostile transferences toward me" (H, p. 234; my translation).

Freud's own daughter who cut the fish in half was critically reduced to a girl of "easy virtuosity." The Rat Man gave also these associations: scales prevent fish from having hair; neither Freud's mother nor his wife, who prepared the meal, had hair; the Rat Man's and Gisela's grandmothers were added in to supplement the split half of the culinary ménage; Freud's science was the child that "peeled off the disguises" of the Rat Man's idea and herring-wishes. Notice the compounded defensive reaction: because of their scales, herring have no hair, but on top of that, even their scales must be peeled off; as if that were not enough, there remains a sufficient quantity of scales to exact a further peeling by psychoanalysis. If Freud did not relate the Rat Man's stripping before the mirror to the overbald fish, it seems rather that psychoanalytic "science" imposed an additional disguise upon their overinvested nakedness.

Our considerations would not be complete if we avoided the possibility of seeing the sequelae of the meal also as derivatives of the unforgettable anal-rat fantasy during maneuvers. On January 4, the revolted Rat Man fantasized kicking Freud's scientific child, psychoanalysis—a fantasy more broadly referring to the infantile belief about anal birth and retaliating for the meal and treatment experienced as an anal rape. The patient went on to remember how, when he cut a biblical lesson at school, he was kicked by his younger brother at the urging of their father. That missed biblical lesson, to be sure, comprised an announcement of the imminent suspension of the analysis between January 3 and January 20, although the connection seems to have been silently passed over. Instead, the rebellious Rat Man disclosed another memory of angry kicking and subsequently complained about losing treatment time through the meal, from which Freud had profited. Then, in a contrasting gesture, which we recognize as all too familiar, the Rat Man thought that he should pay for the meal the sum of seventy kronen, that is, seventy rats. He associated that with a joke from a Budapest music hall: a weakly bridegroom offered seventy kronen to a waiter if he would undertake the first coitus with the bride. Truly, then, the meal had a castrating effect on the Rat Man, all the more so in that Freud was figured to be a Budapest waiter like his supposedly murderous brother. Whereas formerly the Rat Man had wanted to pay Freud twenty kronen as a belittling fee for each session (p. 298),[22] he now was ready to pay three and a half times that amount for a session combined with a biting ritual. A further indication of the Rat Man's revolt was his fear about being swayed by his confidant, Dr. Palatzer, who had expressed antagonism to the treatment.

Reports of the next two sessions in January further lead us to suspect that the Rat Man was planning to interrupt treatment:

> He was smiling with amusement, as though he had something up his sleeve. (p. 315)

> He himself had a feeling that his sly illness had something up its sleeve. (p. 316)

Meanwhile, the puzzled Freud ignored the transferential relevance of the Rat Man's affair with the dressmaker (perhaps, though, in Freud's comment regarding the patient's coitus interruptus—"He is clearly looking for ways of spoiling the affair"—there was an unconscious inkling of the imminent psychoanalysis interruptus). Another precarious sign of the psychoanalytic interruption was the Rat Man's dental dream, in which a dentist erroneously pulled out a large and dripping tooth adjacent to the ailing one. Symbolically interpreting the dream as referring to the subject's masturbation as well as his vengeful castration of his father, Freud swerved away from the negative transference about

---

22. A surviving letter indicates that Freud's hourly fee in 1907 was thirty kronen (see Eissler, 1965, p. 545*n*).

a psychoanalyst-dentist both fulfilling the patient's dreaded wish to be castrated and depriving a rat imago of vital biting power.[23]

It is fitting to give separate attention to the final recorded session of January 20. Additional material pointed to the patient's mounting suppression of anger, but once more Freud appeared not to have transferentially faced the recurrent anal punishment, this time in a dream where a dirty waiter was hit in the behind by an officer. And it is hardly accidental that, just as in the feeding hour, we come upon the Rat Man's restraining his impulses to challenge an oppressive other to a duel. Why do Freud's notes end here? Is there a mere coincidence between their final course and the Rat Man's increasing anger? Did the repercussions of the meal, culminating in a three-week break and the sequel of abundant negative transference in the last recorded hour, finally disrupt the therapeutic alliance? The absence of other notes might well be continuing evidence of how undigested was the present of the repast.

Our preceding investigations have gradually equipped us to outline the Rat Man's treatment in its general course and outcome. Notwithstanding his critical condition and his far-reaching ambivalence in object-relationships, he was able to establish a good therapeutic alliance for at least the initial portion of the treatment. Then he evinced sufficient developmental achievement and object relatedness to regress, to contend with the return of repressed conflicts, and to undergo frustration and deprivation proper to the analytic situation (initially, as we remember, the Rat Man's defensive collapse under an anally cannibalistic rage showed itself in panic and altered states of consciousness). An intense transference neurosis quickly arose, but it did not create that rigid kind of dependence that would have prevented the

---

23. Beigler (1975, pp. 279–80) is the only critic who stresses a positive interpretation for the tooth-pulling dream, linking it to Freud's skillful postprandial interventions and the Rat Man's fantasized pregnancy with a new self; Beigler is influenced by Zetzel's minimizing the bad effects of the meal (1968, p. 129).

expression of negative feeling toward Freud. The Rat Man became joyous and could laugh on certain occasions, and in a positive identification with his paternal analyst, the patient after a while was able to stand up "rather manfully" to his domineering mother.

Yet in spite of Freud's theoretical remarks about there being a new edition of the patient's illness in analysis, he conceived the transference as an intermittent rather than a pervasive phenomenon—hence, we constantly read in the process notes of "*a* transference" or "transference*s*." Freud's transferential references, furthermore, occur only in response to some explicit association made about him or his family; and even then, Freud neglected to interpret the maternal and the negative transference, including anti-Semitic manifestations. Nor do we come across any interpretation by Freud directly addressing the Rat Man's homosexual wishes to penetrate the father-analyst anally. That interpretive omission is all the more critical in view of the Rat Man's need for a strong object of identification and for a supporter against his threatening mother; his anxiety therefore increased when he criticized Freud. In other words, the patient's distressful devaluation of Freud was a measure of his conflicts between a regressed wish to reestablish a passive preoedipal father-son relationship, on the one hand, and oedipal rivalry and the quest for a lost heterosexual object, on the other.[24]

Within the void of the transferential interpretations, we notice the lack of convincing material about any maturation in the Rat Man's heterosexual relationships. Specifically, we are left in the dark about the extent to which the Rat Man reconciled his bisexual conflicts, his entrenched castration anxiety, and his wide-

---

24. For various statements in this paragraph, cf. Zetzel (1966a, pp. 127–28; 1966b, p. 45), Hawelka (1974, pp. 179, 253–54), Viderman (1977, pp. 270, 275), Kanzer (1980, p. 418), Weiss (1980, pp. 207–11), Blacker and Abraham (1982, p. 718), and Gill (1982, p. 168). For Weiss's charge that Freud did not perceive the defense of identification with the aggressor (p. 213), see Zetzel (1966a, p. 125).

spread depreciation of women, including Gisela and his mother, as whores. Although at first he identified Gisela as the object of the rat punishment and only reluctantly added that his father was also a fantasied victim, the Rat Man for some time afterward spoke more freely of his father than of Gisela and his mother. We remember that he resisted revealing Gisela's name. Only much later did he substantially allow his mother into his associations, and his criticism of her came even later (incidentally, Freud's first expressed linking of the two women was noted only on December 23). It was two years after the analysis that he finally married Gisela, but there are no data indicating an appreciable gain in modifying his narcissistic and greatly conflictual attitude toward her. Apposite here is the Rat Man's dream about Japanese swords, which to him meant the prohibition against marrying or having intercourse with Gisela (pp. 267–68, 271).[25] Attention was not paid to the passing description that the swords were made of coins. As a matter of fact, the issue of money, which had a central and overdetermined meaning in the Rat Man's life, hardly received analysis (minted in pathological turmoil, the private and brutal rat currency was a far cry from legal tender); he did, we know, entrust his money-rats to his mother, who acted like the decision-making broker for the analysis.

It was also during the analysis that financial cost, libidinal discharge, and problems with impotence seemed to be the salient factors in the Rat Man's liaison with a dressmaker, who rapidly became his kept mistress. There is no evidence that he was potent with a woman whose social status was respectable to him, and we meet with no demonstration that he attained the level of maturity and tenderness of genital sexuality. In this developmental connection, there are no traces to indicate that Freud's potential

---

25. Silently emending Freud's slip, Strachey (p. 271) translated the word *Schwestern* (sisters) instead of *Schwertern* (swords) (H, p. 122). This parapraxis may stem from a countertransferential reaction to the specifically incestuous role of the Rat Man's sisters.

role as paternal "disturber" and "interferer" in filial sexuality had been analyzed adequately.

The Rat Man generally remained in a passive, masochistic position before Freud as a transferentially paternal authority. Within that position the Rat Man appears to have had an analysis that was quite lively, but it became too anxiogenically so—he could take flight either inside Freud's office or seemingly away from the treatment itself. Did the Rat Man case count among those that came to an untimely end because Freud prematurely revealed the solution (Freud, 1913b, pp. 140–41)? A solution bearing on the meal and a homosexual transference and compounded by maternal interference? We do not, in any event, come across any indication of resolution of the Rat Man's transference neurosis, but we rather find abounding evidence against Freud's claim that he brought about a "complete restoration" of his patient's personality.

The overall tally is that Freud's narrative of the Rat Man's case qua narrative is neither complete nor consistent. There was no lifting of infantile amnesia about the early misdemeanor that provoked the father's punishment, installed him permanently as interferer, and ended infantile masturbation. (Incidentally, Mrs. Lanzer, the sole surviving witness who remembered the misdeed, thought it had simply to do with biting.) A longer analysis would have afforded the occasion for the patient to fill in his story and to bring up explicit memories and fantasies about related primal scenes and early parenting. On the other hand, we should also remember that Freud's conception of the Rat Man's later, adult pathology is somewhat confused. For instance, what was the specific precipitating cause of the patient's later decompensation? the death of an aunt? his mother's marriage plan for him? And how much was the Rat Man's hesitancy before marriage due to Gisela's infertility? How much to his reluctance to transgress his father's wishes by marrying a poor woman? These unanswered questions testify to Freud's explanatory confusion in "The Precipitating Cause of the Illness," one of the ten sections constituting the case history.

Regardless of Freud's excessive claims for his treatment, we have yet to explain its circumscribed progress.[26] Quite relevantly, major credit has repeatedly been given to the impact of Freud's personality and to his genuinely warm interest in his patient, even though it is impossible to determine these factors satisfactorily. Still, Freud's quick insights, awesome intellectual fertility, simultaneous awareness of multiple facets of the conscious and unconscious, strong self-conviction, and engaging sensitivity—the sum of these qualities must have helped unsettle the patient's skepticism, convey confidence, and raise self-esteem.

The cure was in large measure a transference cure, owing greatly to the imposing Freud's accepting attitude and his reassuring technique of reconstructing the infantile as well as the recent past. Mixed with Freud's accepting approach of praise, encouragement, and gratification was his use of suggestive metaphor and indoctrination, even to the point of once repeating a recent lecture on perversions (p. 283). Consequently, the genetic enterprise of the analysis was largely directive: the Rat Man "had to be forced into remembering what he had forgotten and into finding out what he had overlooked" (p. 232). If Freud here did not create an analytic space in which archaic fantasies could be constructed and win deep conviction, he nevertheless managed to communicate that he would clearly understand much of the patient's psychic confusion, thus holding out an anchor to the pa-

26. Cf. Kris (1951, p. 240), Kanzer (1952, p. 143), Grunberger (1966, p. 163), Morgenthaler (1966, p. 206), Hawelka (1974, p. 269), Beigler (1975, p. 283), Viderman (1977, pp. 280–82, 352), Kestenberg (1980, pp. 156, 171), Muslin (1979, p. 574), and Coltrera (1980, p. 296). I should also record Lacan's singular defense of Freud's indoctrination (1960, pp. 290–91) as well as the position of another Lacanian: the Rat Man improved and became more joyous because he was putting Freud's theories to the test and finding them ineffectual; accordingly, the patient was convinced that all his difficulties came from his mother, and he was increasingly stimulated to see Freud as falsely pursuing a paternal etiology (Melman, 1980, p. 138).

tient in his bewildering sea of despair and maddening obsessions. In this matter, a short example of Freud's rapid resoluteness suffices. Within the first seven sessions, Freud declared that the Rat Man's illness had arisen mainly from unresolved mourning for his father's death, a pathological mourning traceable to parricidal wishes from the patient's sixth year. By the second week, Freud thought he had discovered the initial incident in the outburst of fury that the three-year-old Ernst had directed against his erotically inhibiting father. The two full reconstructions found in the case by Strachey (Freud, 1937, p. 256), then, are largely traceable to material concerning hostility to the punitive father and emerging in the treatment's initial fortnight (pp. 182, 205–06).

Thus, by offering himself as a reassuring, internalizable model for attention, exploration, and intelligible confrontation, Freud promoted adaptive secondary process and reorganization of the ego and superego. Realizing that Freud could not be killed by his hostility, the Rat Man became more disposed to speak of the weaknesses of his father, whom he had idealized and unconsciously wanted to destroy. There was also the analytic demystification of the Rat Man's so-called prophetic hunches and dreams, which helped to tame their omniscient strivings; he was helped as well by Freud's attempt through the treatment to draw up a grammar of irrational obsessions, which complemented his grammar of dreams, and a semiotics for translating verbal syntax into the pictorial medium (Mahony & Singh, 1975). Not least of all, once the crippling rat symptom was remitted, there was correspondingly a reinforcement of the ego, better enabling the patient to deal defensively and adaptively with other psychic turmoil and partly to resume his maturation, which had been impeded by his neurosis.

We shall temporarily close our survey by considering something peculiar, which will set us off in a new direction. Although the Rat Man related quite a few dreams and believed that they played a crucial part in his life, they seemed to draw less interpretive attention from Freud than, say, those in Dora's analysis. The official case of the Rat Man refers to only two of the many dreams, and just in passing at that (pp. 193, 200). His obsessions, which were apt to be less clear than their oneiric versions (pp. 267–68, 271), appeared to be more challenging to Freud, and analytic work devoted to them helps us account for the patient's symptomatic remission. One gets the further impression that just as the famous nightmare served as a guiding thread in the Wolf Man's analysis, so the Rat Man's obsession about seeing naked women and fearing his father's subsequent death were main points of orientation in his analysis. In the former case, the nightmare referred to the traumatizing primal scene; in the latter, obsessions led back to a traumatic scene between father and son.

But precisely in what verbalized way Freud succeeded in dealing with his patient's symptoms is an intriguing question that merits exploration in its own right. Freud's verbal responses to the Rat Man's obsessions will be the subject of our next chapter, which will take a historical detour along with performing some textual analysis. Some surprisingly complementary answers await us.

5

Freud's Technique
The Rationale of a Particular Practice

The mouth is the cradle of perception.
—René Spitz, 1965

The letter kills but the breath giveth life.
—2 Corinthians 3:6

We shall change our tempo and broach a historicocultural subject that at the start will seemingly never be able to take us back to the Rat Man. I beg my readers' indulgence, asking them to suspend a demand for immediately apparent relevance and to engage, for a short while, in an attention that floats freely. First of all, I call attention to the surge of modern research on the question of oral versus written culture. In this connection I readily endorse the tenet that orality can enter into and modify the production, transmission, reception, and conservation of information.[1] This leads me to propose a vantage point, other than the usual exclusive one of written culture, from which we might look at psychoanalysis in terms of its discovery, nature, transmission, and even technique.

To be sure, an exhaustive treatment of my subject would mean relating orality and its involvement with visuality to three factors: the congenital and constitutional factor (for example, the visual

---

1. To cite one dramatic example from ancient history: Eric Havelock (1963) showed that the final domestication and internalization of the Greek alphabet influenced Plato to turn against the orality of Homeric Greece and thus banish from his ideal republic the race of poets who were representatives of the old oral-aural world.

theatricality of Charcot's clinical "performances" as etiologically traceable to his noted strabismus); an individual's development and psychosexual experience (for example, auditively pronounced primal scenes); and the social factor proper to the means of communication. We need no prolonged reflection to realize that an analysis of the interaction of all three factors is fraught with imponderables, and this undeniable fact should temper any investigative zeal for premature synthesis. Nevertheless, in the course of concentrating on the orality of media, I shall not eschew the opportunity to bring in some synergistic considerations.

A primary orality typifies cultures untouched by print or writing. Psychoanalysis, however, was born in the Era of Second Orality, ushered in by new means of communication such as the telephone and radio, which introduce a sensorial shift from the previous scriptorial and typographic traditions. Unfortunately for us, the historical impact of the development of communication media upon the human sensorium has yet to be fully charted. Closer to the matter at hand, such a history would enlighten the fundamental nature of psychoanalytic terms. To be more precise:

> For purposes proposed as scientific, psychoanalysis made use of the very "proximity" senses which Freudian thought itself has advertised as prescientific and full of danger for abstract thinking. For psychoanalysis has pointed out that for the rise of civilization, taboos must be imposed on the senses providing greater bodily pleasures (touch most of all, as well as taste and smell), and more attention must be given to the more sublime (abstract, distancing) senses such as hearing and, especially, sight. The relationship of the rise of psychoanalysis to the history of the sensorium and concomitantly of the communications media certainly deserves more attention than there is room or reason to give it [in a general survey].
>
> *What we need is a phenomenology of psychoanalytic concepts.* (Ong, 1967, p. 110; italics mine)

Of course, in the Era of Second Orality, sensorial shifts are gradual and uneven in development. In this regard, we cannot overevaluate the significance of the belated progress of psychoanalytic theory from the topographical model in *The Interpretation of Dreams*, conceiving the psyche as a mechanical apparatus, to the structural model of *The Ego and the Id*, using an organismic metaphor to describe the mind. The vocal implications of the latter, let us note, were to some extent borne out subsequently in Isakower's etiological study of the superego, entitled "On the Exceptional Position of the Auditory Sphere" (1939). Bearing the foregoing in mind, we may wonder how much the distorted idea of psychoanalysis in certain circles—pharmacological, behavioristic, psychiatric—is based on a distrust of orality and a predilection for visual, kinetic, and other models shaping their scientific formation.

Among all disciplines originating in the contemporary period, psychoanalysis is preeminently the most oral—not only in terms of clinical treatment but also in the education and supervision of analytic candidates. Moreover, what other professional organization in its annual meeting devotes a section to its oral history, as does the American Psychoanalytic Association? Then again, even within the larger history of discourse, psychoanalysis stands alone. Prior to the psychoanalytic "talking cure," there was never an enunciatory form, literary genre, or social ritual in which the four basic types of discourse (the referential, rhetorical, expressive, and aesthetic) figured saliently. Even more than that, each of these four discourses takes on new traits in the psychoanalytic setting, and then, most important, a certain dynamic interaction among the four contributes to the uniqueness of psychoanalytic treatment and even comprises one of the verifications of its therapeutic success (Mahony, 1979).

Although steeped in vocalization, psychoanalysis as a discipline has yet to realize fully the intrapsychic as well as transcultural influences of sound. For instance, might Otto Rank not have modified the *universal* importance be attributed to birth trauma if he had known what Margaret Mead (1964) revealed years ago, that there was a South Pacific society in which a special woman was designated to adjust immediately to the neonate's distress and to cry in unison with him? Along the same line, among the Zulus each child is given a cradle song especially composed for him and staying like a name or motto with him for life.[2] Actually it is only very recently that an analyst postulated a sound image of the self which developmentally initiates the body image (Anzieu, 1979); and it is quite to the point that the same author also observed that the editors of the *Standard Edition* of Freud's works did not index such capital terms as voice, sound, and audition! As I have said elsewhere, such editorial neglect would not have occurred

> if psychoanalysis had been invented in a tonal language such as Chinese or in an African language such as Khosi, which mixes words and a tongue-clacking that up to now has defied transcription. In such languages, psychoanalysts would be likely to devote more attention to nonverbal sounds and noises which, after all, increase as the treatment progresses (patients feel freer to make more noises as analysis goes on). I have searched the literature for a psychoanalytic article on patients whispering and can find none, despite the fact that verbalizations during lovemaking are almost always whispered. (Mahony, 1982, p. 4)

Using a transcultural perspective, we can gain insight into the functions of the analyst as recorder or speaker. Freud's counsel that the analyst not write during sessions is glossed by the impatient rebuke of a Maya storyteller to a research anthropologist: "What I tell—did you *see* it or do you only write it?" (Zumthor,

---

2. See Zumthor (1983, p. 91). Zumthor's magisterial study and Walter Ong's *Orality and Literacy* are the two recent books that have decisively advanced my thinking about oral communication. Anyone desiring to pursue the subject will profit from their complementary and highly suggestive bibliographies.

1983, p. 239). It is as if the storyteller demands a full attention and internalization that would be otherwise diminished by scriptive mediation. The voice of the unseen analyst might at times be suggestively considered alongside the fascinating or terrifying role that Occidental mythologies assign to a voice without body, such as the Hellenic Echo or the voices of revenants, earth, and clouds, which appear in French folklore. And as if to subdue the voice, some cultures codify the link between it and posture; for instance, in one of the ethnic groups in Volta, the reclining person manifests confidence, whereas seated he speaks seriously and standing he talks trivialities (Zumthor, 1983, p. 14).

I might briefly add here four other oral-aural subjects that have been neglected in psychoanalysis for reasons of cultural or other limitations. First, it is germane that although the primal scene is mainly visual and auditory, we have no lexical terms for the auditive counterparts of *voyeurism* and *exhibitionism*. Next, analysts should give more organized attention to that function of discourse called phatic (Jakobson, 1960), whereby the message chiefly serves to establish, prolong, or discontinue communication (hello . . . um-hum . . . that's that), or to attract notice or confirm its continuation (wow . . . you got that?). Third, we might duly reflect on the sensorial adjustments that psychoanalytic patients, who by and large are well educated, must undergo. The therapeutic process involves rerouting such analysands, molded for years by the solitary visual experience of book culture, into an intense oral-aural interchange such as they have scarcely had before—designedly bringing them into contact with the endopsychic visual world of dreams, fantasies, and memories, which then must be verbalized and understood primarily within the verbalizable significance of the transference. Finally, the oral nature of psychoanalysis is also distinguished in the sense that within the clinical hour most analysts of orthodox persuasion would rarely address the patient by name. No other personal, secret-sharing discourse of appreciable duration possesses this vocal peculiarity. And since, as Freud says, one's name is intimately bound up with one's personality, the analyst's hesitation toward the name contributes phonetically to the narcissistic privation characterizing the psychoanalytic hour, activating the most intimate memories and fantasies during it. Worthy of future examination is how the analyst's and patient's names may phonetically reappear to determine the patient's dreams and fantasies.

We may now turn our attention to Freud's complex sensitivity to sound, which, along with the historical vicissitudes of the sensorium, played an essential part in the origin and development of psychoanalysis. First of all, given Freud's open reserve toward music, we are most fortunate that the nature of dreams is visual and verbal rather than musical, for otherwise the creative discovery of *The Interpretation of Dreams* would have remained for another day. Less well known than Freud's musical handicap is his stunted acoustic sensibility. As a matter of fact, this deficiency was so acute as to prevent him from understanding the treatment of tone relations in Lipps's *Grundtatsachen des Seelenlebens* (Freud, 1985, p. 325). Nonetheless, inner vocalized language was a significant characteristic of Freud's psychic functioning, as is shown in the following biographical passage from *On Aphasia* (a passage, by the way, not cited by either Jones or Schur):

> I remember having twice been in danger of my life, and each time the awareness of the danger occurred to me quite suddenly. On both occasions I felt "This is the end," and while otherwise my inner language proceeds with only indistinct sound images and slight lip movements, in these situations of danger I heard these words as if somebody was shouting them into my ears, and at the same time I saw them as if they were printed on a piece of paper floating. (Freud, 1891, p. 62)

In keeping with the phenomenon of his inner vocalization, Freud's hallucinations in Paris during 1885–86 were of an auditive nature: "I often heard my name suddenly called by an unmistakable and beloved voice" (Freud, 1901, p. 261).

We might not be surprised to learn, then, that Freud's memory was exceptionally "phonographic." As he said, "Shortly before I entered the University I could write down almost verbatim popular lectures on scientific subjects directly after hearing them" (1901, p. 135). He also remarked that as late as 1916 his "phonographic memory" was still powerful enough that he was able subsequently to record faithfully the improved lectures he gave at the University of Vienna (1933, p. 5). In this context, perhaps we should understand that Freud's decision to study natural science came upon hearing a public recitation of the essay "On Nature." Wrongly attributed by scholars in the past to Goethe, the short three-page essay adulating nature contains this sentence that might have particularly impressed the young Freud: "She has neither language nor speech, but she creates tongues and hearts through which she feels and speaks."[3]

Undoubtedly the oral nature of the Viennese milieu too had a decided influence on Freud. If different eras and cultures vary in taciturnity and prolixity and hence in a redistributed speech mass (Steiner, 1975), we may safely presume that nineteenth-century Vienna enjoyed a remarkable atmosphere of verbalized expression and oral communication, to judge from such interconnected phenomena as the literary resurgence, the intense social life of the famous and not so famous cafés, and the extraordinary waves of Jewish immigrants from diverse cultures into Vienna. More exactly: in 1855, the year before Freud was born, there were 6,000 Jews in Vienna, composing 1 percent of the population; in 1870 there were 40,000 (over 6 percent of the population); and by 1900, when *The Interpretation of Dreams* was published, Jews numbered nearly 147,000, or about 9 percent of the demographic

---

3. This essay, along with some enlightening commentary, conveniently appears in Kaufmann (1980, pp. 32ff.).

total. Pertinently, most of these Jewish immigrants went to Vienna's Leopoldstadt district, where Freud lived for many years (see Klein, 1981, esp. pp. 2, 9, 12). No wonder that one of Freud's books was based largely on his extensive collection of Jewish jokes—and jokes, Freud (1905) reminds us, are the most social of all discourses. As the Germanist Heinz Politzer (1969, p. 740) incisively remarked, "The manner of speaking of Austrian Jews before the turn of the century, their wit and their penchant for ambivalences and ambiguities of every kind, had left traces in Freud's work."[4] On another score, can it be an accident that Freud's last great treatise dealt expressly with the oral tradition of the Bible (1937, pp. 40, 43, 68–69, 94), the very text in which he was precociously immersed very soon after he could read (1925a, p. 8)?

With some justification, we might regard the foregoing comments as a leisurely though essential preparation for us to examine the vital presence in Freud's postures both as speaker and as writer. I can scarcely overrate this weighty claim, for it is not a matter of tracing in a superficial manner merely one of many determinants in Freud's prose. Rather, orality personalizes Freud's expressive mode and renders it consonant with his lifelong subject, the human being.

Appropriately, Freud was faithful to the etymology of his first name, *Si(e)g Mund*, "victory mouth," and his style was ever attuned to the qualities distinctive of oral communication. Among the various reports on Freud's oral delivery by his contemporaries, we may single out Wittels's resonating contention that the persuasive force of Freud's living voice far exceeded that of the cold print by which future generations must appreciate him. Let us now listen to Wittels's irreplaceable description of Freud talking to his Viennese associates:

  4. This is my translation of the German: *Die Sprechweise der österreichischen Juden vor der Jahrhundertwende, ihr Witz und ihre Neigung zu Ambivalenzen und Ambiguitäten aller Art, hat im Werk Freuds Spuren hinterlassen.*

In this circle of intimates, Freud's method was far more audacious than it was in a public lecture. He would begin by enunciating his main contentions categorically, so that they were apt to repel; then he would provide such a wealth of argument in support of them that his hearers could hardly fail to be convinced of their truth. Those who know Freud only through the written word will be far more ready to differ from him than those who listened to the magic of his speech. Not that he is an orator, for he rarely raises his voice. . . . I find his later writings less admirable than I found the earlier ones. But I am perfectly willing to admit that they are no less excellent, and that the reason why they please me less is that I have to read them in cold print, whereas before I used to learn from Freud's living speech. (Wittels, 1924, pp. 134–35)

We might and I think we should question Wittels's emphasis on separating what Freud said from what he wrote, for there are many similarities if one looks for them. Did not Freud dislike some of John Stuart Mill's writing because it was not aphoristic (Freud, 1960, p. 90), a virtual hallmark of oral style? Indeed, Freud's own assimilation of proverbial lore and his ability to create oracular statements and enticingly quotable expressions (everyone has his own favorites) set him apart from so many analysts who neglect the vital oral element and who simply write in and for silent reflection.

For Freud's importation into print of elements of thinking aloud and live speech, we must not neglect the avowed influence of one of his great teachers Jean-Martin Charcot. It is of interest that Freud so admired Charcot's lectures that he translated a number of them that had been gathered into a volume. Here is Freud prefacing his translation of the *Tuesday Lectures* and telling us approvingly about authorial improvisation and audience appeal:

These lectures owe a peculiar charm to the fact they are entirely, or for the most part, improvisations. . . . [Charcot] is obliged to behave before his audience as he ordinarily does only in medical practice, with the exception that he thinks aloud and allows his audience to take part in the course of his conjectures and investigations. (Freud, 1892–94, p. 133)

As if in mimetic response, the oral qualities of Freud's translation itself are manifest in his unique interruptions of Charcot's exposition to put forward not only explanations and additional references but also "critical objections and glosses such as might occur to a member of the audience" (p. 136).

The improvised freedom that Freud admired in Charcot was also evident in aspects of his own vocal and written expression that were to gain widespread praise. Surely a mechanical factor promoting spontaneity was Freud's unusual speed in handwriting,[5] which closed the frustrating temporal gap between his thinking and recording, for most people write by hand at less than one-tenth the rate of their speech (Chafe, 1982, esp. pp. 37–38); such cursive slowness fosters a bent for premeditation, as is evident in the publications of print culture. Freud, on the other hand, admittedly preferred to speak or write to find out where his thoughts would lead him, a practice in harmony with the oral sensitivity of his spontaneous expression. Typically in this spontaneous and expressive discourse there is a tendency to some degree of inconsistency and illogical generalization: hence Freud's *never* might become *sometimes, possibly* might unexpectedly become *definitely*, or vice versa (Mahony, 1982, esp. ch. 4).

Another oral element in Freud's prose is redundancy, which

---

5. Jones's remarks (1957, p. 130) about the relationship between Freud's psychomotricity and handwriting are worth quoting. Jones begins by quoting from a letter in which Freud complains: "I find it very hard to substitute Latin characters for Gothic handwriting, as I am now doing. All fluency—inspiration one would say on a higher plane—at once leaves me." Here is Jones's gloss: "It is evident that the mere physical act of writing, which he performed at an unusually swift speed, had for Freud some special emotional significance."

lends it a certain fluid ease. We may think of this consequential link in the following way:

> Since redundancy characterizes oral thought and speech, it is in a profound sense more natural to thought and speech than is sparse linearity. Sparsely linear or analytic thought and speech is an artificial creation, structured by the technology of writing. Eliminating redundancy on a significant scale demands a time-obviating technology, writing. (Ong, 1982, p. 40)

We must not confuse the measured redundancy in Freud's prose, however, with the accidental feature of repetitiveness, which he himself assigned to the oral tradition. That is to say, with the founding of the *Jahrbuch für psychoanalytische und psychopathologische Forschungen* in 1909, Freud felt that in psychoanalytic circles a written tradition emerged alongside the oral one. Relying on the typographic contribution to communication, Freud no longer had to repeat in every paper the fundamental psychoanalytic premises or to refute elementary objections. As he put it to Jung in 1910: "In the meantime the printing press has been invented so to speak for our benefit; we are no longer dependent on the oral tradition" (Freud, 1974a, p. 282; see also p. 254).

In order to forestall any possible misconceptions, perhaps a statement of caution is necessary at this stage: Freud's style is markedly oral though not exclusively so. But insofar as it is oral, Freud's manner of communicating is a far cry from the detached stance of a goodly number of analytic authors whose publications smack of the lifeless spatiality of print. To make this point clearer, I may allude to the research of the ethnolinguist William Chafe, who studied two maximally differentiated styles, the informal spoken and the formal written. Among other things, informal speakers refer more extensively to themselves and their own mental processes and have greater involvement with their audience—making sure that the message is comprehensible, and so on. On the other hand, formal writers, using a detached kind of language, resort extensively to the passive voice and to nominalization (for example, using *treatment* instead of *treat*). Such nominalization, Chafe (1982, p. 46) continues, "suppresses involvement in action in favor of abstract reification." A little way along this path of thought leads us to conclude that many psychoanalytic articles are deadening to read precisely because—if I may mock the nominalizations—they are in subjection to an infection of impersonalism and manifest an inundation of reifications that are keynoted by their qualities of abstraction and superabundance.

Perhaps the oral qualities of Freud's style will become easier to see if we momentarily tend to those analysts who studiously avoid the pronoun *I* in their writings and rely instead on a grammatical expletive or dispensable filler, an impersonal *it* conjoined with the passive voice; for example, "it was interpreted by the analyst to the patient that," "it was repeatedly observed that." In these authors there is a covert ideology whereby the *it*, or *das Es*, that vibrates throughout Freud's writings gives way to a driveless *it* that is subversive, silently referring to the privileged position, impersonality, and unerringness of mechanized calculations. The overdetermined *it*[6] appears to be a concealed trace of nostalgia for the methodology of "objective" psychology and away from the person-ness of transference and countertransference, away from the orality and pronominal trace of the living human voice.

A short step brings us to examine the orality in Freud's written prose in terms of two interconnected factors, namely, tone and the fictionality of the addressee. The writer-reader relationship indeed has a great deal of fictionality—by the time what I am writing is published, I or some of my intended readers might be dead or incapacitated, and at any event I cannot realistically con-

---

6. This grammatical trait (the overdetermined semantic status of *it*) is particularly suited to the devitalized depersoned printed page, which, beyond being a communicative medium, seems to be a deanimated totem and reified ideal for objective psychology. Accordingly, to sprinkle the totemic page with personal pronouns would be to use desecrating ritual, to violate a taboo.

ceive of the infinite variety of moods and settings in which my future readers will approach this book. Moreover, since finished texts are existentially in the past, they involve the reader with the past, present, and future in a fundamentally different way than a living voice of the present does—clearly "there is no visual equivalent of speech but only a set of visual patterns relatable to speech."[7] Whereas the written text qua text is primarily an experience of visuality and *space*, speech (fleeting) by nature is one of orality/aurality and *time*. In a sense, print is more suited to express the conscious discontinuity of objective time than the subjective one of *durée* that is composed of memory, perception, and desire and that is the experience proper to unconscious and preconscious processes (Jaques, 1982; Mahony, 1984, p. 98). Freud's eminent achievement was to offset the visual quiescence of the printed text: in his processive style he verbalized his unconsciously felt simultaneity of past, present, and future; his frequent retrospections and anticipations involved both himself and his reader in an undercurrent of temporal flow. In this venture Freud engaged himself intimately with the unseen audience, a locutory mastery that few if any analysts have equaled. Collaterally Freud succeeded in the baffling task of communicating the semblance of tone. I stress *semblance*, for the use of tone in textual criticism is metaphorical; since tones of course are auditory in nature, their detection in writing comes from inference, not from a direct sensorial process.

Freud's sensitivity to the oral tradition was manifest not only in his expository manner of writing and lecturing but also, as we shall see, in his clinical technique with the Rat Man. In the evolution of psychoanalytic writing, the Rat Man case was one of the first hybrid specimens spanning the oral and written traditions. But in other ways, the Rat Man case was an eminently oral

---

7. See Ong (1977, pp. 233, 267, 269, and also his second chapter entitled "The Writer's Audience Is Always a Fiction").

one. It is quite to the point that Freud spoke about the patient at no less than six meetings of the Vienna Psychoanalytic Society;[8] he never spoke there about Dora, and spoke only once about the Wolf Man. I have already mentioned that Freud chose to give a lecture on the Rat Man to the First International Congress of Psychoanalysis and that the lecture was his most memorable oral performance.

We can observe a series of oral distinctions about the Rat Man case that at first glance may seem to have fortuitous import. As opposed to the Dora and Wolf Man case reports, which were organized around visual dream events, the Rat Man text centers on obsessional acts and sayings. For Freud, the first clinical problem to be solved was the patient's reaction to the captain's "two speeches" (p. 210)—the rat story and the reimbursing request. Freud ascribed considerable import to an oft-repeated family "tale" about Ernst's raging outburst toward his father (p. 205), which, however, the patient did not believe. More significant is Freud's particular verbal technique in dealing with the obsessional ideation accompanying the Rat Man's compulsive acts. While interpreting the general meaning at various strata underlying those acts, Freud also strove to coin orally marked, aphoristic formulas of which those acts were the immediate translation.

I suggest that part of the contemporary unawareness of Freud's technique of specifically translating is reflected in Strachey's English rendering of one of the subheadings in the Rat Man case: "Some Obsessional Ideas and Their Explanation"; in truth, however, "explanation" should be "translation," which in the German is *Übersetzung* (186/409). The later Freud spelled out his technique this way:

> But there is no doubt that before becoming conscious they [unpleasant obsessive ideas] have been through the process of

---

8. October 30, November 6, and November 20 of 1907; January 22, March 4, and April 8 of 1908.

repression. In most of them the *actual wording* of the aggressive instinctual impulse is altogether unknown to the ego, and it requires a good deal of analytic work to make it conscious. (Freud, 1926, p. 117; italics mine)

Since the Rat Man's obsessional sayings were characterized by temporal isolation, rapid articulation, and ellipsis, they themselves naturally tended to be short and detachable—in a word, aphoristic. Freud's correspondent interpretation was to translate the impulse into verbal terms; when the defensive truncations were minimal, the translation was aphoristic, but when the truncations were more considerable, the translation tended to be like a reconstruction.

A distinctiveness of Freud's technique, then, was that it took account of the psychically structural difference in the obsessional and thereby traced the exact nature of the obsessions. Perhaps Freud worked with an inkling of his later idea that in the obsessional neurotic, censorship functions between the conscious and the unconscious rather than between the unconscious and the preconscious (Jones, 1955, p. 183). In his sensitive pursuit of internal monologue, Freud noted the lexical and grammatical transformations of the obsessional's sayings: patients do not know the wording of their obsessions (p. 223); the Rat Man's adult obsessions supposedly emerged in 1899 as mere hypotheses ("If . . ."), and by 1903 the hypotheses were followed by positive command (pp. 301, 304); obsessional sayings, known consciously only in truncated form, may appear with their actual text in a dream (p. 223); a number of obsessions succeeding one another, even though the wording may vary, are ultimately one and the same (p. 223). There is more. Informed by both analytic observation and empathy, Freud's therapeutic translations were sounded out in the first person or the self-addressed second-person point of view. Such translations, as we shall see from the upcoming examples, were experience-near, assimilable, eminently recitable, and far different from what is often practiced by modern analysts—a wordy paraphrase laid out in the differentiated second or third person and removed from the immediacy of the inner monologue. By empathically filling out ellipses into recitable expansions, Freud aimed to deprive obsessions of their mysteriously frightening and despotic force and to give the patient a stance of self-assured analytic comprehension and self-reflection. Incidentally, my offhand impression of various works is that Jones and Fenichel, more than Ferenczi, Abraham, or any of the earlier analysts, resemble Freud in this practice of translating unconscious impulses into recitable formulas.

An example from the second session enables us to follow Freud's therapeutic aim of reestablishing the exact wording of the obsession. First we break into the hour in the midst of the Rat Man's retrospection:

> There were certain people, girls, who pleased me very much, and I had a very strong wish *to see them naked*. But in wishing this I had *an uncanny feeling, as though something must happen if I thought such things, and as though I must do all sorts of things to prevent it.*
>
> (In reply to a question he gave an example of these fears: "For instance, *that my father might die.*") (p. 162)

As a second step we listen to Freud explaining his way back to the obsession's original, recitable wording:

> If the patient can once be induced to give a particular instance in place of the vague generalities which characterize an obsessional neurosis, it may be confidently assumed that the instance is the original and actual thing which has tried to hide itself behind the generalization. Our present patient's obsessive fear, therefore, when restored to its original meaning, would run as follows: "If I have this wish to see a woman naked, my father will be bound to die." (p. 163)

Perhaps it is more fitting to follow Freud applying his technique to the great rat idea. The patient reported that upon hearing the tale of Oriental punishment, he had a thought in the indicative mode: *"This was happening to a person who was very dear to me"* (p. 167). But Freud suggests that the thought about the father was personally more complicated and should be "translated" into the hortative mode:

> The idea which came into his consciousness for a moment, to the effect that something of the sort might happen to someone he was fond of, is probably to be translated into a wish such as "You ought to have the same thing done to you!" aimed at the teller of the story, but through him at his father. (p. 217)

Concerning the request to repay the post office lady, Freud entertained three responses on the part of the Rat Man (pp. 168, 218–20):

1. Lieutenant Lanzer might have thought, " 'Will I, though?' or 'Pay your grandmother!' or 'Yes! You bet I'll pay him back the money.' " But then Freud immediately excludes the possibility of such answers for they would not have been subject to compulsive force.
2. Lieutenant Lanzer actually avowed thinking that he would not defray the money and that he then said half-aloud to himself: "You must pay back the 3.80 kronen to Lieutenant David."[9] Freud expanded this moral stricture to: "Yes, you must pay back the money to Lieutenant David, as your father's surrogate has required. Your father cannot be mistaken."
3. According to Freud's construction, on a deeper unconscious level a defiance predominated, expressed in some such answer as: " 'Yes! I'll pay back the money to Lieutenant David when my father and the lady have children!' or 'As sure as my father and the lady can have children, I'll pay him back the money!' "

---

9. In German the Rat Man of course is addressing himself as *du*, the familiar form of "you" (*G.W.*, 7:393).

Summarily, Freud shows us that empathy with his patient involved nearness of all kinds, including making sustained efforts to approximate obsessional wording on various psychic levels.

As I look back on what I have expressed, I am all too aware that I have traveled but a few of many paths, and I hope that other voices will soon come to help sound the outlying area. In such expectation, I can scarcely do better than refer to the resounding timeliness of the two citations with which I began this chapter: "The mouth is the cradle of perception"; "The letter kills but the breath giveth life." These adages serve as reverberating oral reminders that forever after we may struggle through the rites of passage. Meanwhile, the pressing venture of making a historical survey bids us on to the pages ahead.

6

Freud's Theory of Obsessional Neurosis

From the clinical material we pass on to Freud's theoretical elaborations, to which he devoted the second though smaller part of "Notes upon a Case of Obsessional Neurosis." In order to enhance our appreciation of that part and its place within Freud's evolution, we shall attempt to map out his prior and subsequent theories of obsessional neurosis. En route we shall observe how Freud developed his relevant conceptions about etiology, symptomatology, defense mechanisms, and so on; perhaps less familiar though unavoidable considerations in our undertaking will be the place of the death complex and the factors of sequentiality and simultaneity in obsessional neurosis as well as Freud's own dynamic involvement in trying to theorize about it.

Our suvey begins with Freud's early, appreciable groping in "The Neuro-Psychoses of Defence" (1894). There we read that an obsession substitutes for an incompatible sexual idea and takes its place in consciousness; the strong affect of the repressed sexual idea, on the other hand, is displaced onto the obsessional idea which has "little intensity in itself." Accordingly, there is in obsessionality a sequential relation between the repressed and its substitute. When, however, the sexual and obsessional ideas are present simultaneously, we meet with evidence of incomplete defensive activity.

We turn next to statements found in "Obsessions and Phobias" and in a relevant section of *Studies in Hysteria,* both written in the early part of 1895 (see Freud, 1893–95, p. xv). In "Obsessions and Phobias" Freud specified that in every obsession there are two constituents: an idea that forces itself upon the patient, and an associated emotional state, such as anxiety, doubt, remorse, or anger, which substitutes for a distressing sexual experience. Later in the same essay, Freud added the modification that in some obsessional cases, the original idea is replaced not by "another idea" but by acts or impulses that had served originally as measures of protection or discharge. In *Studies in Hysteria* we encounter a single new though unelaborated thought: whereas the memories of hysterical patients usually return in pictorial form, the memories of obsessionals return as thoughts (p. 280; cf. Freud, 1896b, p. 184).

Toward the end of 1895, as we can see in a series of letters to Fliess, Freud was preoccupied with the comparative etiology and nature of hysteria and obsessionality. Perhaps a combination of frenetic mental exertion, self-doubt, and guilt about discovery caused Freud's uncertainty as to whether he had already shared his findings with Fliess:

> Just think: among other things I am on the scent of the following strict precondition for hysteria, namely, that a primary sexual experience (before puberty), accompanied by revulsion and fright, must have taken place; for obsessional neurosis, that it must have happened, accompanied by *pleasure*. (letter of 10/8/95; Freud, 1985, p. 141)

> Have I revealed the great clinical secret to you, either orally or in writing? Hysteria is the consequence of a presexual *sexual shock*. Obsessional neurosis is the consequence of a presexual *sexual pleasure*, which is later transformed into [self-] *reproach*. (letter of 10/15/95; Freud, 1985, p. 144)

> I have begun to have doubts about the pleasure-pain explanation of hysteria and obsessional neurosis which I announced

with so much enthusiasm. The constituent elements are correct beyond question, but I have not yet put the pieces of the puzzle in the right place. (letter of 10/31/95; Freud, 1985, p. 148)

Have I already written to you that obsessional ideas invariably are *reproaches*, while at the root of hysteria there always is *conflict* (sexual pleasure along with possibly accompanying unpleasure)? (letter of 12/8/95; Freud, 1985, p. 154)

Freud began the year 1896 by sending off to Fliess the so-called Draft K, an amazingly compact paper carrying the ironic subtitle "A Christmas Fairy Tale." In it Freud proclaimed, "The course of events in obsessional neurosis is what is clearest to me, because I have come to know it best" (in spite of his having analyzed far more cases of hysteria, his knowledge of obsessional neurosis was superior) (Freud, 1896a, p. 219). But the draft is especially significant for what it reveals of Freud's genius at work—it shows his exceptionally nuanced perception of temporal processes and his narrative readiness to describe their complexities in obsessional neurosis. He traced in detail the sexual etiology of the neurosis to a time predating sexual maturity, with heredity determining whether the affect would be one of pathological intensity; more specifically, he laid out an intriguing four-stage development of obsessionality. First, at a very early age and before the experience of pleasure, there is a purely passive experience. Next comes the primary pleasurable experience, active in boys and passive in girls. In a third stage, owing to the convergence of the initial passive experience and succeeding pleasurable experience, unpleasure becomes added to the meaning of that pleasurable experience; conscious self-reproaches result (the chronological relationship of the unpleasurable and pleasurable experiences to each other and to the date of sexual maturity is the determining factor). Fourth, both the memory and the self-reproach are repressed and replaced in consciousness by a primary symptom of defense—that is, the antithetic idea of conscientiousness. But in reality, the return of the repressed in the fourth stage may itself be broken down into successive periods. For a while the returning self-reproach emerges as a pure sense of guilt, without content. Then, as an ideational compromise, the self-reproach links up with a substitute content characterized by the chronological distortion of relating to a contemporary or future action. As an affective compromise, self-reproach is transformable into forms that then can enter consciousness more clearly: anxiety, hypochondria, and so on, and it is at this point that the conscious ego withholds belief in the obsession by resorting to antithetic ideas of conscientiousness formed long before. Also, the ego may now produce secondary symptoms of defense, such as brooding and rituals. Eventually, all the sexual tension generated daily in obsessionals may turn into symptoms issuing from self-reproach. To cure the neurosis, we must undo substitutions and affective transformations until the experience of the primary self-reproach can be submitted for rejudgment by the conscious ego.

In a matter of weeks, Freud revised Draft K into "Further Remarks on the Neuro-Psychoses of Defense" (1896b), and, as might be expected, the published elaboration is more precise in some respects. Freud traced a substratum of hysteric symptoms in obsessional neurosis to a primary scene of sexual passivity in which the child was seduced (the later Freud retained the idea of hysteria as being at the core of obsessionality—see Freud, 1918, p. 75, and 1926, p. 113). Subsequently, especially in male children, there occurs a pleasurable participation in precocious acts of aggression against the other sex, the active nature of which disposes boys more than girls to obsessional neurosis (see also Freud, 1896c, p. 155; 1896a, p. 220; and 1926, p. 143). This initial period of childhood immorality closes with a sexual maturation that is often premature. In the second period self-reproach becomes linked to the memory of these pleasurable actions and the deferred impact of the original passive experience. In a third period of apparent health, the repressed memories are replaced by primary symptoms of defense such as conscientiousness, self-distrust, and shame. The fourth period, that of illness, is distinguished by the return of repressed memories and the self-reproaches associated with them. To become conscious, the content of the repressed idea is distorted so that a contemporary nonsexual idea replaces a sexual one of the past; the affect of self-reproach or one of its formations may emerge with the compromise ideas in consciousness. The compromise, let us note, negotiates between "repressed" and "repressing" ideas. Next, seeking now to fend off derivatives, the ego resorts to symptoms of secondary defense which are all protective measures. Freud insisted that when these measures genuinely succeed, they become obsessional in themselves and stand as pure defenses without aggression. He proceeded to propose three forms of obsession: obsessional ideas, affects, and actions. The nature of the last of these is secondary and defensive, thus obviating direct expression of aggression.

Freud made two other points that are worth mentioning. Generally the subject does not believe his self-reproaches in that their related obsessional ideas are repressed and yield to the masquerading of defensive conscientiousness. Second, Freud restated that cure is effected by merely rendering conscious the connections between the obsessional idea and the repressed early memory. Later in 1896 Freud tried to pinpoint more exactly the etiology of obsessional neurosis: it is traceable back to scenes between the ages of four and eight that are verbalizable. When those scenes are awakened in memory after the age of eight, "psychical obsessional symptoms" emerge (Freud, 1985, p. 188).

From 1897 to the time of the Rat Man case, Freud wrote only two pieces on obsessionality (1907 and 1908); the rest of his pertinent comments are scattered passages, mostly in letters, and can be reviewed in the following way. Although positing that compulsive movements substitute for abandoned masturbation and that, proper to obsessionality, compromises break through into consciousness as perverse impulses (Freud, 1985, pp. 227, 239), he went on to conceive of impulses in obsessional neurosis as generally being "independent of erotogenic zones" (Freud, 1905d, p. 169). Essentially obsessional neurosis is alloerotic and manifests an identification with the loved person; on the other hand, conscious hostile wishes toward parents are also part of the neurosis (Freud, 1985, pp. 390 and 250, respectively). In marginalia written for his private use, Freud spelled out the latter notion in its relation to superstition and to his self-analysis:

> Rage, anger and consequently a murderous impulse is the source of superstition in obsessional neurotics: a sadistic component, which is attached to love and is therefore directed against the loved person and repressed precisely because of this link and because of its intensity. My own superstition has its roots in suppressed ambition (immortality) and in my case takes the place of that anxiety about death which springs from the normal uncertainty of life. (Freud, 1901, p. 260*n*)

In one instance, Freud made a passing remark that came quite close to structural theory: in obsessional neuroses we find "a super-morality imposed as a reinforcing weight upon the fresh stirrings of the primary character" (Freud, 1900, p. 251). Freud also foreshadowed the elaboration of primary process in his analysis of verbal condensation in obsessionality:

> With regard to obsessional neurosis, I have found confirmation that the locality at which the repressed breaks through is the *word presentation* and not the concept attached to it. (More precisely, the word memory.) Hence the most disparate things are readily united as an obsessional idea under a single word with multiple meanings. The tendency toward breaking through makes use of these ambiguous words. . . . Obsessional ideas frequently are clothed in a characteristic *verbal* vagueness

in order to permit such multiple deployment. (Freud, 1985, pp. 287–88)

But going into the twentieth century, perhaps the greatest change in Freud's general understanding of obsessional neurosis was his idea that most children were not really seduced in their early years. Accordingly, he shifted his belief from widespread "infantile sexual traumas" to the effect of fantasies and the "infantilism of sexuality" itself. Although this new position made him reject the passivity of hysterics and the activity of obsessionals in actual seductive scenes, he still held to some correlation between hysteria and passivity, on the one hand, and between obsessionality and activity, on the other (Freud, 1906, p. 275).

Freud's essay of 1907, "Obsessive Actions and Religious Practices," represents his first incursion into the psychology of religion and contains as well his first reference to "an unconscious sense of guilt."[1] While admitting the present impossibility of defining obsessional neurosis, Freud could grandly proclaim that its underlying "primary fact" is the repression of a component of the sexual drive and, through reaction formation, its surfacing in conscientiousness; also, the mechanism of displacement "domi-

---

1. Everywhere in this essay we can detect Freud at his most artful. We watch him as he moves the idea of ceremonial through his comparison of obsessionality and religion, acknowledging the difference between the two and then collapsing that difference—a legerdemain reminiscent of the thaumaturgic incantation, "Now you see it . . . now you don't." Here is Freud in a close-up:

> It is easy to see where the resemblances lie between neurotic ceremonials and the sacred acts of religious ritual. . . . the differences are equally obvious, and a few of them are so glaring that they make the comparison a sacrilege. . . . But it is precisely this sharpest difference between neurotic and religious ceremonial which disappears when, with the help of the psycho-analytic technique of investigation, one penetrates to the true meaning of obsessive actions. (pp. 119–20)

If we x-ray the text, we realize that Freud focused on the double theme of congruity and process: (1) "In the course of . . . [psychoanalytic] investigation, we shall efface the differences between religion and obsessionality"; (2) "As the illness progresses," obsessional actions asymptotically return to their forbidden prototypes; (3) just as obsessional action evolves in a displacement from an im-

nates" the psychical processes of obsessional neurosis. Yet this displacement asymptotically narrows in the life of obsessive actions:

> As the illness progresses, indeed, the actions which were originally mostly concerned with maintaining the defence come to approximate more and more to the proscribed actions through which the instinct was able to find expression in childhood. (Freud, 1907a, p. 125)

In terms of the progress of psychoanalytic technique, Freud could show, as he did earlier with hysterical symptoms, that obsessional actions could be translated into verbal formulas (pp. 120–23).

"Character and Anal Eroticism" (1908a) marks the next *public* step *toward* Freud's full understanding of obsessional neurosis. I stress *public* because two years previously Freud had anticipated the kernel of the essay in a letter to Jung (Freud, 1974a, pp. 8–9); I stress *toward*, because, although Freud saw the origins of orderliness, parsimony, and obstinacy in the anal erotogeneity of early childhood, he ascribed those traits only to character formation. True, he was on the verge of making his epochal discovery that the nature of obsessional neurosis lies in the fixation to sadistic anal eroticism, but what actually kept Freud from making that discovery until 1913, when he wrote "The Disposition to Obsessional Neurosis"? We do not have to look far before we come

---

portant thing to a trivial one which in turn assumes importance, so petty religious ceremonials gradually replace their essential underlying meaning and are eventually subjected to reforms aiming at a reestablishment of original values; (4) whereas "a progressive renunciation" of drives characterizes civilization, an apparently similar progression characterizes religion, for within the development of religion, some of the officially abandoned pleasures could be entertained if done in the name of the deity. Then, in terminating his essay, Freud works the themes of congruence and process into the very textuality of his prose as he logically resorts to an irony-laden distinction that undoes an objectionable loophole in his argument: "it is surely no accident that all the attributes of man, along with the misdeeds that follow from them, were to an unlimited amount ascribed to the ancient gods. Nor is it a contradiction of this that nevertheless man was not permitted to justify his own iniquities by appealing to divine example."

upon two revelatory and interrelated facts. First, of all the startling claims in *Three Essays on Sexuality* (1905d), it was those concerning anal eroticism that most scandalized readers (Freud, 1908, p. 171*n*). Second, Freud's paper on anal eroticism had provoked more derision than any of his previous works (Jones, 1955, p. 53).[2] I suggest then that the unprecedented hostile response was influential in shunting Freud away from earlier discovery of the anal etiology of obsessionality. Yet I do not feel that I have acquitted my obligations to this subject unless I grapple with the question undoubtedly in the minds of my readers: why was it that of the myriad statements pronounced by Freud up to 1908, those about anal eroticism elicited the greatest hostility of the public? In response, one may readily think of the hippie communes in recent years whose cohesion was often eroded not by the daily oral-related tasks of preparing food but rather by contested assignments dealing with cleaning and garbage disposal. We are on surer historical grounds, however, when we refer to the zeitgeist of Freud's contemporary world and its overdetermined concern for anal eroticism. More particularly:

> It is a human tendency to neglect things that are too obvious, and to pay attention to them when they disappear. Thus the folklore of European peasants remained unknown to scientists or was despised by them, until it began to decline, and only then did folklorists arise to record it. In a similar way, for centuries mankind had taken the sight and smell of excrements for granted, but when, at the end of the nineteenth century, plumbing became general, when men began to live in a dulcified and deodorized world, attention was drawn to this matter. The new preoccupation was illustrated by a 600-page compilation by Krauss and Ihm, giving a general survey of the roles of excrement in various populations of the world, with a lau-

---

2. The negative reaction was anticipated by both Freud and Abraham (see the letters of 3/1/08 and 4/4/08 in Freud, 1965, pp. 29, 32).

datory foreword written by Freud in which he speaks of coprophilic manifestations in children, their repression, and their connection with the sexual instinct. (Ellenberger, 1970, p. 504)[3]

These factors, I am sure, had some bearing on Freud's separation of obsessionality from anal eroticism. One of Freud's letters around this time clarifies his perspective: whereas hysteria arises through fixations and repressions in the area of erogenous components, obsessional neurosis stems from disturbances in the area of "object components" or "dependent drives" (*angelehnte Triebe*), that is, the drives to see, know, and possess, the last being sadistic (Freud, 1974a, p. 128; 1974b, p. 142).

In our journey through Freud's theoretical progress the case of the Rat Man suddenly towers so high before us as to make us think that up to now we have covered only plain terrain. But as we decide to pause and settle down among the various regions of the case, much of what gave the initial appearance of being a mountain of sturdy completion dwindles to shifting formations. Let us go closer, keeping in mind that some of the shifting formations will not be seen until the next chapter.

Freud contended that the relationship between love and a nearly equally powerful hatred is among the most recurrent and "probably, therefore, the most important characteristics of obsessional neurosis" (p. 239).[4] Constitutionally its sadistic element is exceptionally strong and with the help of reaction formation undergoes "premature suppression" (p. 240); constitutionally as well, this neurosis nearly always reveals an early development and

---

3. Actually Krauss and Ihm were the German translators of John Bourke's *Scatologic Rites of All Nations*. The uncanny resonance of the beginning of the volume's title in the German translation can hardly escape us: *Der Unrat*.

4. Cf. the exchange of letters between Freud and Jung concerning theory in the Rat Man case (Freud, 1974): 12/14/08, pp. 274–76; 12/19/09, pp. 276–78; 12/25/08, pp. 279–81). Freud criticized Jung for disregarding the libido and taking a position similar to Adler's (p. 278).

"premature repression" of the sexual instinct of looking and knowing, a fact probably related to the high average intellectual gifts among obsessional patients (p. 245 and *n*).[5] The development and strength of the drives, then, help shape obsessional formations: these, standing as a compromise between love and hate, are transformed self-reproaches "which always relate to some sexual act that was performed with pleasure in childhood" (p. 221). Relative to this dynamic factor, we find in the case history a special temporal parallel between the evolution of obsessions and their psychoanalytic treatment. Both harken back: the progress of psychoanalytic treatment is inversely commensurate with an ever-recessive dating of neurotic etiology (p. 229), and the persistence of obsessional acts over time brings them ever closer to resembling infantile masturbation (p. 244).

Freud went on to expound on the obsessional's attitudes to the triad of superstition, reality, and death. In the first place, the superstitious person represses causal connections, then endopsychically perceives them "in some kind of shadowy form," and finally projects them onto the external world (pp. 231–32); the superstitious trait of the omnipotence ascribed by obsessionals to their thoughts or feelings (pp. 233–35) is actually a relic of infantile megalomania functioning with an overpowering hate.

Superstition aside, the need for doubt especially turns the patient away from reality (incidentally, *doubt* is cognate with *double*;

---

5. There is a terminological obscurity in the case history that calls for some elucidation. Most often Freud spoke of the "premature" (*vorzeitig*) development of the Rat Man's sexuality and hostility (165/390, 182/405, 205*n*/426*n*) and also their premature suppression (215/434, 240/456). True to his processive thought, in his last summary statement, Freud distinguished between the early (*frühzeitig*) development of the sexual drive and its premature (*vorzeitig*) repression (245/460); cf. the single preceding instance when Freud referred to Ernst's "early" (*frühzeitig*) developed erotic life, which is changed by Strachey into "prematurely" (201/423). Even if one agrees that Ernst's biting incident between the ages of three and four had erotic significance, neither the biting nor the subsequent outburst of rage should be appraised as "premature"; but whether there was prematurity in the thorough suppression or repression of his anger is another matter.

cf. the German *zweifeln* [to doubt] and *zwei* [two]). The conflict between love and hate paralyzes his will and results in indecisiveness and uncertainty extending to all his behavior. That extension arises from two sources: the doubt of his love and the awareness of the untrustworthiness of memory (pp. 241, 243). Compensating for doubt, compulsion succeeds in bringing an inhibition by means of substitutive intention to a decision. Last, by virtue of their death complex, obsessionals need the possibility of the death of a significant other as a solution to their love conflicts; when the person does eventually die, then obsessive fears about the next world may ensue as a compensation for the death wishes.

Starting from his discussion of doubt, Freud resumed his fascinating preoccupation with time as he rendered an account of the extraordinary temporal and intrapsychic complexity in obsessions. In effect, he gave a metapsychological explanation of what the Rat Man subjectively experienced as "efforts of thought." Doubting one's love leads to a paralysis of the will with respect to certain actions; next, the doubt is diffused over the whole mind, ending in the paralysis of the whole will and the inability to carry out even protective measures. After that, an original intention will compulsively break out in the guise of a substitute intention, and if the actualization of that intention is blocked, anxiety ensues. On the other hand, the intention may be carried through in a substitutive act, which, however, is regularly in the guise of a protective measure; this itself brings some satisfaction to the original impulse warded off. Concomitantly, in all obsessional neurosis there is some conflictually determined inhibition at the motor end of the psychical system, a situation effecting some degree of regression from acting to a thinking process that itself is sustained with an energy normally reserved for actions (p. 246). A lesser or greater amount of regression from acting to thinking distinguishes a case of obsessionality in its correspondently manifesting the characteristics of obsessive acts or of obsessional ideas.

In cases where acting is more marked, there is also a libidinal regression; that is, the obsessional acts tend to resemble infantile masturbatory acts more and more. In cases where the obsessional thinking per se is more marked, the *Wisstrieb* or epistemophilic drive (whose early development and premature repression occur nearly always in obsessional pathology) is a preponderant constitutional feature. When this is so, brooding emerges as the principal symptom, and the thinking process becomes sexualized; as such, the thinking process both acquires the sexual gratification shifted from thought contents[6] and attracts energy that vainly tries to find a sexually gratifying release in the motor sphere. By obtaining an energy normally reserved for actions, obsessive thoughts regressively replace those actions. Aided by distortion and "excessive violence," obsessive thoughts may then make their way into consciousness; but to stay there, they must undergo isolation and generalization of contents. If a distinction were to be made between distortions of content and wording, one would say that the obsession in conscious thought is distorted into indefinite or ambiguous wording that finds its way into the patient's deliria, which themselves form new connections with that part of the obsession's wording and content that have been left proliferating in the unconscious.

The foregoing explanation about the thinking process contained, for Freud, the "psychological characteristic" that gave the products of obsessional neurosis their very quality of compulsion (p. 245). Hence, when he later said that what distinguishes obsessional neurosis lies not in the drive life (*Triebleben*) but in the "psychological field" (p. 248), we are to understand his more restricted use of the term *drive*: that is, we are to understand the nature of obsessionality as relating to a drive-assisted thinking process per se rather than to the functioning of drives as they

---

6. It is as if the taboo of touching in the external world becomes internalized (cf. Freud, 1913c, p. 27) so that, so to speak, representations may be flushed clean of their erotic content. The internalized taboo, in my opinion, relates to the obsessional fantasy of fearing control by an anal penis and its matter.

bear on object relations or on external perception.[7] Similarly, any phasic aspect of the drives is excluded as an explanation of obsessionality. In fact, although dramatic evidence of anal eroticism appears in so many pages of the clinical section of the Rat Man case, anality is mentioned only once within the theoretical section, and nowhere does Freud see it as essential to obsessional neurosis.[8] Seemingly reflecting the very pathology he was trying to explain, Freud "isolated" anality and thereby disturbed its intrinsic, "contiguous" relation to obsessional neurosis.

Actually, at the start of the theoretical section of the Rat Man case, when Freud reviewed his stance on obsessionality promulgated in 1896, he avowed that his former theorizing had been partly infected by the pathology itself. He specifically objected to his having defined the products of obsessionality solely in terms of "ideas." That early definition, Freud asserted,

> was aiming too much at unification, and took as its model the practice of obsessional neurotics themselves, when, with their characteristic liking for indeterminateness, they heap together under the name of "obsessional ideas" [*Zwangsvorstellungen*] the most heterogeneous psychical formations [*Bildungen*]. In point of fact, it would be more correct to speak of "obsessive thinking" [*Zwangsdenken*], and to make it clear that obsessional forms [*Zwangsgebilde*] can correspond to every sort of

---

7. Viewed from another perspective, Freud ascribed the essential nature of obsessionality not to id regression but rather to the ego's regression to the stage of action-thoughts. Cf. Freud's comment in the *Minutes of the Vienna Psychoanalytic Society*, 1:137: "The obsessional neurosis is particularly suited to throw light on the nature of intellectual performances and processes. From the analysis of obsessional neurosis one learns how the psychic apparatus is structured in its higher strata."

8. To repeat: nothing in the text supports Gedo and Goldberg's belief (1973, p. 30) that Freud was explaining obsessionality as a libidinal regression from phallic to anal sadistic aims. See also Anna Freud (1966, p. 119): "In 1909 when Freud published his 'Notes upon a Case of Obsessional Neurosis,' it was a pioneering achievement to look behind the apparent pathogenic importance of recent events, such as the father's death, difficulties in love affairs, etc., and to unearth the upsetting events of the anal-sadistic stage as preceding them."

psychical act.⁹ They can be classed as wishes, temptations, impulses, reflections, doubts, commands, or prohibitions. Patients endeavour in general to tone down such distinctions and to regard what remains of these psychical acts after they have been deprived of their affective index simply as "obsessional ideas" [*Zwangsvorstellung*]. Our present patient gave an example of this type of behavior in one of his first sessions, when he attempted to reduce a wish to the level of a mere "train of thought" [*Denkverbindung*]. (pp. 221–22/439–40; see also p. 167*n*)

If we read the entire Rat Man case in the original German, we notice that it is shot through with Freud's own use of *Zwangsvorstellung* instead of *Zwangsdenken*—hence, a notable inconsistency with the pronouncements in the passage cited above. A concentrated example of Freud's inconsistency appears in the subsection entitled "Some Obsessional Ideas [*Zwangsvorstellungen*] and Their Translation" (pp. 186ff.). More than that, Freud himself went on to use *Zwangsvorstellung* and *Zwangsdenken* synonymously (see esp. p. 244), forcing us thereby to follow but one path of conclusion: Freud furnished us with an explanation of the psychical mechanisms of obsessionals that can help us understand Freud himself and thus detect obsessional traces contaminating his very explanation.

Other examples also expose the impact of obsessionality on Freud's analytic attempt to grapple with it. Thus, as we have seen, Freud attributed the Rat Man's adult incapacity to work to two different precipitating causes, one dealing with death and the

---

9. Seeking an equivalent for the English and French word *obsession*, Krafft-Ebing introduced the term *Zwangsvorstellung* into German in 1867. One of the three essays that Freud wrote in French, "Obsessions et Phobies" (1895), reveals that Freud accepted Krafft-Ebing's neologism as a reading for the French *obsession* (see Strachey's note in the *Standard Edition*, 3:72). Thus the Rat Man case testifies to some shift in Freud's terminology.

other with marriage[10]—the illogical accordance of primacy to two distinct and polarized events seems to distort further the conflict between love and mortal hate which the patient felt toward each of the two events. In this way, Freud left us a countertransferential manifestation of ambivalence and an instance of how obsessionality makes "the fullest possible use of the mechanism of *displacement*" (p. 241). There is also the indicative occurrence of the epithet "omnipotence of thoughts," first used by the Rat Man and then gratefully adopted by Freud as a clinical term (Freud, 1913, p. 85). Although the term reflects intellectualization and defensive isolation in the Rat Man's stress on the omnipotence of his thoughts rather than of his wishes, and although Freud in a postscript to the case said that it would be analytically more proper to say "omnipotence of wishes" (p. 235*n*), he continued to employ the more "obsessional" term ("omnipotence of thoughts") until the end of his life (Freud, 1925a, p. 66; 1929, p. 250; 1933, p. 165; 1935, p. 255; 1939, p. 113).

On a more positive note, we might finally attend to the theoretical achievements of the Rat Man case in its concern for defense, structural theory, and semiotics. Freud drew up a whole gamut of defense mechanisms in obsessional neurosis: regression, rationalization, undoing, isolation, reaction formation, repression, and projection (p. 232). He also distinguished between primary and secondary defensive struggle. With the partial failure of the patient's primary defensive struggle, obsessions force their

---

10. On a personal side, Freud might have been led to stress the marital factor because of the disquieting situation of two unmarried members within his own family. On March 19, 1908, Freud wrote a letter to his eldest daughter, Mathilde, which was partly designed to allay her depressive worry about still being single (Freud, 1960, pp. 280–82). She did get married, on February 7, 1909 (Freud, 1974a, p. 174*n*), the very day on which Alexander, Freud's only surviving brother, also married (Clark, 1980, p. 284). Born two years before the Rat Man, Alexander had to share in the physical support of his own parents and sisters. Freud's "Autodidasker" dream exposes his early concerned desire for his brother to marry (see Freud, 1900, pp. 299–300; 1985, p. 399). Moreover, the Rat Man's sister Olga said that the eligible Alexander would be the right husband for Gisela (p. 285)!

way into his consciousness; then a secondary defensive struggle takes over. The resultant formations or "deliria," such as protective formulas, are infiltrated by the obsession itself and give rise to further misapprehension on the part of consciousness. Hence, in time, warded-off material "regularly"[11] finds its way into defensive measures.

One of the more salient passages in Freud's case occurs at its very end, where the reader will not miss the anticipation of the later structural theory of 1923:

> [The Rat Man's] unconscious comprised those of his impulses which had been suppressed at an early age and which might be described as passionate and evil impulses. In his normal state he was kind, cheerful, and sensible—an enlightened and superior kind of person—while in his third psychological organization he paid homage to superstition and asceticism. (p. 248)

Bearing this and other indications in mind, one should observe how much of the Rat Man's psyche Freud was able to explore without the formal help of his subsequent description of the id, ego, and superego.

Some contemporary theorists of rhetoric have ascribed a primacy to metaphor and metonymy among the multitudinous figures of speech and described the essential nature of metaphor as one of similarity, and of metonymy as contiguity. By taking this one more step, we may bring in the mechanisms of dream work and ally condensation with metaphor and displacement with metonymy. With an additional step ahead, we might consider the basic relationship between hysteria and the simultaneity in condensation as opposed to obsessionality and the sequentiality (contiguity) of displacement. Freud himself contrasted the com-

---

11. Cf. Strachey's "invariably," which mistranslates *regelmässig* (225/443): in this connection, see Ornston (1982).

promises of hysteria, which simultaneously satisfy opposing impulses, and obsessional behavior, which satisfies opposing impulses through sequential acts (p. 192; cf. 1917, p. 301); thus defensive undoing by virtue of its diphasic nature is a particular manifestation of the link between obsessionality and contiguity.[12]

When it comes to obsessional language, we should first note that some of Freud's linguistic ideas in the Rat Man case were different from those he had previously postulated and from what he would say subsequently. In the case at hand, we come upon evidence that words can be repressed and hence driven past the preconscious and into the unconscious; likewise, the repressed words may travel back to the conscious. For this surprising notion, let us listen attentively to Freud talking to us of his patient:

> If he said "May God protect him," an evil spirit would hurriedly insinuate a "not." On one such occasion the idea occurred to him of cursing instead, for in that case, he thought, the contrary words would be sure to creep in. His original intention, which had been *repressed* by his praying, was forcing its way through in this last idea of his. . . . a hostile "not" suddenly darted out of his *unconscious* and inserted itself into the sentence. (pp. 193, 242; italics mine; cf. Mannoni, 1965)

---

12. In a letter to Abraham, Freud again took up the notion of contiguity, which he exemplified in an unnamed reference to the Rat Man: "From the beginning they [obsessional neurotics] have to express both contradictory voices, generally in *immediate juxtaposition* [italics mine]. Hence also their vacillation, because of the equal weight of both sides of the motivation. A patient, for instance, sees a stone lying in the roadway and has compulsively to remove it. But it leaves him no peace, and he has to put it back again. The explanation is that the girl he is in love with is going away that day and will be passing along that street in a cab. The cab might jolt over the stone, so he has to remove it. But his next thought is: No, let the cab overturn, with her inside it. So he has to put it back in its place. In his unconscious he simultaneously combines excessive affection for his beloved with hatred of her" (letter of 1/19/08; Freud, 1965, pp. 23–24). For Freud, the obsessional inhibition about touching had other spatial implications: "There are types—the obsessional neurotics, in particular, are such people—who have a much more solid relation with space than with time" (*Minutes of the Vienna Psychoanalytic Society*, 4:67). Note that with the increasing return

Apposite to the same context, Freud found a simple exception to his belief that speeches in dreams did not come from words heard or spoken by the dreamer. That exception of course concerned the Rat Man, the original texts of whose obsessional ideas appeared in his dreams but reached his waking consciousness only in distorted form (Freud, 1900, p. 304*n*). Nowhere else, I think, do we come upon such explicit claims by Freud for the possibility of a verbally dynamic unconscious.[13]

Still, Freud felt obsessionality to be more readily comprehensible than hysteria in that it selects a language resistant to conversion and closer to the expressive form of our conscious thought (pp. 156–57). Nonetheless, obsessional neurotics do not know the wording of their compulsive ideas and in some cases are ignorant even of the content of their obsessions. In terms of procedural understanding, Freud suggested that often a number of successive obsessions are basically the same despite divergent wording; collaterally, the original appearance in the obsessive series bears the correct wording, which is subsequently manifested in verbal distortion, which in turn is misapprehended by "waking thought" (pp. 223–24).

Freud next took up obsessionality in *Totem and Taboo* (1913c), where he drew up the now well-known parallels with taboo usage; he also continued his comparative differentiation of neuroses. But whereas obsessionality had been considered a dialect of hysteria, now they stand equally as two dialects of the unconscious: the thought-language of obsessionality, and the gesture-language of

---

of the repressed, obsessional acts resemble more and more the originally forbidden acts; hence, obsessional acts evolve toward lessening the difference between contiguity and similarity (cf. Freud, 1913c, p. 88). On the other hand, see the following passage in the *Minutes* (1:287): "In an obsessional neurotic, excessive tenderness is combined with hate; these two currents within him must find release either *simultaneously* or *alternately*" (italics mine).

13. Freud's stance may be explained by a thought he shared only with Ferenczi, namely, that censorship in the obsessional functions between the conscious and the preconscious and not between the unconscious and the preconscious (see Jones, 1955, p. 183).

hysteria, which is similar to the picture-language of dreams (pp. 177–78). On a wider scale, if a paranoiac delusion is a caricature of philosophy, and hysteria a caricature of a work of art, then obsessionality figures likewise with regard to religion. Appearing in the same year as *Totem and Taboo*, "The Disposition to Obsessional Neurosis" innovatively proposes a pregenital organization of the libido in the development of which a component drive may dominate at a regular stage that afterward persists as a point of fixation; in particular, the passive anal erotic and active sadistic component drives underlie a disposition to obsessional neurosis. But whereas formerly Freud was apt to conceive of obsessional neurosis as arising from the precocity of sadistic drives followed by repression, now he ever more firmly reversed the causative sequence and posited an ego development outstripping the libidinal ones. Along similar lines Freud also noted that the sadistic element may yield its place to the drive for knowledge, the latter in turn being repudiated in the form of doubt. A final interesting point concerns Freud's conclusion that whereas hysterical symptoms can appear in the earlier years, obsessional ones usually appear in the second phase of childhood—that is, between six and eight years of age. That observation accords well with the Rat Man's initial illness (p. 162) but not with the onset of obsessional piety in the Wolf Man at the age of four and a half (Freud, 1918, p. 85). This discrepancy becomes all the more curious when we realize that at the time Freud wrote "The Disposition to Obsessional Neurosis," the Wolf Man was well into his third year of analysis with him.

For the next years, we may selectively follow Freud's expatiation on what he had already discovered as well as his relatively few new ideas about obsessional neurosis. When a libidinal regression to the sadistic-anal organization dominates symptoms, the love impulse must then disguise itself by sadistic wording such as "I should like to kill you" (1917, pp. 343–44); such reliance on reaction formation points to an often stronger stress on the repressing functions in obsessional symptoms than in hysterical symptomatology (1923b, p. 247). Within the realm of anal eroticism proper, an unconscious equation holds between baby-penis-money-feces; that series can play an important narcissistic part in the castration complex and process of identification in obsessionality (Freud, 1917; 1918, pp. 72ff.).

In discussing the resistances of his female homosexual patient (1920b), Freud indicated that there were similar ones, in the manner of "Russian tactics," in obsessionals. Given the fact that in the same year that Freud wrote this short case he had the Russian-born Wolf Man back in treatment, I have no doubt about the reference in Freud's mild irony. The passage in question is worth quoting in full for its timely relevance:

> The resistance [in hypnotic treatment] very often pursues similar tactics—Russian tactics, as they might be called, in cases of obsessional neurosis. For a time, consequently, these cases yield the clearest results and permit a deep insight into the causation of the symptoms. But presently one begins to wonder how it is that such marked progress in analytic understanding can be unaccompanied by even the slightest change in the patient's compulsions and inhibitions, until at last one perceives that everything that has been accomplished is subject to a mental reservation of doubt, and that behind this protective barrier the neurosis can feel secure. "It would be all very fine," thinks the patient, often quite consciously, "if I were obliged to believe what the man says, but there is no question of that, and so long as this is so I need change nothing." Then, when one comes to close quarters with the motives for this doubt, the fight with the resistance breaks out in earnest. (1920b, pp. 163–64)

Following his proclamation of the death drive, Freud elaborated on the "death complex" which he had described in the Rat Man case (p. 236). Thus "The Ego and the Id" refers to regressively induced drive defusion and underscores the notable activity of the death drive in obsessionals (Freud, 1923a, p. 42). No longer limited to the disguise of hostility, love impulses may now be transformed into impulses of aggression against the object. Although attempting to control the id's destructive intentions by measures of defense and identification, the innocent ego is held accountable and punished by the superego through the use of aggressiveness mixed with libido (1923a, esp. pp. 42, 53, 55).

Not altogether surprisingly, "Inhibitions, Symptoms and Anxiety" (1926) emerges along our path as one of the more paramount texts. Here we read that the strong affinity between masculinity and obsessionality and its dominant fear of the superego are matched by the strong affinity between femininity and hysteria and its related dominant fear of loss of love; in obsessional neurosis, then, the trigger of all subsequent symptom formation is the ego's fear of punishment by the superego (pp. 128, 143). To be sure, there are instances of obsessional neurosis in which no sense of guilt is present, a condition made possible by the ego's creation of masochistic symptoms (pp. 117–18); attendantly, a narcissistic secondary gain stems from the obsessional's self-flattery that he is cleaner or more conscientious than most other people (pp. 99–100). Developmentally there are two explanations for obsessional neurosis: in order of preference, either the constitutional factor that a feeble genital organization promotes regression (accompanied by instinctual defusion) or the temporal factor that the ego resists too early, while the sadistic phase is at its peak (pp. 113–14). Defensively, hysteria and obsessionality differ in that reaction formations in the former do not have the generality of a character trait but are limited to particular relationships. As well, the coupling of regression and external anticathexis (scotomization) in hysteria contrasts with the linking of regression and internal anticathexis in obsessionality. Two other defenses are again singled out in obsessional neurosis—undoing and isolation; the latter, because of the high tension between the superego and ego, makes it exceptionally difficult for the patient to associate freely in analysis.

We may finally bring in a pair of other observations although, strictly speaking, they do not directly pertain to obsessional neurosis. Freud distinguished three libidinal types: the erotic, the narcissistic, and the obsessional (1931). Overpowered by a fear of conscience instead of by a fear of losing love, the pure obsessional type shows an internal, not external, dependence. The mixed narcissistic-obsessional type has a capacity for forceful action and enjoys an ego strength that contends against the force of the superego. In the erotic obsessional (recalling the Rat Man), the superego restricts the preponderance of the instinctual life, and there is an extreme dependence on the residues of parental and other exemplary objects. Last, in the *New Introductory Lectures* (1933), Freud lists as a contribution Abraham's division of the anal-sadistic phase into two subphases: the first marked by destroying and expelling objects, the second by a friendly attitude of possessing and retaining.

Looking back on the evolution of Freud's theories, we might again remark on the capital importance of the Rat Man case. Some of its glories remain to be discovered by a literary analysis, which at the same time will undercut a few of the certainties that have comforted us up to now. But if in the course of scrutiny the demystification of our assurance proves unsettling, we could yet gain solace in the thought that we might be correspondingly that much nearer to elusive truths.

7

The Art and Strategy of Freud's Exposition

Yf they smell a ratt
They grisely chide and chatt.
—John Skelton, "The Image of Hypocrisy"

The case history stands as the most adequate representation of clinical treatment, and yet, of all the genres in psychoanalytic literature, it is the most difficult to write. This is one reason—there are others—that our discipline has such a limited body of verifiable primary source material of a sustained narrative nature. Those who want to maintain that psychoanalysis is a science rather than a discipline must then contend with the uneasy reflection that among the sciences psychoanalysis would be the one with the least amount of verifiable data narratively corresponding to the nature of the laboratory experiment (the clinical situation). From any point of view, however, there reigns a textual vacuum at the center of psychoanalysis. But can it be otherwise?

Whether on first or successive readings, this question is disconcerting, for the analytic situation resists satisfactory representation. Upon even slight consideration one could advance many reasons supporting Freud's belief that "a real, complete case cannot be narrated but only described" (Freud, 1974a, p. 141). Language is quintessentially linear—one word coming after another—and can only falter in the task of adequately representing both the sequentiality or simultaneity of external events and the kaleidoscopic complexities of endopsychic life, such as regression,

The Art and Strategy of Freud's Exposition 175

deferred effect, partial or full regression, and so forth. Language is further defied by the various orders in psychoanalytic treatment, among which number the order of the patient's fantasying and remembering, the order of his narration of what he remembers or might even experience somatically at the time of his narration, the order of his repeating rather than recalling his past life in the transference, the order of his understanding and his cure, the order of imparting or withholding that knowledge through memories or dreams or spontaneous associations, and the order of the analyst's understanding and his communication of that understanding to the patient. Finally, there is the order of exposition, its footnotes, anticipatory and retrospective remarks, and diverse work drafts of that exposition.

No wonder Freud could lament after he attempted to write up the reimbursement episode in his process notes: "Not well reproduced; many of the characteristic beauties of the case are omitted, effaced" (H, p. 62; my translation—the comment itself is "omitted" in the published case!). As Freud was writing up the case, he complained to Jung:

> I am finding it very difficult; it is almost beyond my powers of presentation; the paper will probably be intelligible to no one outside our immediate circle. How bungled our reproductions are, how wretchedly we dissect the great art works of psychic nature! (letter of 6/30/09; Freud, 1974a, p. 238)

Jung, a prolific author in his own right, read Freud's manuscript shortly thereafter and concurred about the expository obstacle:

> I understand perfectly your impressions of your own paper. This is something that also holds me back from presenting my cases. We just cannot do things as beautifully and as truly as Nature does. (letter of 7/13/09; Freud, 1974a, pp. 240–41)[1]

---

1. Cf. Jung's letter of January 3, 1908, to Abraham: "Seldom in my analytical work have I been so struck by the 'beauty' of neurosis as with this [hysterical] patient. The construction and course of the dreams are of a rare aesthetic beauty" (Jung, 1973, p. 5).

Shortly after this exchange of correspondence, from August 20 to September 21 to be precise, Freud and Jung made their famous trip to the United States, and it is tempting to speculate on how they resumed discussion of the Rat Man and his case history. We do at any rate have a letter from Freud shortly after his return home, expressing dissatisfaction with his corrections of the Rat Man proofs and asking somewhat anxiously about Jung's reaction:

> I am sure you will approve of what I did yesterday (Sunday). I corrected the Rat Man. I still didn't like it. Let me know as soon as you have seen it if you get a different impression. (letter of 10/4/09; Freud, 1974a, p. 249)

Jung's buoyant approval was not long in coming:

> Your Rat Man has filled me with delight, it is written with awesome intelligence and full of the most subtle reality. Most people, though, will be too dumb to understand it in depth. Splendid ingenuities! I regret from the bottom of my heart that I didn't write it. (letter of 10/14/09; Freud, 1974, p. 251)[2]

Three days later, Freud replied: "You are the first critic of the Rat Man. . . . I am overjoyed at your praise" (Freud, 1974a, p. 254).

Up to now I have been concerned with Freud's general success as a writer of case history in spite of its formidable intrinsic difficulties. Now I turn momentarily to the circumspect aspects of Freud's endeavor, keeping in mind meanwhile that no other an-

---

2. Cf. Jung's horse of a different color when he addressed Ferenczi: "Freud's paper on obsessional neurosis is marvellous but *very hard to understand*. I must soon read it for the third time. Am I particularly stupid? Or is it the style? I plump cautiously for the latter. Between Freud's speaking and writing there is a 'gulf fixed' which is very wide. Most of all I have disputed with Freud 'the symptoms of *omnipotence*' (!) because the term is too clinical. Naturally he is right, and the term is artistic too. But if you have to *teach* that kind of thing in a systematic context, you get goose pimples and take to swearing" (letter of 12/25/09; Jung, 1973, p. 14).

alyst has ever composed a more impressive case history. I should also make clear at the outset that my somewhat reserved attitude toward Freud's case history does not extend in the same way to his oral delivery at the Salzburg congress in 1908. Even though Freud feared that he would utter there "a potpourri of particular observations and general remarks" (Freud, 1974a, p. 141), his performance was a memorable triumph, according to the reports of such listeners as Jones and Jung. My guess is that the physical presence and commanding personality of Freud as speaker were able to counteract the disconnected or "potpourri" nature of his remarks.

When he began afterward to write up the case, he again was aware of its disconnectedness and twice considered qualifying it by putting "Aphorisms" in the general title (Freud, 1974a, pp. 145, 159), but finally decided for the more modulated label "Notes upon a Case of Obsessional Neurosis." Going beyond Freud's self-criticism, one reader has insightfully appraised the Rat Man case as "one of the richest, most complex and opaque pieces" in the Freudian corpus, the piece "most difficult to read and the most resistant to serial interpretative schematization." The clinical text in particular he found to be lacking in "the coherence, expository fullness, narrative virtuosity, and sustained sinuosity of episodic, incremental development" of the other major cases (Marcus, 1984, pp. 87, 89, 164).

How are we to explain such deficiencies of the Rat Man case, which at times moves like an ill-coordinated puppet before our eyes? In justifying the disconnected fragmentariness, Freud brought up the ethical need for discretion, his limited literary talents, and his relative ignorance of obsessional neurosis; yet those reasons, slightly adapted, could apply equally to his other, more skillfully written cases. We are left to venture the answer that the Rat Man's obsessionality influenced not only Freud's clinical focus but also his understanding and exposition of the material. For instance, in spite of the importance accorded by the

Rat Man to dreams in his life and in spite of the many dreams reported during the treatment, Freud was guided by a therapeutic rationale that appeared to some extent to redirect his interventions. He even said at one point: "The dream was not interpreted. For it is in fact only a more distinct version of the obsessional idea which he did not dare to become aware of during the day" (p. 267; cf. p. 274). In retrospect, it seems that after having given major semiotic importance to dreams in the Dora case, Freud went on to extend his interest to verbal lapses and faulty actions in *The Psychopathology of Everyday Life* and then concentrated on the wording of obsessions in the Rat Man case. Upon his entrance into this clinical territory, the indefatigable Freud focused on the aphoristic nature and dynamics of obsessional acts and sayings, bringing them into consciousness when the patient did not know their wording and filling in their ellipses, thereby attempting to reconstruct them into larger units of discourse. The noted fragmentation and disconnectedness of the Rat Man's associations and Freud's therapeutic attentiveness to that factor might have rubbed off on his attempts to present a synthetic picture of his patient's life story and obsessional neurosis.

A supplementary explanation for the disarticulateness of the Rat Man's case history as compared to Freud's other writings is that Freud's own obsessionality was countertransferentially activated, leaving traces on his expository control. That is, Freud's expression was infected by its contents, obsessional neurosis, which, by severing causal connections by defensive isolation, is after all a pathology that affects the contiguity of psychic material as well as the verbal expression of that material. Perhaps in that sense, instead of encountering the familiar Freud, with his consistent expository and theoretical articulateness, we come upon an author who confuses precipitating causes; who elaborated but little on the oedipal links among the heterosexual object choices in the patient's oedipal and postoedipal life; who did not firmly enmesh the clinical and theoretical considerations as much as he did in his other cases; who did not integrate his principal explanatory perspectives (in this instance, anality, ambivalence, and economic theory); and who did not succeed in neatly tying together child and adult symptomatology. A consideration of Freud's case history of the Wolf Man can enlighten us at this juncture. With the childhood animal phobia of the Wolf Man, Freud established a forward-moving coherence in his narrative, whereas he was unable to do that in the reverse direction with Dr. Lanzer's rat symptomatology erupting in childhood. At the risk of forcing the issue, we might say that Freud did not sufficiently trace the ratlines, the symbolic lineage, of his patient's symptoms back to childhood. In this and other ways, isolation is analytically enacted as well as described, inscribed in Freud's very text, with the result that the text is a mixture of literary failure and overwhelming achievement.

It is that mixture we shall now analyze as we follow the course of the case history. The style of its sections varies in formalistic features and intrinsic merit so that we shall change our examination correspondingly—now dealing with noteworthy verbal usage, now with more general organizational pattern. We shall also discover the functioning of time in Freud's style, some of whose richness is unimaginable if we rely only on Strachey's translation.

In turning to Freud's Introduction (pp. 155–57) to his case history, we are struck by the contrast he draws between his consummate therapeutic results and limitations of various sorts. There is the sharp contrast between the heralded removal of the Rat Man's inhibitions (*Hemmungen*) by the treatment and the persistence of external and internal inhibitions, which affects Freud himself in his desire to give a representative account of the case. A second contrast, this time of more pronounced proportions, obtains between the proclamation about a *complete* restoration of Dr. Lanzer's personality and the sundry repeated references to the fragmentary, the disconnected or isolated or individual or detail (these last four terms being *[das] einzeln[e]* in German): Freud proposes to furnish in Part One some "fragmentary extracts" of clinical material; in Part Two he will theoretically share some "isolated, aphoristic" (*einzelne, aphoristische*) statements; he is impeded from going "into detail" (*im einzelnen*) about his patient's life.[3] Up to now the psychoanalytic investigation of obsessionality has managed to have but "isolated" (*einzelne*) results; Freud hopes that his work as an individual (*einzelnen*) may contribute to the common scientific enterprise. Curiously, the diverse references to the limited and the disconnected make Freud's claim about effecting a complete restoration of personality stand out as an even greater and yet "isolated" accomplishment. There are other strategic artifices involved in Freud's claim, but they must await a retrospective clarification toward the end of our stylistic analysis.

The German language lets one appreciate other differences and nuances in Freud's discourse in the Introduction. He tells us that obsessional language, by surpassing hysterical language in its resemblance to the expressive forms of our conscious thought, yields more easily to our empathy (*Einfühlung*, which Strachey periphrastically translates as "find our way about"). In his unique way, Freud continues his clinical empathy into the writing of his text, constructing his expository vocabulary partly out of references to sight and military life, thus subtly preparing us for the voyeurism and soldierly life of his patient in the pages ahead. Thus, after signaling the "burdensome attention" (*belästigende Aufmerksamkeit*) that his private practice draws in Vienna, Freud admits having never been able to "see through" (*durchschauen*) a severe case of obsessional neurosis; furthermore, even if he had, he still would not be able to render the psychoanalysis of its struc-

---

3. Although Freud asserts that the revelation of the patient's most intimate secrets is less likely to violate discretion than is the disclosure of harmless facts, little data of any sort appear in the case history about his patient's mother.

ture visible (*sichtbar*) to others. Freud's martial allusions are even more pronounced:

> Obsessional neurotics of a severe caliber [*Kalibers*] present themselves [*stellen sich*—also a military verb, meaning "to enlist"] for analytic treatment far less seldom than do hysterics. . . . just as with the chronic infectious disease, we can point to a file [*Reihe*] of brilliant healing successes in light and severe cases of obsessional neurosis when combated [*bekämpften*] early. . . . The crumbs [*Brocken*, also slang for military clothes or uniform] of knowledge here . . . may in themselves prove less satisfying. (157/383; my translation)[4]

What emerges clearly from this passage is Freud's tendency to let his critical language be infiltrated by the everyday language of its subject matter, an infiltration undone by Strachey, who, along with most psychoanalytic writers, wished to impose a "scientific" policy of lexical apartheid between critical commentary and clinical material. (Their invention of such a rigid lexical borderline, one surmises, often implies the conception of a more "purified" and autonomous ego than Freud would have been ready to grant.)

In the case history proper, Freud's expository maneuvers in presenting the clinical material are fascinating. Part One, "Extracts from the Case History," opens with the preliminary interview followed by a series of labeled sections, the first four of which report and comment on the first seven analytic sessions. Schematically, Part One looks like this:

The Preliminary Interview
(A) The Beginning of the Treatment
(B) Infantile Sexuality (session 1)
(C) The Great Obsessive Fear (sessions 2 and 3)

---

4. Cf. Strachey's translation of *Kalibers* (degree), *Reihe* (number), and *bekämpften* (taken in hand).

(D) Initiation into the Nature of the Treatment (sessions 4 to 7)
(E) Some Obsessional Ideas and Their Translation
(F) The Precipitating Cause of the Illness
(G) The Father Complex and the Solution of the Rat Idea

The schematic outline, however, is not so coherent as it appears on first glance, prompting us to wonder about the peremptory and even unconscious factors underlying the expository organization. On closer look, for example, we may be drawn to ask why there are seven general sections instead of six, since "Some Obsessional Ideas and Their Translation" might well have gone into the theoretical Part Two. Equally pertinent is the question as to why Freud chose to give seven day-to-day reports. As far as patients directly treated by Freud are concerned, the only other case history containing the organizational device of a day-to-day report is that of Emmy von N., a patient with a rodent phobia to whom Freud recounted the rat story of Bishop Hatto (Freud, 1893–95, pp. 51–53, 62–63, 73).[5] But whatever the value of the associative link between the cases of Emmy von N. and the Rat Man, we might find it more profitable to note the heptadic pattern throughout Freud's works: *The Interpretation of Dreams, Jokes and Their Relation to the Unconscious,* "The Unconscious," *New Introductory Lectures, Beyond the Pleasure Principle,* and *The Question of Lay Analysis* each has seven chapters; *The Introductory Lectures* are twenty-eight in number; the first two of the *Three Essays on the Theory of Sexuality* have seven sections each, as does Freud's personal favorite among all his writings, Part Four of *Totem and Taboo* (Freud, 1913c, p. xi). Relatedly, Freud thought his life was

---

5. Cf. Freud's diagnostic appraisals of the symptomatic reactions of Fräulein Elisabeth and the Rat Man: "if one pressed or pinched the hyperalgesic skin and muscles of her legs, her face assumed a peculiar expression, which was one of pleasure rather than pain. . . . it could only be reconciled with the view that her disorder was hysterical" (Freud, 1893–95, p. 137); "At all the more important moments while he was telling his story [of the rat torture] his face took on a very strange, composite expression. I could only interpret it as one of *horror at pleasure of his own of which he himself was unaware*" (Freud, 1909, pp. 166–67).

marked by seven-year cycles; he specifically linked seven to a prediction of death and the effort of his seven internal organs to usher his life to an end; and he eventually visited the forbidden city of Rome and its seven hills for a total of seven times after having phobically avoided it for years (Mahony, 1982, pp. 66–67). *Pace* Freud's contention, the presentation of the first seven sessions does not constitute "the expository portion of the treatment" (p. 186), for the published account of the fifth to the seventh sessions contains little new in relation to the preceding and subsequent ones. To account, therefore, for the not altogether successful heptadic pattern in Freud's case history, we must be ready to recognize the persistent influence of his superstition, which might have been activated by the treatment of the Rat Man, who himself was remarkably superstitious. So much for the overall compositional structure of "Extracts from the Case History"; let us now proceed to its analysis, section by section.

Freud's abrupt presentation of the initial interview disarms us, propels us into the immediate scene, an immediacy unfortunately lost in Strachey's translation. The larger fact is that Strachey characteristically turned into the past tense the present tense which Freud often used for narration, more often to convey patients' associations, and invariably to transcribe their dreams. Here, then, is a sampling of Freud as he dramatically lifts the curtain on his initial contact with the Rat Man:

> A youngish man of academic education introduces himself with the statement that he suffers from obsessional ideas since his childhood, but with particular intensity since four years ago. The principal contents of his suffering are *fears* that something might happen to two persons whom he loves very much—his father and a lady he reveres. Besides this he feels *compulsive impulses*—for example, cutting his throat with a straight-razor; he further produces *prohibitions*, which deal also with unimportant things. (*G.W.*, p. 384; my translation)

Here is Strachey:

> A youngish man of university education introduced himself to me with the statement that he had suffered from obsessions ever since his childhood, but with particularly intensity for the last four years. The chief features of his disorder were *fears* that something might happen to two people of whom he was very fond—his father and a lady whom he admired. Besides this he was aware of *compulsive impulses*—such as an impulse, for instance, to cut his throat with a razor; and further he produced *prohibitions,* sometimes in connection with quite unimportant things. (p. 158)

In passing we can appreciate Freud's intimate talking of the patient's *suffering,* a verbal form of everyday use which we may heuristically compare with Strachey's technical substantive, *disorder.*

But Strachey's Olympian stance toward time is heuristically even more revealing for us; it is as if he resorted to the past tense in order to control, to contain the living present by inserting an antiseptic distance between it and himself, and as if his idea of scientific objectivity demanded the guise of a chronological remove in the very reporting. Freud does not need such posturing; he quickly opens the door to let us into the consultation room. But wait an instant—is that true? Or is it rather that he invites us into his study where he is writing up his process notes at night?[6] Not quite either, for the interview account is a slight revision of the process notes and therefore comes from a different moment of writing. What then? The fact is that, with a majestic daring never attempted by any other analyst, Freud uses the pre-

---

6. In his process notes on the interview Freud terminates by mentioning the patient's return on the next day and his acceptance of the practical conditions; hence at least part of the write-up occurred on the following day. One can find other such discrepancies, including deferred addenda, which undercut Freud's initial declaration about writing down notes at the end of each day (cf. p. 159*n*).

sent tense to merge three different temporal scenes—the clinical scene and two separate scenes of Freud as note taker and revisionist. Fused with a dreamlike vividness into the present tense, clinical event and its successive descriptions become one. We arrive then at a precious conclusion about the psychological makeup of Freud's creative genius: he could relive the past intensely and dramatically express that experience in the immediate present in which all dreams take place; likewise, he had the ability to bypass the conscious perception of time as discrete units in order to express his unconscious perception of it as duration. This extraordinary feature, manifest in his German text, counters to some extent his aphoristic disconnectedness, which we have previously discussed.

We pass on to the first analytic session to read how Freud makes a bold gesture: he starts out under the heading "The Beginning of the Treatment," and then, where the Rat Man is proceeding without any apparent transition, Freud scriptively intrudes to give the indented label "Infantile Sexuality" to the subsequent associations. In effect, Freud expositorily benefits from the Rat Man's packaging, which, however, is not interpreted as such. The fact of the matter is that, despite the Rat Man's love affair with words, he usually has problems giving a long narrative unit (the first analytic session and those of December 23, 27, and 28 are exceptions). Freud, in sum, is confronted by two stylistic factors: Dr. Lanzer fits into that category of patients who have a greater aptitude for the lyric style of association by similarity than for the epic style of association by contiguity (Rosen, 1977, pp. 138–39); and in a pathological sense, owing to the considerable disruption of causal connections by defensive isolation, he cannot give a sustained narrative either of his own "real" life or of that subtending his personal myth.

Nevertheless, in Freud's discussion of the first session, he masterfully infiltrates his expository language with visual references, a lexical element suggesting an empathically analytic stance to his scopophilic patient. Freud begins by announcing that we "see" little Ernst driven by the pleasure of looking (I have translated somewhat literally in order to bring out the visual references):

> We *see* the child under the domination of a sexual drive-component, the *desire to look*, whose result is the ever recurrent wish of great intensity to *see naked* female persons who please him. . . . As often as he wishes something of this kind, he must fear something dreadful would happen. This dreadful thing already *clothes* itself in a characteristic indeterminateness which henceforth will never be lacking from the expressions of the neurosis. Yet in a child it is not hard to find out what is *veiled* by such indeterminateness. If one can come to learn an example from any one of the blurred generalities of the obsessional neurosis, then one can be sure that the example is the original and actual thing itself which must be *hidden away* by the generalization. . . . The distressing affect [of the obsessional neurosis] *clearly* takes on the *tinge* of the uncanny, the superstitious. . . . We shall scarcely go astray if we perceive in this childlike quest for *enlightenment* an inkling of those remarkable psychic processes which we call unconscious and which we cannot dispense with [*entraten*] in the scientific *illumination* of the *dark* circumstances. (162–64/388–89; italics mine)

Freud and Ernst, drive and defense, analysis and exposition, all meet in the eye. Another example of Freud's typical flair for permitting a conflictual theme to invade his very exposition of it concerns little Ernst's lascivious wishes and his defensive reaction; in his clinical comment Freud says that one can hardly "resist" (*sträuben*) qualifying sexual experiences as especially consequential.

We should also remark that three times Freud speaks of "our patient," which Strachey rendered as "the patient." The discrepancy is far-reaching in that Freud pronominally conjoins us with him and thereby turns us as readers into cotherapists in the analysis. Thus a fourth track announces itself in Freud's stereophonic prose—the analytic treatment, the writing of the process notes, their revision, and the public reading experience are now copresent. But the alert German reader detects even a fifth track, for Freud discusses Ernst's life in childhood as also transpiring in the present. As a way of contrastively highlighting this effect, I shall first cite Freud, then Strachey's Freud:

> ... *wollen wir noch als ein wahrscheinlich nicht gleichgültiges Zusammentreffen betonen, dass die Kindheitsamnesie unseres Patienten gerade mit dem 6. Jahre ihr Ende erreicht.* (. . . yet we want to emphasize a coincidence which is probably no accident: *our* patient's amnesia about his childhood end*s* precisely with his sixth year). (p. 390; my translation and italics) . . . stress may be laid on the fact, which is probably more than a mere coincidence, that the patient's infantile amnesia ended precisely with his sixth year. (pp. 164–65)

The temporal and pronominal indicators of Freud's closeness to Ernst and his readership were displaced by Strachey, who interposed his scientific ideology of clinical reportage between Freud and his patient, between Freud and us, and between us and Ernst. Let us further note the diametric opposition of the fictive simultaneity of Freud's five-track stereophonic prose to the pathological simultaneity of the Rat Man's fear, expressed in the first session, that his already dead father might die.

Countering the potentially monotonous typography found in the presentation of the clinical material, Freud precedes the second session with the title "The Great Obsessive Fear." He then sets out by citing his patient at length; Lanzer interrupts himself, we read in the second paragraph, and several sentences later we come upon the most unusual stylistic irregularity in the entire case history and, I would risk saying, in the Freudian corpus. Freud's stereophonic style breaks down next to our very ears as he inconsistently switches to the past tense, thereby expressing a defensive reaction to the interpersonal intrication and his intrusive interventions marking the exchange. By such temporal withdrawal, Freud tries to undo the rat penetration which has already been enacted in and through his enunciatory interplay with Lanzer (my italics stress the significant irregularities in the use of tense):

> Here he breaks off, stands up and asks me to spare him the description of the details. I assure him that I myself have no inclination whatever for horror and certainly have no desire to torment him, but that naturally I cannot grant him something over which I have no ordinance. He may just as well ask me to grant him two comets. The overcoming of resistances is a precept of the treatment which we could in no way disregard. (I *had expounded* on the concept of "resistance" to him at the beginning of this hour, when he said that he had many things in himself to overcome if he were to relate his experience.) I *continued*: but what I could do is to guess fully, from something hinted by him, about what ought to happen. *Is* he perhaps thinking of impalement?—"No, not that, but the condemned *is being* tied up"—(he *expressed* himself so indistinctly that I could not immediately guess in what position)—"over his buttocks a pot *is* turned upside down, in which then rats *are* let in, and they"—he *was* again standing up and *gave* all signs of horror and resistance—"*bored* in."—"Into the anus," I *permitted* myself to complete it. (166/391–92; my translation)

Freud then brings us into his presence: "At all the more important moments one notes on him [*merkt man an ihm*] a very strange composite facial expression." Soon thereafter, although one shifts tense more freely in German, we can find no reason for Freud's inconsistent use of past and present in his exposition (relative to his customary practice), unless we see projection in Freud's account that the Rat Man is "confused" and "bewildered." Seemingly the Rat Man's disowning of his obsessions as "foreign," his enticing reluctance to narrate the torture, and

Freud's guessing (*erraten*) his way into the narration all indicate disturbances of intrapsychic and analytic space, overflowing into the irregular temporal nearness and distancing of Freud's account that significantly starts with the antiphonal construction of the rat story.

Freud's report of the third session has three long paragraphs. In the first, he resumes the description of the Rat Man's madness, starting from near the end of maneuvers to his arrival in Vienna, where he and Dr. Palatzer finally dispatch the famous payment. Thankful for this last detail, Freud says in the second paragraph that he can begin to straighten out the distortions in the Rat Man's story—that is, Ernst must really have known for some time his actual creditor at the post office. Freud then clarifies the imbroglio over the payment for the rest of the second paragraph and, in the third one, traces the Rat Man's life from Dr. Palatzer's consoling companionship to the consultation on Berggasse.

We must note first that the sequence of events in paragraphs one and two is reversed in the process notes, which begin with clarifications and in which Freud's moment of clear perception occurs not with the final detail about Dr. Palatzer in Vienna but with an earlier detail concerning a medical officer during maneuvers.[7] Now why, one may ask, does Freud reorganize the sequence? The answer is readily found in his own qualification of the Rat Man's actions as a "comedy" (*Komödie*), with the result that, with appropriate artistry, Freud restructures the session like a comedy. Thus he eliminates clarifications at the beginning; a partial denouement is saved for the middle; and in a final remark, he maintains the traditional open-endedness of comedy by alluding to the Rat Man's subsequent temptation to resume his maddening quest. Also, like a typical comic dramatist, Freud depicts his questful protagonist as ensnared in a maze of both fate and

---

7. On the other hand, and to Freud's credit, the number of male personnel in the original account (nine) is trimmed by two, thus facilitating the comprehensibility of the published version.

fortune—obsessive wishes, a demand for cure "woven up" (*verwoben*) into a delirium, and a "chance" discovery of Freud's book on chance (*The Psychopathology of Everyday Life*), with the effect of directing the Rat Man's "choice" to Freud. We should note, however, that Freud did not present his drama but narrated it; with few exceptions as this juncture, he set the action in the past, the distancing effect of which is nevertheless offset by his thrice referring to Ernst Lanzer as "our patient."

As opposed to the previous session, with its narrated comedy, the fourth is mostly a dramatic presentation of the Rat Man, with the changing turns of the speakers signaled in the present: "he asks," "he says," "I reply," and so on. This dramatic effect befits Freud's aim, stated at the outset of the sessions, to eschew omniscient remarks in order to sustain the reader's curiosity just as he and Ernst Lanzer do in pursuing free association:

> Let no one expect to hear so soon what I have to bring forward in the clarification of these strange, senseless obsessional representations (about rats); correct psychoanalytic technique requires the physician to suppress his curiosity and leaves the patient the free ordering of the sequence of themes during the work. I therefore received the patient in the fourth session with the question: "How are you going to start off now?" (173–74/ 398; my translation)

It might also be noted, incidentally, that Freud inconsistently carries out his advocacy of suppressed curiosity, for midway through the session he instructs his patient in basic psychoanalytic principles instead of letting him curiously discover them for himself.

I have little to say about the next three sessions except that Freud enters further into a dramatic style; accordingly, the reader is seldom addressed, and the change in speaker is indicated by a dash, thereby enabling the report of the sessions to be laid out like a theatrical text. I should mention, however, one of those rare instances in which Freud turns from his patient to address us: in the main text Freud asserts, "I take the opportunity of urging my case" (p. 185) and then self-reflectively adds in a footnote, "I only produce these arguments so as once more to demonstrate to myself their inefficacy" (Strachey, of course, translated *take* and *produce* in the past). This is another superb example of how Freud's stereophonic style in German creates the impression that the scenes of the ongoing treatment and his subsequent write-up and self-reflection all take place concomitantly on the same dramatic stage.

In the last three sections of Part One of his case history, Freud adopted a new expressive mode. In the references to former events he largely left behind the dramatic present for the narrative past tense (two notable exceptions are the renditions of the Rat Man's dream [p. 193] and fantasy [pp. 194–95], both transcribed in the present tense and hence in conformity with Freud's firm contention that the intrapsychic activities of dreaming and fantasying are preeminently and intrinsically occurrences of the present). Section E is interesting for some verbal complexity, starting with a spatial referent in its title: "Some Obsessional Ideas and Their Translation." The last word in German (*Übersetzung*) also means "carrying over"—in translating unconscious ideas, the analyst also effects a carrying over from the unconscious to the conscious and "brings" (*bringt*) obsessional ideas into a temporal connection with the patient's experiences; in that way he finds out the pathological "derivation" (*Abkunft*, literally, coming away). Later on, Freud playfully voiced the hope that his explanation of an obsessional idea (*Zwangsidee*) is itself not "forced" (*gezwungen*), a humorous self-reflection set in motion by the *zwang* and *gezwungen*, which are respectively the past and past participle of the main verb *zwingen*. Freud also let a note of compulsion enter his exposition when, after expounding on the obsession for protecting, he wrote, "and it bore other fruit besides this"; the English here does not capture the German *Blüten trieb* (literally, put forth flowers), especially in that as a noun *Trieb* means drive. In a more amusing wordplay, Freud compared his patient to Balaam, the self-defeating biblical soothsayer, and then to an incantatory alchemist. Lanzer saw,

> like an inverted Balaam, that something always inserted itself into his pious formulas, which turned them into the opposite. . . . In such affliction he found the way out by putting aside the prayers and replacing them by a short formula that was brewed together [*zusammengebraut*] out of initial letters or syllables of different prayers. (193/415; my translation)

Both the beginning and the end of Section E mention Ernst's ambivalence toward Gisela's absence (pp. 187, 195), and as a matter of fact, Freud resorted to a complex use (and nonuse) of language to deal with that ambivalence. When we hunt up the source in the process notes for Freud's initial assertion that Ernst's suicidal obsessions were occasioned by Gisela's absence (187/410), we are forced to give the following a rereading:

> He lost several weeks through the *presence* of the lady, who went off when her very old grandmother became ill. (H, p. 92; my translation and italics)[8]

In his terminal remark (195/417), Freud expressed his patient's feelings of affection and revenge toward Gisela this way:

> These impulses were silent mostly in her presence and came out in her absence. (my translation)[9]

But within the main part of his elaboration, Freud made more involved distinctions: Ernst's obsession for protecting took place

---

8. Yet that very word *presence* (clearly *Anwesenheit* in my copy of the holograph) was silently changed by Strachey into *absence* (which is *Abwesenheit* in German; p. 259)—presence itself was textually sent into exile!

9. Cf. Strachey's rendering: "These impulses were mostly in abeyance when she was there, and only appeared in her absence." Perhaps in a moment of absentmindedness Strachey unwarrantably inserted an "only" before the last verb, thereby giving rise to a nonsequitur.

during Gisela's presence at his summer resort, whereas his obsession for understanding broke out after her departure. Both obsessions, though, derived from a common circumstance. When he was taking his leave of Gisela before departing for the summer resort, she said something that he understood as her repudiating him before "the present company" (190/412). During her belated stay at the country resort, Gisela cleared up that misunderstanding; prior to that clarification, according to Freud, Ernst's obsession to protect must have broken out. On the other hand, Freud linked the obsession to understand (which occurred after Gisela's departure) to Ernst's ambivalence, which was exemplified by his removing and subsequently replacing the stone in the road several hours before his lady's departure. Yet that replacing, in Freud's words, would be incorrectly classified as a critical repudiation of a pathological action: since putting the stone back was accompanied by a sense of compulsion, that very act was part of the original pathological action. Hence the first stage of the compulsive act was not "neutralized" (as Strachey [p. 192] would have it) by the second stage but rather was both "annulled and conserved" (*aufgehoben*, p. 414). Through his brilliant use of this primal word of antithesis, therefore, Freud showed that the first stage was annulled by what followed and was also conserved in that the compulsion continued into the second stage. In this context, then, the perceptual difference betwen Gisela's presence and absence was collapsed in the Rat Man's ambivalence and compulsion.

From the foregoing, one is driven to conclude that Gisela's fate was to move with equal ease in and out of Ernst's life, and in and out of both Freud's and Strachey's texts. Let us give another example: Ernst uttered two juxtaposed, ambivalent statements about Gisela's presence and absence in his very first analytic session (p. 255); yet those statements are absent from Freud's published report of the first session (p. 158) as well as from Strachey's generalizing account that Freud published the first third of the process notes "almost verbatim" (p. 254). In sum, the matter of absence and presence appears like a series of Chinese boxes, during the unpackaging of which, nuisance turns to new sense as one discovers that by virtue of a dwindling absence, the containers themselves are the only presents.

The outstanding feature of the next section, "The Precipitating Cause of the Illness," revolves around time. Freud settled on Mrs. Lanzer's plan for her son's marriage as the one precipitating cause of illness, seeming to forget for the moment the other explanations: Gisela's infertility and Ernst's aunt's death. In support of his thesis, Freud drew all his clinical material on the Rat Man from the process notes of one session, December 8, whose brevity, however, went against Freud's narrative concerns. As a countermeasure, he opted for the following strategy. In the first of the section's six paragraphs, Freud began in his storylike way with the most traditional of epithets, "One day," and alluded briefly to the Rat Man's unwitting mention of the immediate cause of his illness. Then for the next two paragraphs Freud dropped the Rat Man and took up the mechanisms of isolation and displacement in obsessionality, disgressing at length on a former case[10] (meanwhile we are thinking about the displacements in Freud's own diagnosis and exposition). Returning to his main story in the fourth paragraph, Freud brought up the decisive marriage plan and, in doing so, made the first and only substantial mention of his patient's mother in the main text of the whole case history; the fifth and last paragraphs further explain the cause of illness but do not refer to her. In retrospect, we can think of perhaps three reasons for Freud's deferred reference to Mrs. Lan-

---

10. Strachey's translation does not capture Freud's wordplay in the description of this self-justifying elderly man who left alone neither little girls nor his own self-reproach (the latter was conveniently displaced): thus, on one hand, he sexually molested girls entrusted in his charge by going into their adjacent room and masturbating them; on the other hand, "if he left alone the [self-]reproach where it belonged, he would have had to renounce a sexual satisfaction to which he was probably pushed by strong infantile determinants" (198/419).

zer: he was uneasy and reluctant to discuss her, and when he did, it was as a deus ex machina; the deferment figures in Freud's expository concern to make the treatment appear longer; and from an artistic point of view, Freud's dilatory tactic mimicked his subject's habit of postponing decisions.

In analyzing the last and longest section of Part One, "The Father Complex and the Solution of the Rat Idea," we may initially study several instances of Freud's engaging wordplay and then the more important overall structure of his exposition. After bringing up the debt incurred by Heinrich Lanzer in his military days as a gambler (*Spielratte*, literally, a play-rat), Freud claimed that Ernst must have heard a paternal reference in the cruel captain's reimbursement request. Thus Freud:

> The captain's words, "You must pay back the 3.80 kronen to Lieutenant A." had sounded to his [Ernst's] ears like an allusion to this unpaid debt of his father's. (p. 211)

What is startling is that not only the captain's words "sounded" (*klangen*) like an allusion to the gambling father (*Spielratte*) but also that the very term *allusion* (*Anspielung*) means as well as enacts itself by virtue of its identical root with *Spielratte*; consequently the difference between language and metalanguage is deftly subverted. In this way Freud blended his expository language with a principal signifier in his patient's story. A double instance of this lexical maneuver is found in the following footnote:

> Since the patient had done everything to confuse the little incident of the repayment of the charges for the pince-nez, perhaps my presentation also did not succeed in making it transparent [*durchsichtig*, literally, looked through] without default [*Rückstand*]. (212n/431n; my translation)

Just as vision and payment dominate the Rat Man's story, so also do those themes enter into the self-reflectiveness of Freud's narrative.[11]

A slightly humorous example of narrative self-reflectiveness occurs in a watery context about the rat:

> The rat is a dirty animal, feeding upon excrement and living in drains that carry waste [*Kanälen die den Abfall führen*]. It is rather superfluous [*überflüssig*, literally, overflowing] to point out that . . . (214/433; my translation)[12]

There is also an instance of perhaps unintentional comic effect accompanied by more successful verbal play. In the course of describing his patient's masturbation upon hearing a postilion illegally blowing his horn or upon reading a poignantly amorous passage in Goethe, Freud labeled those occasions as "uplifting" (*erhebenden*) and continued the spatial reference, which disappears when rendered in fluent English:

> But I could not help stressing [*herausheben*, literally, to lift out] what was common in these two examples: the prohibition and a defiance of [*Sichhinaussetzen über*, literally, putting oneself outside and over] a command. (204/425; my translation)[13]

Then Freud resonantly went on to mention the Rat Man's ritual of midnight masturbation which would begin by his defiantly opening the front door as if his father were standing outside. In this way, Freud's phraseology skillfully united father and son as

---

11. *Rückstand* is commonly used in the sense of arrears, a financial reference missing in Strachey's translation: "perhaps my own account of it may also have failed to clear it up entirely."

12. The richness of Freud's text is blotted out by Strachey, who translated *Kanälen die den Abfall führen* simply by sewers, and *überflüssig* by unnecessary (p. 214).

13. Cf. Strachey's translation on page 204. In passing, I might briefly allude to Freud's portrayal of the Rat Man's efforts to bring military colleagues "into his combination" (*Kombination*, 212/431). The richer German term also carries the meanings of reasoning, deduction, conjecture, and guesswork, all applicable to the present context.

being outside, one in a perceptually external space, the other in the intrapsychic space of moral defiance.

Freud saved some of his most extensive punning, however, to depict his patient's itinerary "along the painful road of transference." I shall use Strachey's translation this time:

> "How can a gentleman like you, sir" he used to ask, "let yourself be abused in this way by a low, good-for-nothing fellow [*hergelaufenen Kerl*, literally, a runabout fellow] like me? You ought to turn me out; that's all I deserve." While he talked like this, he would get up from the sofa and roam about [*herumlaufen*] the room. . . . If he stayed on the sofa he behaved like someone in desperate violence; he would bury his head in his hands, cover his face with his arm, jump up suddenly, rush [*lief*, past tense of *laufen*, to run] away, his features distorted with pain, and so on. He recalled that his father had had a passionate temper, and sometimes in his violence had not known where to stop [*gehen*, literally, to go]. (209/429)

We cannot fail to marvel at how this text runs together Ernst's self-evaluation (a runabout fellow), his expression of fear (running about the room), and his father's expression of anger (not knowing where to go). Although it is an open question as to how much Freud himself contributed to the pertinent chain of signifiers, his condensed recording of them is in itself a response to the poetry of the unconscious.

In terms of the larger focus of thematic organization, we find that Freud enlivened the pace of his discourse by constantly referring to events as mediated by tales, by literal hearsay. He saw his first reconstruction confirmed by a tale his patient heard but could not remember (p. 205); the Rat Man's obsessions were activated by the captain's two speeches (p. 210); it seemed as if fate, when the captain told the torture tale, had "called out" (*zugerufen*, 216/435) a "complex stimulus-word" to the Rat Man; the Rat Man identified with his father in his novel about marriage

(*Eheroman*, 211/431);[14] parallel to the captain's erroneous remark that was transformed into paternal infallibility in one of the Rat Man's obsessional sayings is the king's magical utterance. As Freud states, "The king cannot be mistaken; if he addresses one of his subjects by a title which is not his, the subject bears that title ever afterwards" (p. 218).[15] It is precisely through further reflection on this tale that we are enabled to make a surprising discovery about Ernst's mother. In the main text of the case history, she is given limited, mediating status as the bearer of a tale or arranger of marriage, whereas it is only in the subjected typography of a footnote that she acquires a fully oedipal role; curiously, it is also in the important footnote, running for three pages (pp. 206–08), that we find Freud's only considerable treatment of the oedipal (nuclear) complex in the case, albeit largely in general terms.[16]

The time is now ripe for us to outline the structure of the section under consideration, which is as follows: some clinical material, taken from the opening sessions of the analysis, about

14. Freud mentioned a series of identifications that the Rat Man established with his father that had different bases: marital choice, military life, money, and punishment/victimization; but rather than be expressed in one condensed passage, the identifications are strewn out in the narration, which thereupon approximates associative flow.

15. The implications of Freud's observation are far-reaching when considered in the light of speech theorists' distinction between constative and performative discourse. Constative discourse merely describes an event, whereas performative discourse not only discloses an utterance of its speaker but, through the very act of its enunciation, accomplishes the action. Thus, given the necessary felicitous circumstances, such utterances as "I bid hearts" and "I promise" or "I do" perform and accomplish actions in themselves; the imperial enunciation given by Freud is also of such an order. What Freud is saying on a deeper level, however, is that obsessional wording assumes the character of performative discourse for the obsessional, who becomes the enunciated victim of his compulsions and omnipotent wishes.

16. In the footnote, Freud discussed at length the thorny difficulty of ascertaining the historical or psychic reality of infantile sexuality. The discussion is a choice illustration of those times when Freud resorted to an expressive mode in which doubts, qualifications, and assertions loop back upon each other; in resuming the topic in the Wolf Man case, Freud wrote similarly (Freud, 1918, pp. 67–70, 102–03).

the conflict between Ernst and his father (pp. 200–04); Freud's construction of an early conflictual scene between Ernst and his father, and the emergence of that conflict within the transference (pp. 205–09); the ensuing solution of the rat obsession and Freud's "restoration of the context" (*Herstellung des Zusammenhanges*, 209–10/429–30). The last subject itself has three parts: a summary account of the deliria during the military exercises (pp. 210–12); the emergence of the rat associations during the analysis (pp. 213–17); and the explanation of the process and the general context informing the nascent rat obsession (pp. 217–20). Even a cursory examination of the foregoing outline shows how it sets in relief the narrative thrust and vitality we familiarly encounter in Freud's prose. The narrative thrust is further strengthened by the frequent usage of such words as *way, course, follow, turn, lead,* and *reach*. Even though these words compose a family of dead metaphors, their original meanings may be reset in motion by a surrounding narrative context and thereby enhance in turn the narrative flow, as we can pursue in the following:

> From the precipitating cause of the patient's illness in his adult years there was a thread leading back to his childhood. . . . To this unimpeachable body of evidence we shall be able to add fresh material, if we turn to the history of the masturbatory side of our patient's sexual activities. . . . Starting from these indications and from other data of a similar kind, I ventured to put forward a construction. . . . To my great astonishment the patient then informed me. . . . And so it was only along the painful road of transference that he was able to reach a conviction. . . . a quantity of material information which had hitherto been withheld became available. . . . In elucidating the effects produced by the captain's rat story we must follow the course of the analysis more closely. . . . Yet, in spite of all this wealth of material, no light was thrown upon the meaning of his obsessional idea until one day. . . . It was only then that

it became possible to understand the inexplicable process by which his obsessional idea had been formed. . . . Only vague intelligence of these events reached the patient's consciousness. . . . Let us, further, picture to ourselves the general conditions under which the formation of the patient's great obsessional idea occurred.

These extracts help us see that, thanks partly to Freud's lexical choices, his exposition takes on a narrative quality, a quality further reinforced by the metaphor of the journey coursing through his prose (Mahony, 1982). Briefly, even in the etymological sense, the conquistadorial prose of Freud is ambitious (Latin *ambulare*, to walk).

Indeed, the virtuosity of Freud's vivid discourse is so captivating that we must beware of being distracted from the recognition of crucial organizational discrepancies. There is one that is as important as anything we have analyzed stylistically up to now. The matter concerns the two main topics of the section at hand—Ernst's relation to his father and the rat phobia. On one hand, the construction given on October 12 about little Ernst's outburst of anger toward his father was supposedly worked through in the transference, a working through that Freud described solely with material drawn from the period of November 21 to December 8. On the other hand, the *subsequent* solution (p. 209) of the rat idea was based on material drawn essentially from the period of November 18 to January 7 (pp. 210–16); but this time, as our outline plainly shows, Freud did not record any working through in the treatment. Instead, he merely imparted to the reader the reconstructed formation of the rat idea (pp. 217–19) and then concluded with an intellectualizing assertion that when he and his patient had reached (not worked through) the solution given to the reader, the rat delirium disappeared. A bare, bold claim with no demonstration, no further explanation.

It is now that the overall structure of Part One of Freud's case history suddenly becomes clearer to us. In his opening remarks,

Freud repeatedly apologized for the fragmentary nature of his report; in both substance and repetition, those apologies starkly contrast with the single, succinctly worded claim by Freud that he effected a *complete* restoration of his patient's personality and a removal of his inhibitions. Gone is any reference to fragmentariness at the end of Part One, for at this late hour any such avowal would spotlight the transparency of Freud's contention. Like a good rhetorician who may resort to aesthetic and other devices, especially in the area where his logical demonstration is weakest, Freud combines dramatic staging and the typographical strategy of a concluding blank space to give the impression of definitiveness and to distract from the defensive closure of his narration. By a stylistic sleight of hand, the father complex in its full recapitulation was apparently tucked under the rat idea, and now, at the final moment, the disappearance of the delirium is announced. Exit rats, exit father complex, and offstage, somewhere, a fully restored man is walking, we are told.

Part Two of Freud's case history, accorded the title "Theoretical" only in 1924, has three short sections. The first, "Some General Characteristics of Obsessional Structures," affords us the opportunity to see in a negative and positive light the possibilities of Freud's processive style, an unfolding style that adapts itself not to *pensée pensée* (thought thought) but to *pensée pensante* (thinking thought). In opting for the spontaneity of *pensée pensante*, Freud risked confusion and inconsistency in areas where he was making an issue about clarity itself. For example, Freud started out the section by trying to correct his use of the term *obsessional ideas* in his essay of 1896; this terminology, he had come to believe, was too extensive and bore the influence of the obsessional neurotic's penchant for indeterminateness.[17] Accord-

17. Rather than refer to his inaccurate usage of 1896, Freud might have brought up Subsection E of Part One of his case history, the title of which begins "Some Obsessional Ideas" (*Einige Zwangsvorstellungen*, 186/409). Strachey, for his part, was given to translating *Zwangsvorstellungen* simply as obsessions (189/412, 191/413).

ingly, instead of *obsessional ideas* (*Zwangsvorstellungen,* 221/438), Freud now proposed the more precise term *obsessive thinking* (*Zwangsdenken,* 221/439), which includes "wishes, temptations, impulses, reflections, doubts, commands and prohibitions." Although Freud preferred *Zwangsdenken* in that it was more properly applicable to the gamut of psychical phenomena, he immediately raised a logical objection to his patient's reductively referring to a "train of thought" (*Denkverbindung,* 222/440). More important, in spite of Freud's *isolated* rejection of the indeterminate, affectless use of *obsessional ideas* favored by obsessional patients, he himself proceeded casually to use the very term; for example, *"patients themselves do not know the wording of their own obsessional ideas"* (*Zwangsvorstellungen,* 223/441).[18] It should also be noted that the foregoing self-contradiction, undermining a critical thesis in the case history, is more serious than the many localized self-contradictions that we are familiar with throughout Freud's work. In this context we find a hallmark of processive style in its often casual use of mutually contradictory qualifiers for the same assertion. Compare, for example, Freud's perfunctory switch from *only* to *occasionally* in the following two statements: obsessive thought processes are known in waking life "only" in distorted form (p. 223); obsessional thought processes break through "occasionally" in undistorted form (p. 228).

The present section offers a few examples of one important aspect of Freud's processive style, the coiling type. Being somewhat reminiscent of a certain kind of free association in analytic sessions, it is a far cry from a rigorously inductive or deductive style (and if anyone were to copy it too closely, he would risk having his article refused for publication in most current psycho-

---

18. In a later passage Freud explicitly pointed to obsessional thinking and ideas as *synonyms:* "According as this regression from acting to thinking is more or less marked, a case of obsessional neurosis will exhibit the characteristics of obsessive thinking (that is, of obsessional ideas) or of obsessive acting in the narrower sense of the word (p. 244; cf. *G.W.,* p. 460: *den Charakter des Zwangsdenkens [Zwangsvorstellung]*).

The Art and Strategy of Freud's Exposition

analytic journals—but that is another oedipal story). As one of the simpler forms of Freud's coiling style, the following skeletal extract shows how the fourth statement reverts to the second:

1. In the year 1896 I defined obsessional ideas. . . .
2. This definition now seems to me to be open to criticism . . . and took as its model the practice of obsessional neurotics themselves . . . with their characteristic liking for indeterminateness. . . .
3. In point of fact, it would be more correct to speak of "obsessive thinking," and to make it clear that obsessional structures can correspond to every sort of psychical act.
4. Patients endeavour in general to tone down such distinctions. . . . Our present patient gave an example of this type of behaviour. (pp. 221–22)

As a complex form of Freud's coiling style, the next example exhibits how a difference posited in the first statement is grounded by a convoluted sameness in the second:

1. . . . an obsessional command (or whatever it may be), which in waking life is known only in a truncated form . . . may have its actual text brought to light in a dream.
2. [The distortion of an obsessional idea] enables it to persist, since conscious thought is thus compelled to misapprehend it, just as though it were a dream; for dreams are also a product of compromise and distortion, and are also misapprehended by waking thought. (pp. 223–24)

Through our attention to these scattered instances of coiling style and its doubling back on itself, we gain a strategic perspective on Freud's manifold sensitivity to time, to origins, even to "prior" origins:

When we have at great pains elucidated an unintelligible obsessional idea, it often happens that the patient informs us that

> just such a notion, wish, or temptation as the one we have constructed did in fact make its appearance on one occasion *before* the obsessional idea had arisen. (p. 224; italics mine)

As Freud's exposition proceeded, he returned to this idea about origins, and that return *in itself* was part and parcel of a concern to record origin as ever receding:

> . . . the patient is obliged to place it [the first occurrence of an obsession] further and further back as the analysis proceeds, and is constantly finding fresh "first" occasions for the appearance of the obsession. (p. 229)

Finally, I cannot forgo the opportunity of quoting what for me is the finest example of Freud's mordant irony, whose measured exasperation reaches its most subtle limit in the unforgettable last sentence:

> It would be a most desirable thing if the philosophers and psychologists who develop brilliant theoretical views on the unconscious upon the basis of hearsay knowledge or from their own conventional definitions would first submit to the convincing impressions which may be gained from a firsthand study of the phenomena of obsessional thinking. We might almost go to the length of *requiring* it of them if the task were not so far more laborious than the methods of work to which they are accustomed. (p. 228)

In the next section, avowedly dealing with issues relatively minor as compared to what will follow (p. 229), we notice the increasing expository disorganization, and we may justifiably surmise that Freud as theoretician was gradually disinvesting in his patient. After announcing in the section's heading that he will examine the psychological attitude of obsessionals toward "reality, superstition and death," Freud went on to look at superstition and, in a second movement, analyzed the need for doubt, which draws the individual away from reality and brings him forcefully to contend with four uncertain subjects: "paternity, length of life, life after death, and memory." Suddenly Freud dropped to a footnote in order to treat the first subject, paternity.[19] Then, in the main text, Freud jumped to the fourth subject, memory, which he dismissed in half a sentence; next, he asserted that the second and third subjects would be preceded by an appropriate transition dealing with the topic of superstition, which was brought up at the outset (p. 233).

Such a strikingly untidy sequence of expression gives the impression that Freud had lost his customary expository control over his processive style. There is no way of telling how much the very subject matter might have caught Freud off guard, activated dormant conflicts, and disturbed his stylistic mastery—but his attitudes toward paternity were undoubtedly unsettled by the complexities of his father's three marriages (one of which was later shrouded in secrecy [Schur, 1972]), and we know that Freud had a superstitious side which extended to an obsessive preoccupation with death and a numerologically oriented anticipation of it. Yet whatever the reasons for Freud's general stylistic disorganization, they did not prevent him from writing some salient lines where again he takes us as co-workers with him in the representation of the Rat Man's analysis:

---

19. Freud's footnote at this point is remarkable for its syntactical disconnectedness as well as for its conception of historical advance as bound up with phallocentricity and the evaluation of inference as tantamount to perceptual evidence: "As Lichtenberg says, 'An astronomer knows whether the moon is inhabited or not with about as much certainty as he knows who was his father, but not with so much certainty as he knows who was his mother.' A great advance was made in civilization when men decided to put their inferences upon a level with the testimony of their senses and to make the step from matriarchy to patriarchy.— The prehistorical figures which show a smaller person sitting upon the head of a larger one are representations of patrilinear descent; Athena had no mother, but sprang from the head of Zeus. A witness who testifies to something before a court of law is still called '*Zeuge*' [literally, begetter] in German, after the part played by the male in the act of procreation; so too in hieroglyphics the word of a 'witness' is written with a representation of the male organ" (p. 233).

> Assuming, without more ado, that this belief [of the Rat Man] is a frank megalomania of infancy, we will proceed to ask our patient for the grounds of his conviction. In reply, he adduces two experiences. (p. 234)

In this passage, as in many others in the case history, we recognize that Freud's prose is truly one of rapprochement—interpersonally, between author, reader, and patient, as well as temporally, variously bringing together past, present, and future.

The final section bears the title "The Instinctual Life of Obsessional Neurotics, and the Origins of Compulsion and Doubt," but the word *origin* only partially conveys the sense of the German *Ableitung*, which might signify *derivation* and which is also a term of physics and engineering meaning, respectively, conduction and discharge (of floods). Hence Freud described compulsion in the sense of an energetic *Ableitung*: energy damned up in an original intention "makes itself felt now in commands and now in prohibitions, according as the affectionate impulse or the hostile one snatches control of the pathway leading to discharge" (p. 244; see also p. 246). A richer specimen of Freud's verbal skill is found in a context where, in theorizing about Ernst's biting rage, Freud suggestively referred to passionate love as having been "eaten up" (*aufgezehrt*, 239/455) by hatred. A little further on, we also can appreciate Freud's lexically orchestrated disclosure that his patient "correctly guessed" (*erraten*, 242/458)[20] that one of his prayers was an attempt at cursing—a fittingly climactic use of the charged verb with the Rat Man as its grammatical subject, as opposed to previous instances when he was exclusively the object of his parents' or Freud's guessing.

I have reserved for special attention a passage—perhaps unequaled for his verbal craft in the Freudian corpus—that concerns the eroticized substitution of obsessive acting by thinking

---

20. Strachey's translation of the verb by "understood" (p. 242) effaces its deeper significance.

(245/460-61). In this process, the epistemophilic drive attracts energy which tries to push its way forward (*durchdringen*) into action, so that soon the substitutive act is replaced by a preparatory act of thought; but in its turn, this procrastination (*Aufschub*, literally, shoving on or toward) in action is replaced by lingering over thoughts. Finally:

> der ganze Prozess ist schliesslich mit Erhaltung all seiner Eigentümlichkeiten auf ein neues Gebiet übersetzt, wie die Amerikaner ein Haus zu "*moven*" vermögen.
> Ich würde mich nun getrauen, den lange gesuchten psychologischen Charakter . . . in Anlehnung an die oben stehenden Erörterungen zu bestimmen.
>
> the whole process, with all peculiarities preserved, is finally translated into the new region, just as Americans are able "*to move*" a house.
> I should now venture, with the support of the preceding discussion, to determine the psychological characteristic, so long sought after. (245/461; my translation)

Expositorily, Freud resorted to a lexical referent of space (*durchdringen, Aufschub*) which becomes richly metaphorical with *übersetzt*. This German word is somewhat complex: when the prefix of *übersetzen* is separable, the verb is used literally (to carry across) and a *ge* marker is interposed in the past participle (*übergesetzt*); but when the prefix is inseparable, the verb is used figuratively (to translate) and the past participle needs no extra marker (*übersetzt*). In the passage cited above, one might have expected Freud to use *übergesetzt* (carried across, or, as in Strachey's version, transferred). Freud, however, was more subtle— he called the transition from expression in action to expression in thought a translation—that is, worded obsessional rumination. The translation is into a new region (*Gebiet*), which is no longer a physical domain—the "region" itself is a metaphorical translation. By then comparing the whole process (the translation from the physical and to the psychical) to a physical carrying across, Freud ingeniously suspended the borderlines between literal and metaphorical, physical and psychical. And as if this complexity were not enough, he artfully coined a neologism for the second part of his metaphorical comparison by taking the English word *move* and transferring? translating? it over to German. *Move* is moved and accordingly comments on itself, much like the previously discussed *Anspielung*. There is more. Freud set off the infinitive in three ways: he gave it the German suffix *-n,* placed it in italics, and put quotation marks around it. I suggest that the two typographical signs are especially significant since Freud did not use them in the case history for the other foreign word, *mésalliance,* which Strachey italicized on his own (175/399). In German, the word for italics is *Kursivschrift,* the first root of which is *Kursive* (running hand, cursive writing or script); quotation marks are colloquially called *Gänsefüsschen* (the little feet of geese). Running hand and feet—*move* is even further on the go. Once more, we are witness to an explanation by Freud that simultaneously describes psychical processes and comments on its textual exposition of them. Put another way, Freud's explanation operates neither solely descriptively nor self-reflectively but rather mimically relates the two activities.

We may also observe that the inferential range of *moving* in the passage extends from the internal to the external, even transatlantic world—the impressive moving of whole houses. This is a feat Americans "are able" (*vermögen*) to perform; the German verb, unfortunately translated by Strachey as "will be," resonates with its substantival meaning of "wealth or property," thus suggestively reinforcing the European conception of America at that time. It is also apt that after the references to psychological lingering and moving in America, Freud himself decided not to linger any longer on the topic. With the next paragraph he himself proceeded to shift his explanation from instinctual to psychological grounds, the latter being "so long sought after," a phrase bearing echoes of the legendary El Dorado and moving us back to America.[21]

There are several issues apart from the lexical that remain to be at least recognized, if not elaborated upon. Hamlet lurks behind so many references to the Rat Man—their ghostly fathers, their brooding, doubts, and superstitions, their grave concerns over mortality and life after death, and so on (Marcus, 1984, pp. 150–51). For another thing, we might observe that in spite of Freud's naming compulsion and doubt, in that order, in his section's title, he proceeded to expatiate first on doubt—a manifestation of reversal that we frequently find in obsessionals. But it is during the more fundamental switches in Freud's thought that our greater surprise breaks out, and it is to this that we must now turn.

The title of the last section does not give any hint of Freud's main effort to choose between what he called a "drive" and a "psychological" explanation for obsessional neurosis (p. 248). What is more, in vacillating between the two explanatory poles, Freud lost the balance that he characteristically maintained between processive expression and expository control. Thus, from a formal renunciation of any attempt on his part to discuss the psychological significance of obsessional thinking (p. 228), Freud moved on to offer an explanation of obsessional neurosis in terms of the drives of "love and hatred":

---

21. As an added reflection I should like to bring Freud's transferred use of *move* into life with his equally brilliant use of an English phrase in his essay "Negation" (1925b). As I wrote elsewhere (1982, p. 142): "Explaining that a repressed image or idea can emerge into consciousness only if it is negated, and that therefore the intellectual substitute of repression is negative judgment, Freud asserts that *no* is the trademark of repression, a certificate or origin like 'Made in Germany.' If Freud had chosen a negative phrase by way of illustration, his figure would have been less momentous. As it is, he rises to the occasion with a *positive* expression, 'Made in Germany,' which is at home in the unconscious, where there is no negation; and yet, those words, being in English in an otherwise completely German text, manifest an expatriation to an alien clime."

> If we consider a number of analyses of obsessional neurotics we shall find it impossible to escape the impression that a relation between love and hatred such as we have found in our present patient is among the most frequent, the most marked, and probably, therefore, the most important characteristics of obsessional neurosis. (p. 239)

But no sooner had Freud pointed to a drive explanation than he shied away from it:

> But however tempting it may be to bring the problem of the "choice of neurosis" into connection with instinctual life, there are reasons enough for avoiding such a course. For we must remember that in every neurosis we come upon the same suppressed instincts behind the symptoms. After all, hatred, kept suppressed in the unconscious by love, plays a great part in the pathogenesis of hysteria and paranoia. (pp. 239–40)

Then, contrary to what he had just said about avoiding a drive solution, Freud followed with a provisional one (p. 240), and thereafter linked the domination of compulsion and doubt in the life of obsessionals to the drives—doubt is rooted in a doubt about one's love (p. 241), and compulsion compensates for doubt (p. 242). At that point, Freud modified his monolithic solution by examining the products of obsessional thinking in the combined terms of a drive-influenced "psychological characteristic" (pp. 245–46).

Freud further changed his viewpoint in the three last paragraphs (pp. 246–48), which constitute a rather loose ending to Part Two and lead us to wonder how far it was anally determined. In the antepenultimate paragraph we come upon a digression on obsessional defensive manifestations, which were treated on earlier pages. Then in the penultimate paragraph Freud once more took up the instinctual life of obsessionals in general and Dr. Lanzer in particular and launched into an olfactory explanation of civilization. Finally, assuming an either-or position in the last paragraph, Freud insisted that what characterizes obsessional neurosis lies not in the drives but in the "psychological field." From there he delineated Dr. Lanzer's three-tiered personality structure and alluded to a similar tripartition in another patient, in whom the deepest part consisted of "ancient and long-repressed wishful impulses." These stand as Freud's ending words, but they are words that return in the direction of a drive explanation for obsessional neurosis! Clearly the many veerings and retractions of Freud's chief thesis testify to the admitted disconnectedness of his theoretical discussion.

In summary, we can look at the overriding organization of Freud's case history in this way. Beginning with apologies for textual fragmentariness offset by the claim that he had completely restored Dr. Lanzer, Freud moved in Part One to a defensively definitive closure with its rapidly repeated claim about therapeutic resolution. In contrast, Part Two begins with a lexical clarification that is thereafter undone, and likewise proceeds to take up expository stances that undergo repeated undoings right up to the conclusion. Here it seems as if Freud hesitated between retaining and eliminating, a dual gesture comprehending both ends of the anal phase and elliptically leaving the impression that there was more to say of both.

8

Conclusions and Reiterations

The Rat Man case is a majestic fragment for many reasons, historical and otherwise. Since Ernst Lanzer had previously been seen by Wagner-Jauregg, Vienna's most renowned psychiatrist, Freud was bent on making the case a psychoanalytic showpiece—much as he was subsequently to do with the Wolf Man, who had previously consulted the foremost psychiatrist in all Europe, Emil Kraeplin. Freud's powers of mind and language are evident in his case of the Rat Man, which, together with his other major cases, remains a memorable classic even though it was composed before he formulated his later theories of psychic functioning:

> The timeless elements in Freud's case histories seem to derive from the fact that the inner workings of the patient's mind are bared for us so cogently and artfully that we ourselves are involved. This is sadly not always the case with the more technically and theoretically correct presentations of the present. Freud once remarked that *Oedipus Rex* unraveled like an analysis and we may say in turn that his analyses develop like great dramas that one never forgets. (Kanzer, 1980, p. 429)

Still, we must never forget that Freud was not analyzed by a second party and that his self-analysis had nothing like the effectiveness of an analytic treatment as is understood nowadays. Even Freud himself said that if self-analysis were really possible, neurosis would not exist. That experiential lack in Freud's life, it hardly needs insisting, could never be filled by his creative and intellectual genius.

Conclusions and Reiterations   213

Like other giants of cultural and scientific history, Freud did not spring fully formed and Minerva-like from the head of Zeus; he had phases in his development, yet only sometimes have his adherents been able to build on them. It follows that although the therapist of the Rat Man might be profitably understood within the perspective of his own and later psychoanalytic development, he should in no way be judged from that perspective. But unfortunately the Freudian movement got caught up in various chauvinisms, in the idolization of heroes and Manichean judgments of enemies as totally bad—a pernicious phenomenon of group psychology that was to some degree activated by countergroups parasitically given to hero-bashing. For my part, I would agree with Eissler that psychoanalysis empirically rests on the pillars of Freud's five case histories and that Freud's specific ability to "perceive a complex phenomenon in its component parts, and as the product of an evolutionary process, as something that has become . . . does not seem to have been duplicated in anyone else as yet" (Eissler, 1965, pp. 395–96).

Bitter contentions endorsed by antithetical factions make it all the more difficult to maintain a balanced appraisal of Freud as clinician and writer. In the case at hand Freud mixed momentous insights with exaggerated claims; obviously some of the latter were due to his lack of psychoanalytic experience, and some of them, we should admit, were made in his zeal to protect and promote a new discipline. In those instances where Freud's case histories did not factually conform to his process notes, we notice that he retained his role as effective storyteller, aesthetically guiding his fabled reconstruction by narrative principles. Such a set of complications, however, should not prevent us from attempting equitably to resume Freud's efforts in the Rat Man case, where his accomplishments play against his inadequacies and where the inevitable inadequacies (given those early days of psychoanalysis) outnumber those few that were wittingly avoidable.

Some accomplishments in the Rat Man case have become so familiar that it is difficult to recapture their individuality near the beginning of our century. For example, Freud took a stand against the majority of doctors and sided with his patients as to their general feeling that masturbation lay at the root of their troubles (p. 202); he also complained about attempts by his contemporaries to explain obsessional neurosis without any reference to affects (p. 163n). We may easily cite other prominent psychoanalytic contributions in "Notes upon a Case of Obsessional Neurosis": the diagnostic comparisons with hysteria; the insightful examination of hatred and love in obsessional neurosis; the clarification of the symptoms of doubt and compulsion; the role of superstition, the portrayal of many obsessional defenses, and the distinctiveness of primary and secondary defense symptoms; technical considerations for the understanding and interpretation of obsessions; the significance of "omnipotence of thoughts (wishes)"; the tracing of the sexualized nature of obsessional thinking processes as a regressive substitute for prohibited sexual activity; and the dazzling uncovery of the meanings of Ernst Lanzer's magical prayers and rat symptoms. Perhaps most memorable of all this is Freud's phenomenological description of the tortured psychic processes of the obsessional neurotic, a description that remains unexcelled in psychoanalytic literature.

In the case history there are also theoretical achievements that on the whole have been neglected and that demand more exploration than I have given. For instance, here and there Freud hinted at a whole semiotic range of contiguity and isolation in obsessional neurosis, from relationships within the body schema, to the separation of affect from ideation, to the substitution of the visual function for physical touching, and finally to the temporal disconnectedness that can keynote obsessional articulation. Freud's idea about a death complex in obsessional neurosis also remains largely unexploited. I have suggested for my part that the ultimate scenes—the intimately related fantasies of conception, birth, and death—may have their own particular constellation in the anally marked body schema of obsessional neurosis.

Conclusions and Reiterations 215

From a strictly clinical point of view, one must admire the concentration, astuteness, and insightfulness of Freud, who discovered so many things single-handedly and without benefit of a sustained conventional analysis. The multifariousness of his recorded observations testifies to the fact that much of what escaped this earlier phase of development in his analytic and synthetic powers fell within the orbit of his indefatigable conscious and unconscious awareness. Another clinical factor that I have labored to describe concerns the nature of Freud's presence with his patient. Freud was all intent to understand the mass of confusing detail, to share that understanding with his patient, and in doing so to make appropriate interpretations with the experience-near pronouns of the first person and self-address—an expression of analytic empathy that could well stand as a model today. This of course is not to deny that other aspects of Freud's stance were not so exemplary, including his indoctrination, encouragements, reassurances, and intrusiveness.

Understandably, because of his lack of experience, his own complexes, and those of society in some instances, Freud could not yet see a whole series of issues that we grasp and contend with more readily today: narcissism, early parenting, body schema, sibling relationships, unresolved mourning, the transference in the here and now, including its maternal and negative varieties, and the resolution of transference neurosis. It is somewhat more mysterious that Freud did not draw on his former discovery of primal scenes in order to interpret his patient's early exposure—and to what extent Ernst's early outburst of anger in a triad of insults, upon which Freud conferred so much importance, might have been a symbolic screen condensation of looking (lamp) at the sadistic primal scene as cannibalistic (plate) and anal (towel).

The regular psychoanalysis of the Rat Man did not exceed several months, despite Freud's claim to the contrary (to my knowledge, one of the very few deliberate distortions he ever made). It is much less surprising, then, that the treatment could not have effected any very profound transformation in the Rat Man's deep-seated relationships to male and female objects in his life. During the course of the therapy, moreover, the highly overdetermined meaning of money was never regulated (could the Rat Man ever have been fully content to pay the piper?). But at least the crippling effects of the rat symptomatology disappeared, and that was a remarkable therapeutic change within such a short period of time; an apparently immediate outcome, we have seen, was that seven months after first seeing Freud, Dr. Lanzer was able to accept work in his legal profession. The extent of that professional success might have been mitigated, however, in the sense that Lanzer's dossier shows that he had some instability—that is, his changing employment an inordinate number of times (a continuation of a homosexual flight from the analysis and the return of a rodent's scurrying?). There is also a serious question as to whether Lanzer acceded to any appreciable quality of mature genital love with women. We know that in 1909, after his psychoanalysis, he became enaged to Gisela and that their twelve-year acquaintanceship finally led to marriage in 1910; nevertheless, we are left in ignorance about the expression of old conflicts in marriage. Did Lanzer have some deep fear of children as being rats? Did he have greater potency with an infertile woman? Was he taking revenge against his father by ensuring that the family name would not be continued, and/or was he oedipally avoiding any effort to rival his father by not having a son? The questions are endless, much as Lanzer's analysis by its brevity was made that much more decisively interminable.

Let us again look at the case history of the Rat Man but this time from the angle of its nature. One can quickly point to a number of ways in which, of all the major case histories, this one is the most inconsistent and disconnected: Freud hardly referred to the mother in the early family constellation; he scarcely connected her to Ernst's late heterosexual choice; little of the adult symptomatology was specifically traced to childhood and the manifestations in adolescence were nearly completely passed over; various precipitating causes for Ernst's adult symptomatology were given in isolation from each other; in spite of having slept in the parental bedroom for years, Ernst did not explicitly relate any primal-scene material and to that degree kept his parents "apart" in his case history. For in none of his other writing, moreover, did Freud complain so helplessly about an aphoristic style, a factor that we would understand more broadly as a disruption of linkage or a disconnectedness among larger units of discourse. That disconnectedness, I propose, must be related in part to the fact that Freud had not yet discovered the essence of obsessional neurosis to be a regression from oedipal conflict to anal eroticism. I suggest, further, that although Freud formally assigned an energetically defined thinking process to be the organizing factor in obsessional neurosis, he unconsciously perceived the centrality of anal eroticism, which, in a return of the repressed, made its appearance as voids, gaps, a disconnectedness between groups of statements. In other words, *the working of a certain kind of defensive isolation was not only secondary to repression but in itself constituted a trace of the repressed.*

Freud's later comment on isolation has a bearing on our line of thought:

> Isolating is removing the possibility of contact; it is a method of withdrawing a thing from being touched in any way. And when a neurotic isolates an impression or an activity by interpolating an interval, he is letting it be understood symbolically that he will not allow his thought about that impression or activity to come into associative contact with other thoughts. (1926, p. 122)

Parallel to the interval of time inserted between the neurotic's vocalized thoughts, various logical gaps or "isolations" disrupted

Freud's written corpus. A short step leads us to the dynamic relation between defensive isolation and the body schema:

> There is good evidence that the isolation of dream elements represents the aperture of the female genital. . . . I tentatively conclude that the two constituents separated by a pause or void as observed in isolation reproduce the image of a traumatic perception of a body aperture. . . . If my hypothesis regarding the genetic relationship between isolation and traumatic perception of the female genital could be verified, an important grasp would be gained on the cumbersome problem of the origin of defense mechanisms. (Eissler, 1959, p. 46)

But might not isolation be etiologically related to the anal aperture? If, in Lou Andreas-Salomé's conception of female psychology the vagina is taken on lease from the rectum (Freud, 1918, p. 133), might not there be an early experiential link among anus, vagina, and castration in the life of the male obsessional? I suggest that the societal hostility to the importance of anal eroticism (described in chapter 6) and the countertransferential reactivation of Freud's anal erotic conflicts mobilized in him an intensely defensive isolation whose traces of anal aperture were reinscribed and at least partly determined the exceptional disconnectedness in Freud's case history of the Rat Man. There is the additional consideration that Freud's brilliant therapeutic focus on his patient's "truncated" and therefore aphoristically brief obsessions might have had a negative effect on the exposition of a coherent clinical interview. Taking a further step ahead, we are on surer grounds to perceive that in Freud's and the Rat Man's disconnected narratives, there is a marvelously economic, overdetermined textuality where, from one perspective, contiguity and similarity, rather than being alternate to each other, are simultaneously interplaying. Thus, if we focus on the principle of contiguity, we see that the isolation of narrative units function to break causal connections. If, on the other hand, we focus on the principle of similarity, we note that the space between the isolated units also has a meaning, much as the very gaps in dreams may symbolize the female genitalia (Freud, 1900, pp. 332–33).[1]

As a last area of investigation, there remains the wider and intriguing issue that Freud's works, much to his credit, maintain a classic stature in spite of their having been faultily translated and read. In clarification of this, I shall proceed to a series of reflections which the reader himself may variously apply to the Rat Man case and beyond that, to the Freudian corpus. First, translation. While acknowledging that Strachey's translation is very good, Ornston in a series of preeminent studies has laid bare the losses suffered by the unilingual reader who must rely solely on the *Standard Edition*. In the heroic achievement of his translation, Strachey nevertheless mistook psychic energy for Freud's most fundamental concept and quantified many of his descriptive metaphors; exaggerated Freud's claims to originality and in that way cut off Freud's roots in the science and literature of his own time; played down motivation and meaning; silently crystallized psychic process and function into psychic structure; condensed Freud's descriptive figures of speech and imagery into fewer concrete terms; and used the factually weighted indicative mode for the unconscious, whereas Freud often used the subjunctive mode of uncertainty. In saying how things "are," Strachey obscured Freud's irony, skepticism, tentativeness, and evocative ambiguities. On another score, where Freud was applying the same vocabulary in his descriptions of the normal and psychopathological in order to indicate their continuity, Strachey tended to use different vocabularies. As well, Strachey nearly always separated the

---

1. It might be remarked here that whereas Freud theoretically considered the Rat Man's rapid speech to be a means of defense, he seemed to understand his patient's interrupted utterances of the second session merely as indicative of horror and self-guilt. In extending Freud's concept of isolation as a defensive way of severing connections, I propose that isolation also applies to the very manner of interrupted articulation characterizing the speech of so many obsessionals; the pace of hysterical discourse tends to be different.

psychical activities of the analyst and patient by availing himself of different words, whereas Freud made use of the same word for the two persons (see Ornston entries in the Bibliography).

One may surmise that Strachey's ideologies of science and of class structure helped shape his level of language, his conception of audience, and his thematic orientation, whence comes the crucial divergence of his translation from the original text. We should also observe that the immediacy of Freud's vivid, experiential language and his general intimacy with his wide audience are in keeping with his dynamic conception of psychic activity as processive. In contrast, Strachey's stilted, reserved language and his imagined audience as composed of well-educated mid-nineteenth-century English scientists (*S.E.* 1:xix) are in keeping with a scientific conception characterized by a reified, quantified, static slant. But even apart from the strictly scientific conception, the elimination of lexical traces of Freud's personal and temporal nearness to his patient and reader reveals Strachey's heroic enterprise to be to some degree a translating–acting out and a monumental displacement.

Still, even to deal with Freud in the original text does not solve the all too frequently overlooked problems of reading him. Traditionally, and quite rightly so, psychoanalytic institutes have offered ample courses on the enclosed *scene of therapeutic communication*—that is, the listening and speaking that go on between patient and analyst; on the other hand, short shrift has been accorded to analyzing the strategic activities of reading and writing that constitute much of the public *scene of professional communication* (the interaction between these scenes of therapeutic and professional communication is even more neglected). To stress one aspect of all this, reading Freud as opposed to reading other colleagues is an especially complicated matter, given the transferences we may have to him, to the human subjects of his writings, to his fictively created interlocutors (Mahony, 1982, chap. 3), and to the psychoanalytic institution. Time willing, diverse readings of Freud will be classified by century and nation, much as has happened with the Bible and Shakespeare (the Spanish Shakespeare, eighteenth-century Shakespeare, and so on). Perhaps the embittered rivalry seen between the interpretations of the "French Freud" and the "Anglo-American Freud" will serve for future reflection on the possible psychopathologies of reading Freud in order to distinguish among hysterical, obsessional, narcissistic, fetishistic, and other kinds of readings. Such possibilities notwithstanding, we should conceive of a reading alliance according to which we as agents participate and observe ourselves in our reading of Freud. He does not just invite us to read him. He involves us as readers in becoming the object of his text so that the reading is something like a "working through" or a "reading through" which complements his "writing through"—that is, his readiness to write on impulse and to observe himself as a participant in that impulsive gesture.

A beautiful balance between impulsive freedom and control typifies Freud's discourse. Rather than choose a pale, superficial medium to convey premeditated thought, he opted for a processive writing in which approximate definitions were in accord with the open-endedness of the subject matter, self-irony, and the expression of his ongoing psychic processes. It is in traveling through that prose that we learn to take in stride the false and trial starts, the wrong turns, the interesting side excursions, the dead ends, the momentary mirage, sudden stops for a comprehensive perspective, anticipation of uncertainties, deferred revelations, and so many other itinerary surprises. One significant upshot of this processive style is that it requires a unique lexicographical attention. As fine as the *Vocabulaire de la Psychanalyse* (Laplanche & Pontalis, 1967) is, the dictionary traces Freud's lexical evolution from work to work but not within any one work. Yet this latter area is crucial, as we have seen just from Freud's groping definitions of obsessionality winding through the Rat Man case.

By broadening our frames of reference and increasing our awareness of the mode in which Freud wrote, we correspondingly learn to appreciate his genius and the way he understood psychoanalysis. In this sense we should single out another profound feature of Freud's style to which we have already referred somewhat loosely: along with its processiveness, it is eminently concordant, seeking to establish, now a commonness, now a complementarity, between disparate entities and realms of experience. In uniting different time frames in the present, Freud's multitrack stereophonic expression is distinctive, even in spite of the greater flexibility about the use of the present tense in German than in English.[2] Temporally, spatially, intrapsychically, interpsychically, and locutorily, Freud's prose posits solidarity without exaggerating differences:[3] we are moved by the blending of expository

2. In further consideration of this point, we might profitably refer to Horace Gregory's remark on his translation of Ovid: "I have removed many of Ovid's uses of the historical present with his apostrophes to his heroes and demigods which are awkward when the mainstream of the story is told in the past tense. The English language, unlike others, does not take kindly to shifts in which the historical present tense is most effective" (Gregory, 1958, p. xxviii). But Freud's exceptionally frequent and therefore distinctive use of the present is not explainable merely in terms of a conventional historical present. For example, in displaying his dream theory that "the present tense is the one in which wishes are represented as fulfilled" (Freud, 1900, pp. 534–35), Freud typically reported dreams and their associations in the present. Strachey's translation regularly put dreams in the past tense and in that way constantly undercut one aspect of Freud's theory of dreams (see also Mahony, 1977).

3. Cf. the similarities in Joyce's novelistic style in *Ulysses* and *Finnegans Wake*. In both books "the language reflects not only the main characters, as when the river is described in words which sound like rivers or when the style tumesces with Gerty MacDowell's sexual excitement, but also the time of day or night, as when, late in the evening at 7 Eccles Street, the English language is as worn-out as the day and can produce only clichés, or when, early in the morning at the end of Earwicker's dream, the style dies away with the night. Joyce even learned to make language reflect aspects of the setting, as when, in a butcher shop, Bloom's mind unconsciously borrows metaphors from meat even when he is thinking of quite other things. This magnetization of style and vocabulary by the context of person, place, and time has its humble origin in the few pages Joyce wrote for *Dana*" (Ellmann, 1959, p. 151). It is interesting to note that the resemblance of Joyce's name to Freud (in German, joy is *Freude*) informed Jung's attack on Joyce as a disguise and displacement of an original hostility toward Freud (see Sollers, 1971).

and enactive discourse; by the vocabulary that resonates at unconscious, preconscious, and conscious levels; by the joining of ourselves as readers with Freud as clinician and author and with his patient; by the mixture of formal and informal, dramatic and narrative, oral and written styles; and by the interfusion of subject and object whereby Freud's own processes become the matter of investigation.

Freud poured all these complexities into his case histories, thereby ensuring their permanent fascination. Since him, no one has stepped forward to solve the problem of writing long cases, which could "easily become boring and lead the reader to resist their impact by not reading them" (Freud, 1974a, p. 234). Nor is anyone comparable to Freud for his rare graphic imagination, his magisterial analytic powers, and his imposing awareness of temporal convolutions and the intricacies of antecedents and consequents in intrapsychic life, all of which, inscribed in a supple and multifaceted prose that surmounts the fundamental linearity of language, proceeds in a series of sentences looping and interlooping, pulsating dystolically and systolically, centrifugally expanding and then contracting toward a burgeoning thesis whose transitory centrality begins to shift—but here, I confess in instantaneous retrospect, my own metaphor is sliding. We return quickly to the Rat Man case and see what rests for a verdict: magnificence in failure.

Restless

i.

A mother said: an eyeless man foresaw
My son would live until great age if he
Should never come to know himself. It came
About one day he went astray amidst
The woods and cried, "Is any body here?"
"Hear" gave back tree-hidden Echo who
Jumped like a sulphurous match to nearby flame.

In vain he looked, reflected shortly, then
Proposed, "We should here meet" but simply "meet"
He heard. Then brusquely she disclosed herself
With open arms advancing, making him
In horror sink: "I'd yield to death before
I'd pray to have your arms about my flesh."
"My flesh," she ever cried, and wasted to a voice.
Observing how he blighted all his kind,
The fateful Nemesis directed him
Near a shaded pool. He bent to slay his thirst
And bent, remained entranced by what looked up—
A match for none. The more he bent it bent;
To his retreat the shade replied in kind.
Tormented by this play he tried at length
Embracing what had seared his heart and eyes
And then unrolled in sudden rings of blurs
Upon the waters which, as he withdrew,
Slipped back to look like him. As sole repose
And nourishment, the shade consumed him still,
A wavering veil and unconsummate love.
Which was the beloved, lover, torturer
And victim? Father, son, self-fathering,
Together unwrought. Only there he would
Have stayed, hung in trance on the mirror face,
A creature without mind or memory
Or pity in its mute fidelity.
His hatred drifted inwards to his dreams
That stole his image from him as they came
And went behind the bidding of his head
On the pillow down turning into pool.
More time took place in sameness until once
He cried, reflexive and dispirited,
"Oh you whose love sowed my undoing"—
"Doing" returned Echo he turned flower.

Before the one more waking in a time
Dream-rooting which child and mother could
Have dreamt, he was displaced. From water drawn
He rose into that sunburst house to know
The Nile's head, Sphinx's noose and Pharaoh's dreams,
The earth's awe. Justice-bound, he killed and fled
To save at well-drawn waters' meeting place
And grace upon the little bird the kind
Of smile that comes from deep inside the face.
Both led and leading, prompt to strike a rock
That broke out waters on the deathly sand;
A book of dreams about his father's bones
Beneath his arm; a face of fire and cloud;
Unbending, gesture unforgettable,
Unconsummated ire, the start and end.
His horns indrawn for cause and golden calf;
Migrating with his sons and ruling stone—
A cut above the rest—until the halt
By the sight of the promised land, uncrossed.

ii.

Beholden nightly in observant rite,
His songbird firmed with the force of a spear
That rises to its tip in readiness—
The spear is always strongest flying. Back
That mirror face addressed his magic want
Sapped by boned rage until the next daze when
Again his father peeringly tried
The worry bead prayer for a ghostly smile,
The desecration of a dream kissed dry.

In exile from one mirror to the same,
Demanding vainly over years that it
Give more than ever what was had, at last

He laid his emptiness upon the couch
And felt an eye, unshuttered, lone
Behind a keyhole, piercing, epicene,
That moved away and back. As he resumed
Dream-rooting, he appeared to feel, to hear,
Or to imagine as interpreted
"Scratch the mirror's back, see metaphors through":
Protruding gargoyles into reddy dawn,
Intestate fathers, infants' timeful sleep
Within the bliss of their still milky tongues,
The world-side window of the hermit's cell
At which the dove's spread wing would lance the need
For sight-letting, fantasies' treadmill
Impelled by ever unsaid, driftwish combed
From mourning, bare shudder of intasy,
The twitched divining rod, inothering,
Asail his father gone from waving arm's
Slow fall, a vessel unrecallable
From the sea gull glutted abandoned pier,
Those dreams turned wishes kidnapped from the past
After birth candled for the clotted yolk,
A grass widow leashed onto her hound
Around cavorting in her sandbox of hopes,
His bodyquake on ghastly vaginal fault
Lines, coral women poisoning the rub,
The boredom of his hanging picture's back:
If, magic want in doubters' paradise,
Like puppeteers' fingers hunching in their tool,
The Altamira herd, evolving rock
Of bison deer goat horse bewildered boar
And symbols which express the eye behind—
Aged tombs, somewhat effaced, remembered, if . . .

It wouldn't have been chance to think at death,
"I solely wish the curse of rats on those

Who start a war, on those who gnaw the young
And old, and suck the blood from out our veins."
The eyes soon closed and touched their dreams inside,
Expectant for a universe of sons.
Infirm in life and legendary, now
Unwitting of the wish of being home
Again, becoming slowly like the rest.

References

Anzieu, D. (1976). The sound image of the self. *Internat. Rev. Psycho-Anal.*, *3*, 253–58.
Bell, A. (1961). Some observations on the role of the scrotal sac and testicles. *J. Amer. Psychoanal. Assn.*, *9*, 261–86.
Beigler, F. (1975). A commentary on Freud's treatment of the Rat Man. *Annual of Psychoanal.*, *3.*, 271–86.
Bessis-Rubin, G. (1979). *Les 4e, 5e et 6e séances de "L'homme aux rats: Journal d'une analyse."* Unpublished doctoral dissertation, Université Paris VII.
Blacker, K., & Abraham, R. (1982). The Rat Man revisited: Comments on maternal influences. *Internat. J. Psychoanal. & Psychotherapy*, *9*, 705–27.
Bradlow, P., & Coen, S. (1984). Mirror masturbation. *Psychoanal. Quart.*, *53*, 267–85.
Brodsky, B. (1959). The self-representation, anality, and the fear of dying. *J. Amer. Psychoanal. Assn.*, *7*, 95–108.
Chafe, W. (1982). Integration and involvement in speaking, writing and oral literature. In D. Tannen (Ed.), *Spoken and written language: Exploring orality and literacy.* Norwood, N.J.: Ablex.
Chasseguet-Smirgel, J. (1967). Diskussionsbemerkung zu dem Beitrag von L. Veszy-Wagner: Zwangsneurose und latente Homosexualität. *Psyche*, *21*, 616–22.
Clark, R. (1980). *Freud: The man and the cause.* New York: Random House.
Coltrera, J. (1980). Truth from genetic illusion: The transference and the fate of the infantile neurosis. In H. Blum (Ed.), *Psychoanalytic explorations of technique. Discourse on the theory of therapy* (pp. 289–314). New York: International Universities Press.
Compton, A. (1981). On the psychoanalytic theory of instinctual drives.

II: The sexual drives and the ego drives. *Psychoanal. Quart.*, 50, 219–37.

Eissler, K. (1959). On isolation. *Psychoanal. Study Child*, 14, 29–60.

———. (1965). *Medical orthodoxy and the future of psychoanalysis.* New York: International Universities Press.

———. (1971). *Talent and genius.* New York: Quadrangle Books.

———. (1983). Victor Tausk's *Suicide.* New York: International Universities Press.

Ellenberger, H. (1970). *The discovery of the unconscious.* New York: Basic Books.

Ellmann, R. (1959). *James Joyce.* London: Oxford University Press.

Erlich, I. (1977). What happened to Jocasta? *Bulletin Menninger Clinic*, 41, 280–84.

Evans, M. (1979). Introduction to Jacques Lacan's lecture: The neurotic's individual myth. *Psychoanal. Quart.*, 48, 386–404.

Ferenczi, S. (1950). Stages in the development of the theory of reality. In *Selected Papers* (Vol. 1, pp. 213–39). New York: Basic Books.

Fliess, R. (1956). *Erogeneity and libido.* New York: International Universities Press.

Freud, A. (1966). Obsessional neurosis: A summary of psychoanalytic views as presented at the 24th International Congress. *Internat. J. Psycho-Anal.*, 47, 116–22.

Freud, S. (1891). *On aphasia.* London: Imago Press.

———. (1953–74). *The standard edition of the complete psychological works* (J. Strachey, Ed. and Trans.). 24 vols. London: Hogarth Press. All the following references to this edition (*S.E.*) will be by volume and page.

———. (1892–94). Preface and footnotes to Charcot's *Tuesday lectures.* *S.E.*, 1:133–36.

———. (1893–95). *Studies on hysteria. S.E.*, 2.

———. (1894). The neuro-psychoses of defence. *S.E.*, 3:43–68.

———. (1895). Obsessions and phobias. *S.E.*, 3:71–82.

———. (1896a). The aetiology of hysteria. *S.E.*, 3:191–221.

———. (1896b). Further remarks on the neuro-psychoses of defence. *S.E.*, 3:162–85.

———. (1896c). Heredity and the aetiology of the neuroses. *S.E.*, 3:143–56.

———. (1900). *The interpretation of dreams. S.E.*, 4 & 5.

———. (1901). The psychopathology of everyday life. *S.E.*, 6.

———. (1904). Freud's psycho-analytic procedure. *S.E.*, 7:249–54.

———. (1905a). Fragment of an analysis of a case of hysteria. *S.E.*, 7:3–122.
———. (1905b). *Jokes and their relation to the unconscious.* *S.E.*, 8.
———. (1905c). On psychotherapy. *S.E.*, 7:257–68.
———. (1905d). *Three essays on the theory of sexuality.* *S.E.*, 7:125–243.
———. (1906). My views on the part played by sexuality in the aetiology of the neuroses. *S.E.*, 271–79.
———. (1907a). Obsessive actions and religious practices. *S.E.*, 9:117–27.
———. (1907b). The sexual enlightenment of children. *S.E.*, 9:131–39.
———. (1908a). Character and anal eroticism. *S.E.*, 9:168–75.
———. (1908b). Creative writers and day-dreaming. *S.E.*, 9:142–53.
———. (1909a). Analysis of a phobia in a five-year-old boy. *S.E.*, 10:3–145.
———. (1909b). Notes upon a case of obsessional neurosis. *S.E.*, 10:155–320. Also in *Gesammelte Werke* (Vol. 7, pp. 379–463). Frankfurt am Main: Fischer Verlag, 1941; and *Collected papers* (Vol. 3, pp. 291–383). London: Hogarth Press, 1957.
———. (1910). The future prospects of psycho-analytic therapy. *S.E.*, 11:141–51.
———. (1913a). The disposition to obsessional neurosis. *S.E.*, 12:313–26.
———. (1913b). On beginning the treatment. *S.E.*, 12:123–44.
———. (1913c). *Totem and taboo.* *S.E.*, 13:1–162.
———. (1914). Remembering, repeating and working through. *S.E.*, 12:145–56.
———. (1915a). Observations on transference-love. *S.E.*, 12:159–71.
———. (1915b). The unconscious. *S.E.*, 14:161–215.
———. (1915–17). *Introductory lectures on psycho-analysis.* *S.E.*, 15 & 16.
———. (1918). From the history of an infantile neurosis. *S.E.*, 17:3–122.
———. (1920a). Beyond the pleasure principle. *S.E.*, 18:7–64.
———. (1920b). The psychogenesis of a case of homosexuality in a woman. *S.E.*, 18:147–72.
———. (1923a). The ego and the id. *S.E.*, 19:12–66.
———. (1923b). Two encyclopaedia articles. *S.E.*, 18:235–59.
———. (1925a). An autobiographical study. *S.E.*, 20:3–74.
———. (1925b). Negation. *S.E.*, 19:235–39.

———. (1926). Inhibitions, symptoms and anxiety. *S.E.*, 20:87–172.

———. (1929). Dr. Ernest Jones (on his fiftieth birthday). *S.E.*, 21:249–50.

———. (1931). Libidinal types. *S.E.*, 21:217–20.

———. (1933). New introductory lectures on psycho-analysis. *S.E.*, 22:3–182.

———. (1935). To Thomas Mann on his sixtieth birthday. *S.E.*, 22:255.

———. (1937). Analysis terminable and interminable. *S.E.*, 23:211–53.

———. (1939). Moses and monotheism. *S.E.*, 23:7–137.

———. (1960). *Letters of Sigmund Freud: 1873–1939* (E. Freud, Ed.). London: Hogarth Press. [*Briefe (1873–1939)* (E. Freud, Ed.). Frankfurt am Main: S. Fischer Verlag].

———. (1965). *A psycho-analytic dialogue: The letters of Sigmund Freud and Karl Abraham* (H. Abraham, Ed.). London: Hogarth Press. [*Briefe, 1907–1926* (H. Abraham, Ed.). Frankfurt am Main: Fischer Verlag].

———. (1974a). *The Freud/Jung letters* (W. McGuire, Ed.). Princeton: Princeton University Press. [*Briefwechsel (1906–1916)* (W. McGuire & W. Sauerländer, Eds.). Frankfurt am Main: S. Fischer Verlag].

———. (1974b). *L'Homme aux Rats: Journal d'une analyse* (E. Hawelka, Ed. and Trans.). Paris: Presses Universitaires de France.

———. (1985). *The complete letters of Sigmund Freud to Wilhelm Fliess (1877–1904)* (J. Masson, Ed. and Trans.). Cambridge, Mass.: Harvard University Press.

Gedo, J., & Goldberg, A. (1973). *Models of the mind.* Chicago: University of Chicago Press.

Gill, M. (1982). *Analysis of transference.* Vol. 1. New York: International Universities Press.

Gill, M., & Muslin, H. (1976). Early interpretation of transference. *J. Amer. Psychoanal. Assn.*, 4, 779–94.

Glenn, J. (1981). *The Rat Man: Historical and contemporary views of Freud's psychoanalytic use of psychotherapeutic approaches.* Unpublished manuscript.

Glover, E. (1931). The therapeutic effect of inexact interpretation. *Internat. J. Psycho-Anal.*, 12, 397–441.

Gregory, H. (Trans.). (1958). *Ovid: The Metamorphoses.* New York: New American Library.

Grunberger, B. (1966). Some reflections on the Rat Man. *Internat. J. Psycho-Anal.*, 47, 160–68.

———. (1967). En marge de "L'Homme aux Rats." *Revue française de la Psychanalyse*, *31*, 589–610.
Guttman, S. (1960). Criteria for analyzability: A panel presented at the annual meeting of the Amer. Psychoanal. Assn., April, 1959. *J. Amer. Psychoanal. Assn.*, *8*, 141–51.
Hartman, F. (1983). A reappraisal of the Emma episode and the specimen dream. *J. Amer. Psychoanal. Assn.*, *31*, 555–85.
Hartmann, H. (1964). *Essays on ego psychology*. New York: International Universities Press.
Havelock, E. (1963). *Preface to Plato*. Cambridge, Mass.: Belknap.
Holland, N. (1975). An identity for the Rat Man. *Internat. Rev. Psycho-Anal.*, *2*, 157–69.
———. (1985). *The I*. New Haven: Yale University Press.
Isakower, O. (1939). On the exceptional position of the auditory sphere. *Internat. J. Psycho-Anal.*, *20*, 340–48.
Jakobson, R. (1960). Concluding statement: Linguistics and poetics. In T. Sebeok (Ed.), *Style in language*. Cambridge, Mass.: MIT Press.
Jones, E. (1953–57). *The life and work of Sigmund Freud*. 3 vols. New York: Basic Books.
Jung, C. (1973). *Letters (1906–1950)*. Vol. 1. (G. Adler, Ed., & R. Hall, Trans.). Princeton, N.J.: Princeton University Press.
Kanzer, M. (1952). The transference neurosis of the Rat Man. *Psychoanal. Quart.*, *21*, 181–89.
———. (1980). Freud's human influence on the Rat Man (pp. 232–40) and Integrative summary (pp. 241–47). In M. Kanzer & J. Glenn (Eds.), *Freud and his patients*. New York: Jason Aronson.
Kardiner, A. (1957). Freud—The man I knew, the scientist, and his influence. In B. Nelson (Ed.), *Freud and the 20th century* (pp. 209–29). New York: Meridian Books.
———. (1977). *My analysis with Freud*. New York: W. W. Norton.
Kaufmann, W. (1980). *Discovering the mind: Freud versus Adler and Jung*. Vol. 3. New York: McGraw-Hill.
Kernberg, O. (1976). *Object relations theory and clinical psychoanalysis*. New York: Jason Aronson.
Kestenberg, J. (1966). Rhythm and organization in obsessive-compulsive development. *Internat. J. Psycho-Anal.*, *47*, 151–59.
———. (1980). Ego organization in obsessive-compulsive development: The study of the Rat Man, based on interpretation of movement patterns. In M. Kanzer & J. Glenn (Eds.), *Freud and his patients* (pp. 144–79). New York: Jason Aronson.

Klein, D. (1981). *Jewish origins of the psychoanalytic movement.* New York: Praeger.
Kris, E. (1951). Ego psychology and interpretation in psychoanalytic therapy. *Psychoanal. Quart., 20,* 15–30.
Lacan, J. (1979). The neurotic's individual myth. *Psychoanal. Quart., 48,* 405–25.
Lagache, Marianne. (1968). "L'Homme aux rats" et "Le petit Eyolf." *Bulletin de l'Association Psychanalytique de France, 4,* 109–21.
Langs, R. (1974). *The technique of psychoanalytic psychotherapy.* Vol. 2. New York: Jason Aronson.
———. (1976). *The bipersonal field.* New York: Jason Aronson.
———. (1978). *Technique in transition.* New York: Jason Aronson.
———. (1980). The misalliance dimension in the case of the Rat Man. In M. Kanzer & J. Glenn (Eds.), *Freud and his patients* (pp. 215–31). New York: Jason Aronson.
Laplanche, J. (1980). *Problématiques (L'Angoisse).* Vol. 1. Paris: Presses Universitaires de France.
Laplanche, J., & Pontalis, J. B. (1967). *Vocabulaire de la psychanalyse.* Paris: Presses Universitaires de France.
Lewis, Harvey. (1958). The effect of shedding the first deciduous tooth upon the passing of the Oedipus complex of the male. *J. Amer. Psychoanal. Assn., 6,* 5–37.
Lewis, Helen. (1971). *Shame and guilt in neurosis.* New York: International Universities Press.
———. (1981). *Freud and modern psychology: Vol. 1. The emotional basis of mental neurosis.* New York: Plenum.
Lipton, S. (1977). The advantages of Freud's technique as shown in his analysis of the Rat Man. *Internat. J. Psycho-Anal., 58,* 255–74.
———. (1979). An addendum to the advantages of Freud's technique as shown in his analysis of the Rat Man. *Internat. J. Psycho-Anal., 60,* 215–16.
———. (1981). Letter to the editor. *Internat. J. Psycho-Anal., 62,* 125.
———. (1971). Freud's analysis of the Rat Man considered as a technical paradigm (abstract). *Bulletin Philadelphia Psychoanal. Assn., 21,* 179–83.
Mahony, P. (1977). Towards a formalist approach to dreams. *Internat. Rev. Psycho-Anal., 4,* 83–98.
———. (1979). The place of psychoanalytic treatment in the history of discourse. *Psychoanal. and Contemporary Thought, 2,* 77–111.

———. (1982). *Freud as a writer.* New York: International Universities Press.

———. (1984). *The cries of the Wolf Man.* New York: International Universities Press.

———. (1985). The oral tradition, Freud, and psychoanalytic writing. In P. Stepansky (Ed.), *Freud: Appraisals and reappraisals* (pp. 199–214). Hillsdale, N.Y.: Analytic Press.

Major, R. (1971). Interpretation 1907: Contribution à l'étude de la technique analytique. *Revue de la Psychanalyse Française, 35,* 527–42.

———. (1974). The language of interpretation. *Internat. Rev. Psycho-Anal., 1,* 425–36.

Mannoni, D. (1965). L'homme aux Rats. *Les Temps Modernes, 20,* 2028–47.

Marcus, S. (1984). *Freud and the culture of psychoanalysis.* London: Allen & Unwin.

Mead, M. (1964). Vicissitudes of the study of the total communication process. In T. Sebeok et al. (Eds.), *Approaches to semiotics* (pp. 277–87). The Hague: Mouton.

Melman, O. (1980). An obsessional neurosis. In S. Schneidermann (Ed.), *Returning to Freud* (pp. 130–38). New Haven: Yale University Press.

Meyerson, P. (1966). Comments on Dr. Zetzel's paper. *Internat. J. Psycho-Anal., 47,* 139–42.

Mirbeau, O. (1957). *Le jardin des supplices.* Paris: Fasquelle. (Original work published 1899)

Morgenthaler, F. (1966). Psychodynamic aspects of defence with comments on technique in the treatment of obsessional neurosis. *Internat. J. Psycho-Anal., 47,* 203–11.

Muslin, N. (1979). Transference in the Rat Man case: The transference in transition. *J. Amer. Psychoanal. Assn.,* 561–78.

Nunberg, H., & Federn, E. (Eds.). (1962–75). *Minutes of the Vienna Psychoanalytic Society.* 4 vols. New York: International Universities Press.

Ong, W. (1967). *The presence of the word.* Ithaca, N.Y.: Cornell University Press.

———. (1977). *Interfaces of the word.* Ithaca, N.Y.: Cornell University Press.

———. (1982). *Orality and literacy.* London: Methuen.

Ornston, D. (1978). On projection: A study of Freud's usage. *Psychoanal. Study Child, 33,* 117–66.

———. (1982). Strachey's influence. *Internat. J. Psycho-Anal.*, 63, 409–26.

———. (1985). Freud's conception is different from Strachey's. *J. Amer. Psychoanal. Assn.*, 33, 337–70.

———. (in press). Book review of *Freud and man's soul* by Bruno Bettelheim. *J. Amer. Psychoanal. Assn.*

———. (in press). The invention of "cathexis" and Strachey's strategy. *Internat. Rev. Psycho-Anal.*

———. *Psychotherapy and translation.* Unpublished manuscript.

———. *On revising the Standard edition of Freud's writings.* Unpublished manuscript.

Peters, H. (1962). *My sister, my spouse.* New York: W. W. Norton.

Pletsch, Carl. (1982). Freud's case studies. *Partisan Review*, 49, 101–18.

Politzer, H. (1969). Book review of *Sigmund Freud's Prosa* by W. Schönau. *German Quarterly*, 42, 739–41.

Rank, Otto. (1910). Summary of Freud's talk on the Rat Man during the Salzburg Congress. *Zentralblatt Psychoanal.*, 1, 125–26.

Reik T. (1949). *Fragment of a great confession.* New York: Farrar Straus.

Rey-Flaud, H. (1983). *Le névrose courtoise.* Paris: Navarin.

Roazen, P. (1971). *Freud and his followers.* New York: Signet, 1971.

———. (1985). *Helene Deutsch: A psychoanalyst's life.* New York: Anchor Press.

Roback, A. (1954). *Destiny on motivation in language.* Cambridge, Mass.: Sci-Art Publishers.

Rosen, V. (1977). *Style, character and language* (S. Atkins and M. Jucovy, Eds.). New York: Jason Aronson.

Rosenfeld, David. (1980). The handling of resistances in adult patients. *Internat. J. Psycho-Anal.*, 61, 71–83.

———. (1981). Letter to the editor. *Internat. J. Psycho-Anal.*, 62, 125–26.

Ross, H. (1966). Depression and object-loss: A panel report on a presentation at the annual meeting of the Amer. Psychoanal. Assn., 1965. *J. Amer. Psychoanal. Assn.*, 14, 142–53.

Saussure, R. (1956). Sigmund Freud. In W. Ruitenbeek (Ed.), *Freud as we knew him* (pp. 357–59). Detroit: Wayne State University Press, 1973.

Schönau, W. (1968). *Sigmund Freud's Prosa.* Stuttgart: Metzlersche.

Schur, M. (1972). *Freud: Living and dying.* New York: International Universities Press.

Shengold, L. (1965). The rat and the tooth: A study of the central clinical significance of overstimulation. *Psychoanal. Quart.*, 34, 477–79.

———. (1967). The effects of overstimulation: Rat people. *Internat. J. Psycho-Anal.*, *48*, 403–15.
———. (1971). More on rats and rat people. *Internat. J. Psycho-Anal.*, *52*, 277–88.
———. (1974). The metaphor of the mirror. *J. Amer. Psychoanal. Assn.*, *22*, 97–115.
———. (1982). Anal erogeneity: The goose and the rat. *Internat. J. Psycho-Anal.*, *63*, 331–45.
———. (1985). Defensive anality and narcissism. *Internat. J. Psycho-Anal.*, *66*, 47–64.
Sherwood, M. (1969). *The logic of explanation in psychoanalysis.* New York: Academic Press.
Sollers, P. (1977). Joyce and co. *Triquarterly*, *38*, 107–21.
Spitz, R. (1965). *The first year of life.* New York: International Universities Press.
Steiner, G. (1975). *After Babel: Aspects of translation and language.* London: Oxford University Press.
Sterba, R. (1982). *Reminiscences of a Viennese psychoanalyst.* Detroit: Wayne State University Press.
Stone, L. (1981). Notes on the noninterpretive elements in the psychoanalytic situation and process. *J. Amer. Psychoanal. Assn.*, *29*, 89–118.
Veszy-Wagner, L. (1967). Zwangsneurose und latente Homosexualität. *Psyche*, *21*, 592–615, 622–23.
Viderman, S. (1970). *La construction de l'espace analytique.* Paris: Denoël.
———. (1977). *Le céleste et le sublunaire.* Paris: Presses Universitaires de France.
Weiss, S. (1980). Reflections and speculations on the psychoanalysis of the Rat Man. In M. Kanzer & J. Glenn (Eds.), *Freud and his patients.* New York: Jason Aronson.
Wittels, F. (1924). *Sigmund Freud: His personality, his teaching and his school.* New York: Dodd, Mead.
Zetzel, E. (1966a). Additional notes upon a case of obsessional neurosis: Freud 1909. *Internat. J. Psycho-Anal.*, *47*, 123–29.
———. (1966b). Additional notes upon a case of obsessional neurosis: Freud 1909. *Bulletin Philadelphia Psychoanal. Assn.*, *16*, 44–47.
Zola, E. (1978). *La joie de vivre.* Paris: Fasquelle. (Original work published 1884)
Zumthor, P. (1983). *Introduction à la poésie orale.* Paris: Seuil.

Index

Abraham, Karl, 83, 94, 148, 173
Adler, Alfred, 100
Adler, Dr., 14
Adler, Gisela: relationship with Ernst Lanzer, 7–17 passim, 24–27 passim, 31–38, 41–46 passim, 49–67 passim, 77, 97, 128–29; same name as Gisela Fluss, 97; use of picture of, 115–16
Andreas-Salomé, Lou, 218
Anniversary phenomena, 45–46
Anzieu, Didier, 136

B., Lieutenant, 14, 15
Brücke, Ernst, 1, 97

Chafe, William, 142, 143–44
Charcot, Jean-Martin, 134, 141–42
Contiguity: as a principle of obsessional neurosis, 56–58, 67–68, 167–68, 178, 185, 214, 217–19. *See also* Simultaneity

D., Lieutenant, 12, 41
David, Lieutenant, 3n, 14–16 passim, 63–64, 102, 108
Dora, 81, 85, 90–95 passim, 132, 146, 178

Eissler, Kurt, 65, 213, 218
Elisabeth, Fräulein, 182n
Ellenberger, Henri, 160
Emmy von N., 182

Ferenczi, Sandor, 83, 148

Fliess, Wilhelm, 88, 95, 152, 153
Fluss, Gisela, 12, 97
Freud, Alexander, 166n
Freud, Sigmund: scientific genius, 18, 153–54, 178, 212–13, 222–23; conceptions of clinical writing as literature, 30, 189–90, 194, 198; clinical achievements, 93–94, 108, 130–33, 147–50, 212–16; shortcomings, 30–35, 43, 47, 53n, 178–79, 190, 213, 216–17; impact of his unconscious on his theory, 47, 94–97, 103–06, 110, 165–66; impact of his unconscious on his clinical writing, 47, 164–65, 178–79, 182–83, 187–89, 205, 209–11, 218–19
—prose style: scope of, 28, 102, 153–54, 157–58n, 177, 212–13; attitude toward lexical apartheid in, 37n, 180–81, 185–86, 195–97, 206; oral aspects of, 140–47; processive, 161n, 201–02; feature of commonness in, 180–81, 186, 222–23; stereophonic, 184–87, 191, 222; enactive, 195, 198, 223; coiling, 202–04; of rapprochement, 205–06; self-reflective, 207–08
Freundlich, Jacob, 3n, 27, 34

German language: key words treated: aber, 58–59; Adler, 63; Anspielung, 195; aufheben, 45n, 193; bohren, 105; dick, 62; Ei, 59n; Einfühlung, 180; ernst, 16, 62–63; Freude, 16, 107; frühzeitig, 161n; Glejisamen,

239

German language (*continued*)
59, 60, 71; Hering, 123; Kneifer, 54; Kniebohrer, 16, 105; kriechen, 61; Lanze(r), 62, 121; Leichenvogel, 63; Lösung, 78, 91; Messer, 62; Nasenbohrer, 105, 117; Sack, 50; Samen, 11, 59; Scherberl, 63n; Si(e)gmund, 140; sterben, 62–63; stören, 114; Topf, 53, 63n; übersetzen, 146, 191, 207–08; verehr(t)e, 42n, 63; verschlingt, 120n; vorzeitig, 161n; Zwangsdenken, 164–65, 201n, 202; Zwangsvorstellung, 164–65, 202
—the "Rat" group: erraten, 21, 104n, 105, 112n, 189, 206; heiraten, 51, 80; Kamerad, 52; Rasiermesser, 62; raten, 51n, 60, 80; Raten, 52, 106; Rätselraten, 21; Rätzche, 51n; Spielratte, 51, 80, 195
Goethe, Wolfgang, 39
Gross, Otto, 86–88

Hans, 82
Hartman, Frank, 95
Hawelka, Elsa, 6n, 10n, 22, 33n, 37n, 62

Ibsen, Henrik, 47, 76–77
Isakower, Otto, 135

Jakobson, Roman, 137
Jaques, Elliott, 145
Jones, Ernest, 18, 20, 83, 94, 138, 147, 148, 159, 177
Julius Caesar, 113
Jung, Carl, 17, 19, 69, 70, 82–88, 143, 175–76, 177

Kanzer, Mark, 66, 96, 212
Kardiner, Abram, 97–98
Kestenberg, Judith, 66
Klein, Dennis, 140
Knöpfmacher, Wilhelm, 1
Kraeplin, Emil, 212

Lacan, Jacques, 55, 130n
Lanzer, Ernst, and family: Heinrich Lanzer (father): historical account of, 3–4, 7, 9, 24, 25; as chastiser of Ernst, 29–30, 32, 43, 45–47, 53, 119, 216; Ernst's reactions to death of, 34, 39–40, 63, 65; Ernst's ambivalence toward, 43–44, 50, 54, 200. Rosa Herlinger (mother): historical account of, 3, 6, 17, 24, 25, 26, 27; oedipal importance of, 32, 37, 65, 195, 198, 216; marriage plan of, 32–35, 194; extant information about, 35–36, 180n; Ernst's dislike of, 36–38, 123, 128; Ernst's phantasies about, 38, 49, 123. Siblings: Robert, 3n, 5, 24, 37, 44–45, 46, 115; Camilla, 3n, 4, 29, 30, 41, 45, 53, 63n; influence of her death on Ernst, 24, 28, 32, 37–42 passim, 44, 63, 65, 119; Olga, 3n, 24, 25, 26, 34, 37, 46, 56, 112, 123; her erotic attraction to Ernst, 40–41; Gertrud, 3n, 24, 40; Rosalie, 3n, 24, 40, 44, 45n; Hedwig, 3n, 24, 41, 45. Deceased aunt, 8, 26, 32–33, 34, 45, 46, 129, 194
Laplanche, Jean, 221
Libitsky, August, 17, 27
Lipps, Theodor, 138

Macbeth, Lady, 46
Mahony, Patrick, 85, 131, 135, 136, 142, 145, 183, 200, 220
Mannoni, Octave, 169
Marcus, Steven, 33n, 177, 209
Mead, Margaret, 136
Mill, John, 141
Minutes of the Vienna Psychoanalytic Society, 92, 109, 116n, 121n, 164n, 168n; citation of the Rat Man in, 31n, 36, 43, 44, 51n, 54n, 90, 146
Mirbeau, Octave, 12, 49
Mondsee, 10, 26
Morgentaler, F., 66
Munich, 11, 27, 116

Nemeczek, Captain, 12, 52, 53, 102

Obermayer, H., 27
Ong, Walter, 134, 143

Ornston, Darius, 22n, 219–20

Palatzer, Dr., 3n, 9, 15–16, 99, 110, 125, 189
Paula, Fräulein, 3n, 24, 25
Politzer, Heinz, 141
Pontalis, J.-B., 221
Primal scenes, 47, 52, 56, 215, 217. *See also* Ultimate scenes
Przemsýl, 15

Rank, Otto, 36, 59n, 135
Ratzenstein, Dr., 16
Richard, 9, 10, 11, 12, 26, 34, 62
Roback, A. A., 61
Rosen, Victor, 185
Rudolf, Fräulein, 3n, 5, 24, 30n, 61, 100

Saborsky family, 3, 32, 33, 34, 55, 56
Salzburg, 27, 33, 82, 83, 86, 177
Saussure, Raymond de, 98
Schick, Alois, 27
Schur, Max, 94, 95, 138, 205
Shengold, Leonard, 13n, 60n, 66
Simultaneity, 187. *See also* Contiguity
Singh, Raj, 134
Sophocles, 19, 35
Sphinx, 19–20

Spielrein, Sabina, 85–88
Steiner, George, 139
Strachey, James: deficiencies or omissions in transcriptions, 6n, 21–22, 33, 51n, 100, 101, 123, 128n, 175, 192n; inadequacies in translation, 9n, 11n, 22–23, 30n, 45n, 69n, 91, 103–04, 112, 117, 146, 161n, 167n, 179–81, 183–87, 198; faulty annotations, 24–26; suggestive annotations, 50n, 53n, 81–82, 131
Swoboda, Hermann, 87–88

Trieste, 41, 66

Ullmann, Ernst, 27
Ultimate scenes, 46–48, 105. *See also* Primal scenes
Unterach, 10–11, 26, 120, 121

Wagner, Richard, 5, 64, 107
Wagner-Jauregg, Julius, 12, 212
Weiss, Stanley, 96
Wittels, Fritz, 140–41
Wolf Man, case of, 171; compared with case of Rat Man, 47, 63n, 64, 65, 85, 94–95, 132, 146, 170, 179, 198n, 212

Zola, Emile, 121
Zumthor, Paul, 136–37